CAMBRIDGE STUDIES IN PHILOSOPHY

Propositional Attitudes

CAMBRIDGE STUDIES IN PHILOSOPHY

General editor SYDNEY SHOEMAKER

Advisory editors J. E. J. ALTHAM, SIMON BLACKBURN,
GILBERT HARMAN, MARTIN HOLLIS, FRANK JACKSON,
JONATHAN LEAR, WILLIAM G. LYCAN, JOHN PERRY,
BARRY STROUD

Propositional Attitudes

AN ESSAY ON THOUGHTS AND HOW WE ASCRIBE THEM

Mark Richard

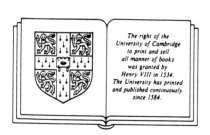

The right of the
University of Cambridge
to print and sell
all manner of books
was granted by
Henry VIII in 1534.
The University has printed
and published continuously
since 1584.

Cambridge University Press

Cambridge

New York   Port Chester   Melbourne   Sydney

Published by the Press Syndicate of the University of Cambridge
The Pitt Building, Trumpington Street, Cambridge CB2 1RP
40 West 20th Street, New York, NY 10011, USA
10 Stamford Road, Oakleigh, Melbourne 3166, Australia

First published 1990

Printed in the United States of America

Library of Congress Cataloging-in-Publication Data
Richard, Mark.
Propositional attitudes : an essay on thoughts and how we ascribe
them / Mark Richard.
p.   cm.
Bibliography: p.
Includes index.
ISBN 0-521-38126-6. – ISBN 0-521-38819-8 (pbk.)
1. Proposition (Logic).   2. Cognition.   3. Attitude (Psychology)
4. Logic.   5. Semantics.   I. Title.
BC181.R5   1990   89–35543
160 – dc20   CIP

British Library Cataloguing in Publication Data
Richard, Mark
Propositional attitudes : an essay on thoughts and
how we ascribe them.
1. Thought processes.
I. Title
153.4'2

ISBN 0-521-38126-6 hard covers
ISBN 0-521-38819-8 paperback

For my friends

Contents

vii

Acknowledgments

I wish to acknowledge the comments and patience of those who read versions of this manuscript. First among equals is Ed Gettier, whose philosophical style and good sense I hope are occasionally reflected in the following pages. Graeme Forbes commented extensively on the manuscript; he and Ali Kazmi commented on a forerunner of Chapter 3 at an APA symposium in 1988. I very much appreciate their attempts to set me straight. David Auerbach, David Austin, Jody Azzouni, Chris Hill, Harold Levin, Bill Lycan, and Sydney Shoemaker read various temporal slices of the book, for which I thank them. Dick Grandy, David Kaplan, Nathan Salmon, and Scott Soames had considerable impact through conversations, comments on my earlier work, and their own work on the attitudes.

I wrote most of this while on leave from Tufts University, at the National Humanities Center in Research Triangle Park, North Carolina. During that time I was partially supported by a Mellon Fellowship from the university, for which I am grateful. I am particularly indebted to the National Humanities Center for its financial support and extraordinary working environment.

Parts of Chapter 2 are adapted from Richard (1988). A very abbreviated forerunner of Sections 2 and 4 of Chapter 3 appeared as Richard (1989); and the first section of Chapter 4 is a rewritten version of the first sections of Richard (1987b).

This book is dedicated to my friends, first among whom is my wife Barbara. She says that I should say that none of this would have been possible without her. Perhaps she is right.

Introduction

This book is about propositional attitudes – believing, saying, desiring, knowing, and so on – and how we talk about them. Its primary goal is to give an illuminating answer to questions like the following: When someone says

Maggie thinks that Odile is tired

or

Maggie said that Clark Kent is Superman

or

Maggie wishes that Greg would leave her alone

how do things have to stand with Maggie in order for what is said to be true? What makes sentences like these true or false?

This, then, is a book about the semantics of attitude ascription. But it would be difficult to say anything illuminating about the meaning of 'believes', 'desires', and their friends without saying something substantive about belief, desire, and the other propositional attitudes. And so this book addresses topics in the philosophy of mind, as well as ones in the philosophy of language. Discussed in the following pages are, for example, the nature of the psychological states that are beliefs and desires; the beliefs and desires (or lack thereof) of speechless nonhuman animals; the distinction between tacit and explicit belief; the idea that the sentences of a natural language play, for all its speakers, more or less the same cognitive or conceptual role.

Here is a summary of the main thesis of the book. Suppose that Maggie thinks that Odile is tired. For Maggie to think that, it is, of course, not necessary that she think to herself, 'Odile is tired'. She could think Germanically to herself, 'Odile ist müde'. Or she

1

might think to herself, 'You are tired', looking at Odile. But for Maggie to think the thought in question, she does need to think of Odile and to think of the property of being tired – and, of course, to think that the one has the other. For Maggie to think that Odile is tired, she must have some representations of Odile and of being tired "put together" in an appropriate way. In some broad sense of 'sentence', she must employ a mental sentence saying that Odile is tired.

Suppose I say, 'Maggie thinks that Odile is tired', attempting to tell you what Maggie thinks. My sentence has a part – 'that Odile is tired' – that itself has parts representing Odile and being tired. On each side of the fence – on the side of the speaker and on the side of the thinker – we find the same sort of thing: a sentence, or sentence-like representation, whose various parts pick out objects and properties:

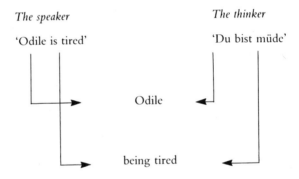

What makes my report true is that my sentence faithfully represents a sentence of Maggie's; what makes it false is not faithfully representing such.

What is faithful representation? Necessary for this is the kind of relation portrayed in the picture above. My sentence and Maggie's need to pick out, component by component, the same individuals, properties, and relations. To use some contemporary jargon, the sentences must determine the same Russellian proposition. Is this sufficient for faithful representation? No. If Maggie utters, 'Clark Kent is Clark Kent', and I say, 'Maggie said that Clark Kent is Superman', there is an isomorphism of Russellian content between my sentence and Maggie's:

2

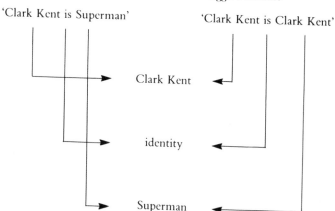

My sentence 'Clark Kent is Superman'

Maggie's sentence 'Clark Kent is Clark Kent'

Clark Kent

identity

Superman

But I did not, presumably, speak truly.

So what else is necessary for faithful representation? Some say that the two sentences must involve the same ways of thinking of objects and properties, in some interesting sense of 'ways of think-ing': They must have the same Fregean sense, or the same concep-tual roles, for speaker and thinker, or they must be united under some other interesting cognitive equivalence relation.

This answer isn't correct. The pithy explanation of why it is wrong is that such ways of thinking are too idiosyncratic. If Jones utters, 'Tully is tubby; Cicero is not', she has said that Tully is tubby, but Cicero is not. If we agree about this, we should agree that the above answer is wrong. For we *know* what Jones has said; we *know* that the report 'Jones said that Tully is tubby, Cicero is not' is correct. But *who knows* whether the ways of thinking of Cicero that Jones associates with the names 'Cicero' and 'Tully' are the same, similar, or wildly different from those we associate with them?

What counts as faithful representation varies from context to context with our interests and expectations. Context places certain restrictions on what can represent what. Sometimes these are very specific – for example, 'Clark Kent' is to represent only 'Clark Kent'. Sometimes they are less specific – a context may say that 'Greg' in 'Maggie wishes that Greg would leave her alone' is to represent terms connected with Maggie's current perceptual ex-perience of Greg. Sometimes context is silent on these matters, and

3

expressions are free to represent any expressions with which they corefer. The upshot is that 'Maggie thinks that Odile is tired' is true in a particular context provided its 'that'-clause (or t-clause) represents, according to the context, one of the sentences that constitute Maggie's thoughts.

Most of this book is devoted to elaborating and defending this view of the matter. The view involves two sorts of sententialism about attitudes: a semantic sententialism, on which what a t-clause names is a sentence-like entity (made up of both the expressions in the t-clause and the things they pick out); and a psychological sententialism, on which the psychological states that constitute our attitudes themselves involve some sort of sentential structure. Both sorts of sententialism have come under heavy fire of late; the first chapter defends them. The view opposes what are probably the most popular theories about attitude ascription – cognitive theories of content, such as those provided by Fregeans and advocates of conceptual role semantics. In the second chapter, I set out the case against some representative theories of this stripe.

The second half of the book elaborates the theory sketched above. Chapter 3 gives an initial statement of the view and applies it to some puzzle cases. It addresses various likely objections: for example, that propositions (what t-clauses name) are individuated too finely, since the words in a t-clause are parts of the proposition named. That chapter compares my view with contemporary Russellian, or "direct reference," views of attitude ascription. I was once a Russellian myself, and I think my view to be kin to Russellianism – though, I hasten to add, I do not endorse the Russellian's idea that, if Odile knows that Superman can fly, she must also know that Clark Kent can. The final chapter is concerned with some broadly logical issues: quantification into attitude contexts and the objectuality of the quantifiers; assigning truth conditions to dialogues and conversations; propositions as truth bearers. And it takes up a few other issues as well: the attitudes of animals; demonstrative thought; the retention of attitudes over time.

Attitudes and their ascription raise many issues that are not addressed in this book. I have said my piece about belief about the self – belief *de se* – elsewhere (Richard 1983); here I ignore it. What is here was written with the conscious resolve to ignore problems raised by the use of empty and fictional names in attitude ascription, as well as ticklish problems involving "quantifiying out" of attitude ascriptions (as in 'Hob thinks the unicorn ate the petunias, but Nob thinks it probably didn't'). I have decided to remain neutral on issues concerning the sorts of semantic contributions definite descriptions make to what we think and to reports about what is thought. Many, myself included, think that a thought or assertion realized by a sentence in which a demonstrative or ordinary proper name occurs in some sense contains the referent of that term. It is a singular thought or assertion, with the individual figuring among its constituents. Some think the same is true, at least some of the time, of thoughts and assertions realized by sentences in which definite descriptions occur. Not having fixed my own opinion on this subject, I preserve a stony neutrality on it. And there are any number of issues from the philosophy of mind concerning attitudes that I ignore.

This book starts from the assumption that attitude ascriptions are what they appear to be: sentences in which a two-place predicate ('believes', 'says', etc.) connects two genuine terms, one typically simple syntactically ('Iago'), the other typically complex ('that Desdemona will betray Othello'). This assumption – that at a certain level of generality

Iago hopes that Desdemona will betray Othello

is on a syntactic and semantic par with

Iago kissed Desdemona

– saddles us immediately with t-clauses as names of entities of some sort. That is, it saddles us immediately with propositions.

I make no apologies for my propositional promiscuity. After all, attitude ascriptions *do* appear relational. We do, for instance, quantify into propositional position, as in 'Everything he says is *meshugge*'. (Bealer 1982 begins with an inventory of relevant evidence.) Provided we can work out a coherent account of what propositions are and how the sentences containing their names work, it seems reasonable enough to take this appearance for reality. This book is an attempt to provide such an account.

Philosophical semantics is a subject that tends to get pretty technical pretty fast. I have tried to keep things as nontechnical as I could. I have not embedded the proposals made here in one or another syntactic theory for English, nor have I spelled out all the

5

details for embedding the semantic proposals in one or another approach to the semantics of natural language. I try to say enough so that it is tolerably clear how one would go about realizing the semantic proposal in one or another such theory. In general, I try to minimize the amount of technical and quasi-technical apparatus I invoke. This leaves the book relatively neutral among various syntactic and semantic frameworks. I tend to spell out semantic details in a possible-worlds framework, in part because the framework is simple and relatively well understood. But those working in other frameworks – for example, situation semantics – could surely adopt the view presented here.

1

Structure

Form ever follows function.
Louis Henri Sullivan, "The Tall Office
Building Artistically Considered"

Assume that in an attitude ascription, that is, in sentences such as

John believes that Patty is pretty,
Jane wishes that Mick were dead,
Hob says that all is right with the world

the 'that'-clause (t-clause) functions as a term.[1] Call what such terms name 'propositions'.[2]

---

1 Somewhat more precisely, an attitude verb is any verb that can take a t-clause as an object and singular terms as subjects in surface realizations; an attitude ascription is a sentence whose principal verb is an attitude verb. To make this perfectly precise, we would have to replace talk of t-clauses with talk about phrases of the form COMP + S, or of some analogous notions, in order for sentences like 'I wonder whether he's touching it' or 'I want to be alone' to turn out to be attitude ascriptions.

2 Of course, a t-clause names a proposition only relative to various things: a context or a use, an assignment to free variables, etc. I generally suppress such niceties if nothing under discussion hangs on them. Or I spell them out in footnotes, as I am doing here.

   I sometimes let myself be somewhat lax in matters of use and mention in the main text. Again, this is in the interest of comprehensibility: My policy has been to be sloppy, provided that no point important to an argument is blurred by the sloppiness and anyone who would notice that I was being sloppy would know how the prolix correction should go.

   The general conventions on use and mention followed in the text are as follows: Italicized roman letters are used as variables over expression types of whatever language is under discussion. For example, 'S' is used as a variable over types of sentences. Context makes it clear when an expression is so functioning, and I usually do not bother to announce it.

   In the text, when expressions are not being displayed, as they are in

This is an example of a displayed sentence,

7

One would like to know what sorts of things propositions are. This chapter makes a start at an account; it takes up the question whether propositions have structure. Two views on this predominate. One is that propositions have no interesting structure, even though their canonical names, 'that'-clauses, do. This view is held, for example, by those who take t-clauses to be names of sets of possible worlds. The other view is that propositions have a structure that more or less recapitulates the structure of a sentence. Those who identify propositions with sentences, Russellian propositions, structured intensions, or certain sets of equiformed sentence tokens are in this pigeonhole.

I think that what a t-clause names is sententially structured; in this chapter I attempt to make a case for that view. I carry on the argument within the framework of possible-worlds semantics. This is mostly for the sake of convenience, although I am sympathetic with the view that the framework is as good a one for natural language semantics as we have. In any case, the issues under discussion cut across various frameworks, and the arguments given could for the most part be adapted by, or applied to, those who favor other frameworks.

The chapter proceeds as follows: Section 1 reviews the main problem with the view that propositions have no structure. The problem is that attitudes turn out to be closed under logical consequence. A recent attempt by Robert Stalnaker to finesse this problem is reviewed and criticized.

Section 2 discusses a compromise between the two predominant views of propositions, one developed by Max Cresswell. I find Cresswell's view ingenious but inadequate to the data.

In Section 3, I argue that a reasonable view of propositions is that they have a structure that for all practical purposes is isomorphic to that of the sentences forming their canonical names.

Section 4 broaches the relation between semantic sententialism – the view that t-clauses name sententially structured entities – and psychological sententialism – the view that the psychological states underlying belief, desire, and other psychological attitude ascrip-

---

italicization is used in the way that Quine's corner quotes are usually used. Thus, I write things like 'John believes that S is true in a context c . . .', instead of '⌜John believes that S⌝ is true in a context c . . .'. When expressions are displayed, I dispense with such italicization. Single quotes are used to form names of expression types; double quotes are used for citation and for "shudder quotes."

tions are relations to sentence-like entities. I argue that, even if the psychological view should prove to be quite mistaken, this wouldn't cast doubt on the semantic doctrine.

However, I don't think that the psychological doctrine is wrong, loud protests by philosophers of mind notwithstanding. Section 5 addresses what is perhaps the most common objection to the psychological doctrine, one based on the claim that many of our beliefs are tacit and that this is inconsistent with psychological sententialism. I argue that this objection is based on a simplistic account of what it is to have an interesting psychological relation to a sentence. I think it important to rebut such objections, since they threaten a relatively simple and, I think, correct approach to the semantics of verbs such as 'believes'.

1. STRUCTURELESS PROPOSITIONS

An elegant construction of propositions proceeds as follows: We begin with a collection of things that "make sentences true." Perhaps we begin with possible worlds, or with what Barwise and Perry call situations. Call whatever truth makers we begin with *circumstances*. We then think of propositions as arbitrary sets of circumstances; a sentence S expresses the proposition consisting of just those circumstances that make it true.

On such a view of propositions, they don't have any internal structure; they are just sets.[3] In particular, they don't reflect the structure of the sentences that are used to form their names in 'that'-clauses.

This is perhaps clearest in possible-worlds semantics. Take the set of worlds S in which either Smith is not asleep or Jones is not asleep. If we identify propositions with sets of worlds, we will say that S is

the proposition that either Smith is not asleep or Jones is not asleep,
the proposition that it is not the case that: Smith is asleep and Jones is asleep,
the proposition that if Smith is asleep, then Jones is not.

3 I am oversimplifying here; it is not just the fact that propositions are identified with sets that makes it appropriate to say that no structure is ascribed to propositions. It is the way in which the identification is made. A view that identified propositions with sets of structured intensions, defining the sets in terms of equivalence classes themselves defined in terms of appropriate structural transformations on the intensions, would be a view that ascribed sentential structure to propositions.

On almost any account of sentential structure, the sentences used to form names of this proposition have different structures, since, on almost any such account, disjunctions, negations, and conditionals have distinct, mutually exclusive structures. These structural differences aren't reflected in any interesting sense in the set of worlds the sentences determine. Obviously, they don't contribute to the individuation of propositions, with, for example, disjunctive sentences naming propositions distinct from those named by negations. The set of worlds S is as much a disjunction as a negation. In fact, in possible-worlds semantics, being a disjunction (a negation) is just a matter of being the union of two sets of worlds (being a complement of some other set). So *every* proposition is both a negation and a disjunction.

It seems that those views about the nature of propositions that (a) don't award propositions a structure more or less like that of the sentences that express them and (b) say something definite in answer to questions like 'When do two t-clauses name the same proposition?' employ a construction like the above. So in considering whether propositions have sentential structure, it seems proper to begin by considering views that employ such constructions.

Such views seem invariably to fall prey to one or another version of the same objection: They require the attitudes to have a particular sort of closure under logical consequence, which they clearly don't have.[4]

Here is how the problem arises in the context of a simple possible-worlds semantics, in which a t-clause is taken to name the set of worlds in which its content sentence is true. (This set is often called the sentence's *intension*.) The argument

Barbers shave only those who do not shave themselves; the barber Jones shaved all the men who attacked Lionel; hence, Jones didn't attack Lionel

is valid. Since the truth of its premises ensures that of its conclusion, the worlds in which all its premises are true are exactly the worlds

---

4 The relevant notion of logical consequence varies according to the construction and the associated semantics. For example, the notion of logical consequence in situation semantics (see Barwise and Perry 1983) is interestingly different from the account associated with standard possible-worlds semantics. For a discussion of this, as well as objections to situation semantics along the lines of that in the text, see Cresswell (1985), Soames (1985), and Soames (1987a).

in which all the premises and the conclusion are true. Thus, the intension of

Barbers shave only those who do not shave themselves, and the barber Jones shaved all the men who attacked Lionel

is the intension of

Barbers shave only those who do not shave themselves, and the barber Jones shaved all the men who attacked Lionel, and Jones didn't attack Lionel.

So in a simple possible-worlds semantics, it turns out to be a truth of logic that

Whoever believes that (barbers shave only those who do not shave themselves, and the barber Jones shaved all the men who attacked Lionel), believes that (barbers shave only those who do not shave themselves, and the barber Jones shaved all the men who attacked Lionel, and Jones didn't attack Lionel).

This doesn't seem to be a truth, much less a logical one.

The point is perfectly general and can be made with respect to any valid argument: In such a semantics, believing (saying, deducing, desiring, etc.) the conjunction of the premises of a valid argument is the same as believing (saying, etc.) the conjunction of the argument's premises and its conclusion. This is simply a consequence of the facts that logically equivalent sentences are true in the same worlds and that a t-clause in such semantics names the set of worlds in which its content sentence is true. A special case of the problem is that in which the premise and conclusion of the argument are necessary truths, as in: $1 > 0$; thus, every integer greater than 1 can be uniquely decomposed into powers of primes.

Suppose we wished to preserve the view that t-clauses name sets of worlds. Then, I think, we would have to adopt one of two strategies to deal with the above problem. First, we could say that, although t-clauses name sets of possible worlds, they do not invariably name the set of worlds determined by their content sentences. For example, we might say that 'that $1 > 0$' usually names not the proposition that $1 > 0$ (viz., the set of all worlds), but the proposition that '$1 > 0$' expresses a necessary truth. If we said this, we could placate the intuition that Mary may believe that $1 > 0$ although she does not believe that every integer greater than 1 can be uniquely decomposed into powers of primes. We could say that one or both of the ascriptions ascribe to Mary a belief, not in a necessary truth about numbers, but in a contingent truth, that a certain sentence expresses a necessary truth. Since the propositions are different, Mary might believe one and not the other.

The second strategy for defending the view that propositions are sets of worlds would say that we tend to make certain kinds of mistakes about what people believe. An extreme (and implausible) version of this strategy would simply insist that *if* Mary believes that $1 > 0$, then she does indeed believe the fundamental theorem of number theory. We are simply mistaken (perhaps as a result of Mary's own mistakes in characterizing what she believes) if we say she believes the one and not the other. As we shall see, there are more subtle (as well as more plausible) versions of this strategy that the advocate of propositions as sets of possible worlds can use.

Stalnaker (1984) has tried to defend the view that t-clauses name sets of worlds by combining these two strategies. Calling our problem the problem of deduction, Stalnaker writes:[5]

There are two... parts to the strategy I am suggesting for treating the problem of deduction. The first... begins with the observation that it may be a nontrivial problem to see what proposition is expressed by a given sentence.... If sentence *s* expresses (according to the standard rules) proposition *P*, then it [also determines]... the proposition that *s* expresses *P*. In cases of ignorance of necessity and equivalence, I am suggesting, it is the second proposition that is the object of doubt and investigation.... For some examples, pointing this out would be sufficient to reconcile necessity with the possibility of ignorance. If someone is ignorant of the fact that all ophthalmologists are eye doctors, this is probably because he is ignorant of the meaning of one of the words in the statement. (pp. 84–5)

This proposal does not really deal with the *general* problem raised above. It is very implausible to think that someone who we would be inclined to say believes that

(A) Barbers shave only those who do not shave themselves, and the barber Jones shaved all the men who attacked Lionel

---

5 The following citations are from passages in which Stalnaker is discussing belief. Stalnaker distinguishes between an account of belief and an account of ascriptions of belief. His remarks on belief ascription are tentative; his remarks about belief itself are more fully developed. So, strictly speaking, the criticisms in the text apply to Stalnaker's views about belief, and not his views about belief ascription. But it seems fair to say that, if the objections in the text are cogent, Stalnaker does not have a strategy to deal with attitude ascriptions.

but who, we would be inclined to say, fails to believe that

(B) Barbers shave only those who do not shave themselves, and the barber Jones shaved all the men who attacked Lionel, and Jones didn't attack Lionel

must fail to see what the sentences say, or be suffering from linguistic confusion. This is perhaps clearest in the case of someone who already behaves like one who believes the two premises of the original argument but has never "put them together." If such a person is a normal speaker, it would surely be wrong to say that he didn't understand the relevant sentences. And his behavior, linguistic and otherwise, may make it obvious that, taking each sentence individually, he knows what it says and believes it true. He may, for example, have a stable set of dispositions to behave as if barbers shave only those who shave themselves, respond affirmatively to the question 'Do barbers shave only non-self-shavers?' and so on.

Suppose that such a person asks himself whether the argument is valid, and is unsure. We don't want to say that he thereby loses his understanding of the sentences. And it seems quite willful to say that, by asking whether the argument is valid, he thereby loses a belief. But this person doesn't seem to be much different from one who (as we would normally put it) understands (A) and (B) but can only use (A) to express his beliefs. Such a poor devil believes what the sentences say, but has simply failed to draw the slightly unobvious consequences of his beliefs. He hasn't put things together.

This last remark is at the core of Stalnaker's second strategy for dealing with the problem of deduction. Stalnaker does not deny that someone who has belief (A) also has belief (B). Instead, he sharply distinguishes between the states

believing *p* and *q*

and

(believing *p*) and (believing *q*),

denying that being in the second implies being in the first. Stalnaker argues as follows: It is somewhat more difficult to have belief (A) [and thus to have belief (B)] than you might think. Simply having the beliefs naturally expressed by the subsentences of (A) does not necessarily do the job. One must integrate these beliefs, a nontrivial

13

matter: This requires coordinating and harmonizing the different complex dispositions to behave that, ultimately, are these beliefs. The cases in which we are inclined to say that someone has belief (A) but not belief (B) are actually cases in which belief (A) is not present, but rather only the belief that

Barbers shave only those who do not shave themselves

and the belief that

The barber Jones shaved all the men who attacked Lionel.

Here is how Stalnaker (1984) puts all this. Note that for Stalnaker a basic notion for explaining belief is that of a belief state, a state whose content is a set of worlds. A person believes a proposition p if it is entailed by (i.e., true in all the worlds in) one of his belief states:

The rational dispositions that a person has at one time [may] arise from several different belief states. . . . an agent may at one time be in separate, even incompatible belief states. . . . it may be a nontrivial problem to put separate beliefs together into a single coherent system. . . . There may be propositions that I would believe if I put together my separate systems of beliefs, but which, as things stand, hold in none of them. These are the propositions whose truth might be discovered by a purely deductive inquiry. . . . The thesis [is] that acquiring deductive knowledge is putting one's separate belief states together. (pp. 83–7)

Presumably, to integrate belief states a and b is to get into a belief state whose content is the intersection of a and b. In general, when one makes a deduction from things one previously believed, one integrates states entailing the premises of the deduction.

There is a problem with this solution. When a collection of premises entails distinct propositions p and q, one may see one entailment, but not the other. It is difficult to see how Stalnaker can account for this.

Here is an example. Smith begins to inquire as to who attacked Lionel. He suspects both Jones and Anderson. After some research, he comes to hold the following beliefs, each of which we may suppose constitutes the content of one of his belief states:

(C) Barbers shave only those who do not shave themselves,
(D) The barber Jones shaved all those who attacked Lionel,
(E) Anderson shaves himself.

At first Smith does not see that he has ruled out Anderson. But after a while he deduces that Anderson didn't attack Lionel.

14

On Stalnaker's view, Smith must have done this by integrating the belief states corresponding to (C), (D), and (E). No proper subset of (C) through (E) entails that Anderson didn't do it, and we may fairly assume that none of Smith's other belief states are relevant here. So it is hard to see how Smith could have arrived at his belief, save by putting (C) through (E) together. But if he did this, then he was in a belief state that entails that Jones did not attack Lionel. So he must have believed this too. But he need not have such a belief. He may continue to suspect Jones, and certainly need have no dispositions to behavior that indicate such a belief.

One might be tempted to defend Stalnaker as follows: What Smith did was to integrate his belief states sequentially. Perhaps he first integrated (C) and (D) and thereby came to be in a state whose content is given by

(F) No one who shaves himself attacked Lionel.

Then Smith integrated this state with (E), thereby deducing that Anderson didn't do it, without ever deducing that Jones didn't do it.

The problem with this is that, when Smith integrated (C) and (D), the state he was thereby in was one whose exact content is given by the conjunction of (C) and (D), not by (F). But (C) and (D) entail that Jones didn't do it. So we still don't have an account of how Smith could deduce one consequence of (C) through (E) without the others.

Since there doesn't seem to be any way to explain how Smith got from (C), (D), and (E) to his belief about Anderson, save via the integration of the relevant states, Stalnaker seems to be stuck with the view that Smith knows that the barber didn't do it. This strikes me as improbable.

In a somewhat different context, Stalnaker (1984) considers accepting such improbable consequences: "William III of England believed, in 1700, that England could avoid a war with France. But avoiding a war with France entails avoiding a nuclear war with France. Did William III believe England could avoid a nuclear war? . . . I am not sure whether it would be literally incorrect to say that William III [did]." But Stalnaker eventually shies away from the idea, suggesting that "perhaps for it to be true that x believes that P, it is necessary that x understand the proposition that P, or that x have entertained the proposition that P" (pp. 88–9).

If we apply this suggestion to the problem about deduction, we would say that, for it to be true that Smith deduced that Jones did not attack Lionel, it must be true that Smith understands or has entertained the proposition that Jones did not attack Lionel. It is not clear how this helps. It seems that Smith could make his deduction concerning Anderson while entertaining the proposition that Jones did not attack Lionel and still not notice that it was a consequence of (C) through (E).

Incidentally, Stalnaker's suggestion has a rather odd result in the case of William III. On Stalnaker's view, the proposition that England can avoid war with France is the conjunctive proposition that England can avoid war with France and England can avoid nuclear war with France. This is just an example of the fact that, in a possible-worlds framework, if p entails q, then p is identical with the conjunction of p and q. So William understood and entertained, and thus believed, the proposition that England could avoid war with France and it could avoid nuclear war with France. At least he did given that he had these attitudes to the proposition that he could avoid war *simpliciter*. It sounds just as strange to say that William had the conjunctive belief as to say that he believed that England could avoid nuclear war. Furthermore, if, from the fact that one has entertained p and q, it follows that one has entertained p and entertained q (understood p and understood q) – something that many would agree to – then Stalnaker's suggestion does not block the consequence it is intended to block.[6]

Stalnaker's problems with deduction are pretty typical of the problems one runs into if one takes the semantic objects of the attitudes to be unstructured. Given this, we have a reason – not demonstrative, but a reason nonetheless – for supposing that propositions have a structure that, to some extent, apes that of the sentences expressing them.

2. STRUCTURED INTENSIONS

Perhaps there are inferences that things with beliefs cannot help but make. For example, perhaps it is true that no one can believe that

---

6 Scott Soames (1987a) stresses the problems these sorts of distribution principles raise for accounts that take propositions to be unstructured or "partly structured." In arriving at the views about structure and propositions that I defend here, I have been influenced by Soames's criticisms of my own earlier views.

snow is white and grass is blue without believing that snow is white and believing that grass is blue. Perhaps any sentence of the form

For any x: If x believes that A and B, then x believes that A and x believes that B

expresses a necessary truth. If so, then in some sense, things with beliefs can't help making an inference that we might call conjunction reduction.

One might argue that there are not very many inferences like this. If you have taught propositional logic, you are probably inclined toward this view. Most students at first don't see the validity of very obvious inferences. For example, they don't see that, from the claim that if the Sox win the Series, Rice will have gone 15 for 18, and Rice will not go 15 for 18, it follows that the Sox won't win the Series. It is not for any want of linguistic understanding that students are unable to draw these inferences. Clearly, students understand, even believe, that

The Sox will win only if Rice goes 15 for 18, and Rice won't.

And they understand

The Sox will win only if Rice goes 15 for 18, and Rice won't, and the Sox won't win.

But they don't believe this.

Thus, whatever account we give of propositions, it has to be one that makes pretty fine grained distinctions among them. For example, it will have to assign one thing to 'that'-clauses with content sentences of the form

If A, then B; but not B

and another to ones with content sentences of the form

If A, then B; not B; not A,

even though the sentences are logically equivalent. For as we just saw, it is not only possible, but common, for someone to believe that (if A, then B; but not B), without believing that (if A, then B; not B; and not A). In general, if it is just *possible* that

x believes that A

be true while

x believes that B

not be true, then we have to assign the terms *that A* and *that B* different things.[7]

What these observations seem to show is that the structure of two t-clauses has a bearing on whether they name the same thing. In general, if the clauses have distinct enough structures, they name distinct things, even if their content sentences are logically equivalent. And it does not take all that much for the structures of two sentences to be distinct enough. The structures of sentences of the forms

A and *B*   *B* and *A*

may not be different enough to require that they name different things on the above grounds, but arguably the structures of

not(*A* and *B*)   not *A* or not *B*

are.

In the preceding paragraphs, the examples have had to do with sentential structure induced by sentential connectives. I hope it will be granted that it is equally plausible that other aspects of sentential structure – in particular, quantificational structure and the presence of terms and predicates – are reflected in the individuation of propositions. Reading such structure into propositions, after all, is the natural way of blocking the identification of what is named by 'that $2 + 2 = 4$' and 'that $7 - 5 = 2$', or of the proposition that all the men here are self-shaving men who shave none who shave themselves with the proposition that there are no men here.

This makes the hypothesis – propositions named by t-clauses of English have a structure more or less like that of sentences of English – a reasonable place to start theorizing. How much like that of sentences? What we have said so far suggests an extreme answer: If the structure of the sentences S and T are distinct, so are the proposition that S and the proposition that T. The sort of structure in question here is (more or less) that which an adequate grammar for English would assign to the sentences S and T.

This sort of answer has had a number of advocates.[8] In discussing

---

7 If you formalize this argument, you see that you need to assume that t-clauses are rigid. This doesn't seem to invalidate the argument. It is also assumed here that, barring any ambiguity in *A* and *B*, the t-clauses will not turn out to be ambiguous.

8 Besides the view of Cresswell discussed below, views along these lines have been suggested in Carnap (1947), Church (1954), and Lewis (1972).

it, we will find it useful to have a more or less specific version of the proposal before us. Since we have been working within a possible-worlds framework, let's spell out some of the details of a possible-worlds version of this approach.

Consider, then, the view that identifies propositions with structured intensions. A structured intension is what you get if you take the phrase structure marker (or PSM) for a sentence – that is, the output of a grammar, which gives the syntactic structure of a sentence – and replace the expressions at the base with their intensions, and the expressions at other nodes with intensions determined by the intensions below. For example, suppose the PSM for a sentence of the form *A and B* is as follows:

(M)

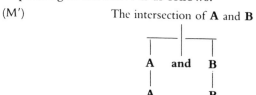

(I am pretending for simplicity that *A* and *B* themselves are structureless.) For the purposes of this section, let's indicate the intension of an expression by boldfacing. Then the structured intension corresponding to the above is as follows:

(M′)   The intersection of **A** and **B**

```
          ┌────┼────┐
          A   and   B
          │         │
          A         B
```

I will sometimes speak of (M′) as an interpretation of (M). [There is an ambiguity in the use of 'phrase structure marker'. Sometimes it is (a) used to name structures that are the output of phrase structure rules and transformations, sometimes (b) the result of inserting lexical items in a PSM in sense (a). Above, and very often below, it is used in sense (b). When I use the term in sense (a), I try to be explicit about this.]

A PSM has something like the structure of an ordered set, as the linguist's practice of naming PSMs with labeled bracketing makes clear. Nothing would be lost if we simply identified PSMs with very complicated ordered sets. Taking a sentence to be a PSM, it is not too great a distortion to say that a sentence is a sort of ordered *n*-tuple, and the structured intension of the sentence is a corresponding ordered set, with expressions replaced by intensions.

Once we start thinking of a PSM as a set, natural simplifications of the view that propositions are PSMs suggest themselves. For example, a natural simplification is to think of the structured intension that a t-clause names as containing only the intensions of the terminal vocabulary from the PSM. Instead of thinking of the proposition that *A* and *B* as containing the intensions

A, B, and, the intersection of **A** and **B**,

we could think of it just containing **A**, **B**, and **and**. In this case, we would think of the structure of the structured intension as telling us how constituents are to be combined to yield the overall intension the sentence determines. Proceeding in this way, we might take the set

$\langle$**and**, $\langle$**A, B**$\rangle\rangle$

to correspond to (M′) and to be what 'that *A* and *B*' names. In what follows, I presuppose that such encoding of tree structure into set theoretic structure has already been done.

Such a view individuates propositions very finely indeed. Consider the propositions that *A* and *B* and that *B* and *A*, for some sentences *A* and *B*. So long as *A* and *B* aren't necessarily equivalent, the structured intensions $\langle$**and**, $\langle$**A, B**$\rangle\rangle$ and $\langle$**and**, $\langle$**B, A**$\rangle\rangle$ with which the view identifies the propositions are distinct. Likewise, the view distinguishes the propositions that $7 + 5 = 12$, that $5 + 7 = 12$, that $12 = 7 + 5$, and that $12 = 5 + 7$. This is a result of reading the *structure* of the sentences onto the propositions. It doesn't matter that the view picks intensions as semantic values. The same would result if we were to, say, make Frege's senses the values of '5', '7', and '12'.

It's actually a little misleading to characterize this approach as one that gets a proposition from a sentence by interpreting *the* structure that a grammar assigns to the sentence. Advocates of this approach often allow that we might have one set of rules to generate the "surface structures" of the language, and a second set of rules that map these structures to some others ("logical forms"), which are what get interpreted to yield propositions.

Even without being very specific about grammatical details or about the relation between surface forms and logical ones, I think it's possible to evaluate this sort of approach. For one thing, the sort of structures that get interpreted are always quite closely related to surface structures. Usually, what is involved in going from surface structure to logical form is a bit of pruning of the surface structures, along (sometimes) with a bit of regimentation, not unlike that involved in translating from English to one or another predicate logic. Almost invariably, the structures we wind up interpreting bear a striking resemblance to the sentences of one or another enrichment of first-order logic.

So even without considering the exact details of the approach, I think it's possible to anticipate most of the objections that might be made to this sort of view. Essentially, we ask ourselves what objections might be made to the view that propositions have the structure of canonical regimentations into a (suitable enrichment of a) first-order language.

I think that a view that reads this much structure into propositions is defensible, and in the next section I will defend it against some objections. But first I want to discuss a version of the propositions-are-structured-intensions view elaborated by Cresswell (1985). Although I don't agree with everything Cresswell says on the subject, it is instructive to consider his view.

In some ways, Cresswell's view is a compromise between the view that t-clauses name wholly unstructured entities like sets of worlds and the view that they name entities with the exact structure of a sentence. The most important claim Cresswell makes is that t-clauses are ambiguous: Sometimes a t-clause in an attitude ascription names just a set of worlds; sometimes it names a wholly structured intension; sometimes it names something in between.

Cresswell thinks that he can explain a good many puzzling facts with this view. For example, he objects to Barwise and Perry's (1983) view that it makes the substitution of

that A and B and C

for

that C and B and A

logically valid. Sometimes, Cresswell argues, the substitution leads from truth to falsehood. An example of a context in which this is so is 'John deduced that . . .'. Roughly, Cresswell argues that, if

John is given that C and A and B, he might immediately deduce that C and B and A, but only after a while deduce that A and B and C. So it might be true at three o'clock that John has deduced that C and B and A, but not that he has deduced that A and B and C.

Cresswell thinks it a virtue of his view that it doesn't require us to say that whoever has deduced that A and B and C has deduced that C and B and A. Now, it seems clear that the two t-clauses are often substitutable *salva veritate* – for example, after 'says'. It's pretty clear that it is only rarely, if ever, true that someone *says* that A and B and C, but doesn't say that C and B and A. If by postulating an ambiguity Cresswell can explain these and other puzzling facts, and there's no compelling reason to reject the claim of an ambiguity, then Cresswell will have given a very persuasive account of t-clauses.

Cresswell works under the assumption that English is a categorial language.[9] Each sentence S of such a language clearly determines

9 It is possible to follow the text without knowing anything of categorial grammar. But for completeness' sake, here are some remarks about the sort of system Cresswell works in.

In the sort of categorial language in which Cresswell works, each expression is of one syntactic type. These types are built up from the basic types 0, the type of sentences, and 1, the type of names. There is one way to build up types: Given any types $t_1, \ldots, t_n$ and s, there is the type $(s/t_1, \ldots, t_n)$. This is the type of expressions that combine with expressions of types $t_1, \ldots, t_n$ to form an expression of type s.

For example, 'Jane' is of type 1, as is 'Mick'. 'is happy' is of type (0/1): It combines with something of type 1 – a name – and yields something of type 0, a sentence. Likewise for 'is sad'. Sentences such as 'Jane is happy' are of type 0. And the connective 'and' is of type (0/00), which is to say that it takes two arguments of type 0 – i.e., takes two sentences – and yields a sentence in return.

Such languages have a large number of syntactic types but a small number of grammatical rules. For our purposes we need only the following rule: If a is an expression of type $(s/t_1, \ldots, t_n)$, and $b_1, \ldots, b_n$ are expressions of, respectively, types $t_1, \ldots, t_n$, then $\langle a, b_1, \ldots, b_n \rangle$ is an expression of type s. For example, using the expressions above, we can construct the complex sentence

$\langle$ and, $\langle$ $\langle$ is happy, Jane$\rangle$, $\langle$ is sad, Mick$\rangle$ $\rangle$ $\rangle$.

And we may suppose that this, or a version labeled with the appropriate syntactic types, gives the syntactic structure of the English sentence 'Jane is happy and Mick is sad'. (In the text, I sometimes add angled brackets to indicate grouping.)

In a categorial language, semantics neatly recapitulates syntax. For each of the basic syntactic types, there is a corresponding domain of interpretations of items of that type. For 1, the type of terms, there is I, which is the set of individuals; for 0, the type of sentences, there is P, the set of sets of possible worlds – call this the set of propositions. Each of the complex functional syntactic types is two intensions. It determines a wholly structured intension, which results from replacing each simple expression in S with its interpretation, and it determines the wholly structureless intension, which results from applying functions to arguments in the structured intension. Thus, the sentence

⟨and, ⟨⟨is happy, Jane⟩, ⟨is sad, Mick⟩⟩⟩,

which can be thought of as a categorial version of 'Jane is happy and Mick is sad', determines the wholly structured intension

⟨and, ⟨⟨is happy, Jane⟩, ⟨is sad, Mick⟩⟩⟩.

It also determines the wholly structureless intension of just the set of worlds in which Jane is happy and Mick is sad.

Actually, a sentence will generally determine more than two intensions. Let p be the set of worlds in which Jane is happy, q those in which Mick is sad. The sentence we have been discussing determines the intensions

⟨and, ⟨p,⟨is sad, Mick⟩⟩⟩,
⟨and, ⟨⟨is happy, Jane⟩, q⟩⟩,
⟨and, ⟨p,q⟩⟩,

as well as the two mentioned above. In general, if we start with the most structured intension a sentence determines, thinking of it as a tree, then the rest of the intensions it determines are obtained by "pruning" away its branches (see footnote 11). I will call the collection of all the intensions that a sentence determines its family.

As noted earlier, Cresswell does not simply propose that a t-clause names the wholly structured intension of its content sen-

---

interpreted by a corresponding function from semantic domains to a semantic domain. For example, corresponding to syntactic category (0/1) – the category of one-place predicates – is semantic category (P/I), the set of functions from individuals to propositions.

Each simple expression of a categorial language receives an interpretation from the appropriate category. For example, 'Jane' receives Jane Doe, 'is sad' receives the function that takes an individual to the set of worlds in which he is sad, and 'and' is interpreted as the function that takes propositions p and q and returns their conjunction (i.e., intersection).

In presenting Cresswell's views I have simplified them considerably. I note that given the above semantics Cresswell's view isn't strictly a view that associates structured intensions with t-clauses, at least as I explained the notion of a structured intension. For individuals like Jane Doe are (presumably) not intensions, but they are constituents of some of what Cresswell assigns to t-clauses. Broaden the notion of structured intension so that these are included.

tence. He claims that sometimes the intensional structure of a t-clause is relevant to the truth value of an ascription that involves it, but sometimes it is not.[10] We noted something that might seem to be evidence for this thesis: Expressions of the forms *that A and B* and *that B and A* seem to be sometimes intersubstitutable (after 'says', for example), and sometimes not (after 'deduces').

On Cresswell's account, 'that' turns out to be infinitely ambiguous. There is one 'that' which combines with a sentence to form a name of the structureless intension of the sentence. For each intension in the family of intensions determined by a sentence, there is a 'that' operator which combines with the sentence to form a name of the intension. Attitude verbs are each assigned a relation between individuals and intensions. For example (and simplifying somewhat), the assignment to 'says' is a function that takes an individual u and an intension s to the set of worlds in which u produces a sentence that has s as a member of its family of intensions.

Thus, the surface form

Jane says that Mick is sexy, and no rock star is sexy

is at least five ways ambiguous. It can be used to ascribe to Jane a relation to any of the five intensions in the family of its content sentence.[11]

---

10 Cresswell gives a positive argument for the view that t-clauses are ambiguous that I don't discuss here. The argument is ably criticized in Gupta and Savion (1987).

11 Here is how Cresswell characterizes t-clauses. The operator that forms the name of a wholly unstructured intension, 'that$_0$', is of the syntactic type (1/0). Where $t_1, \ldots, t_n$ are any syntactic categories, then *that $(0/t, \ldots t_n)t_1, \ldots t_n)$* is in category $(1/(0/t_1, \ldots, t_n)t_1, \ldots, t_n)$. The assignment to such an operator is a function that takes a sequence of arguments of appropriate types to that very sequence. "The idea is that any 'that' operates separately on expressions that by themselves can combine to form a sentence, making out of them a name of a sequence consisting of the meanings of the separate parts" (Cresswell 1985, p. 102). For example, **that((0/1)1)** is a function that takes a pair consisting of a one-place predicate intension x and an individual y and returns $\langle x,y \rangle$. The term

$\langle \text{that}_{((0/1)1)}\langle \text{is sad, Jane} \rangle \rangle$

refers to the result of applying **that((0/1)1)** to $\langle$ **is sad, Jane** $\rangle$, which is $\langle$ **is sad, Jane** $\rangle$. In general, if the syntactic type of a 'that'-operator is $(1/a_1 a_2, \ldots, a_n)$, then it names the function that takes a tuple $\langle \mathbf{b}_1, \ldots, \mathbf{b}_n \rangle$, each $\mathbf{b}_i$ a member of the semantic domain of a_i, to itself.

There is a minor problem here. Suppose that Jane says, 'seven is not even'. Cresswell himself (p. 85) suggests that, when we report,

It seems to me that there are two problems with this view. Suppose that Jane utters the sentence, 'Mick is sexy, and no rock star is sexy'. Abbreviate the constituent conjuncts of this sentence with 'M' and 'R', respectively. Surely it normally makes no difference to the truth of a report of Jane's dictum whether we say

(1) Jane said that M and R

or

(2) Jane said that R and M.

Unless circumstances are exceptional, either of these would be correct. Indeed, many would say no matter what the circumstances, (1) and (2) are equally correct reports.

Cresswell can accommodate this fact, but only at a rather high price. Consider, for example, the reading of (2) that takes its t-clause to be a name of

(3) $\langle$**and, R, M**$\rangle$.

Jane says that seven is not even,

our sentence should be capable of an interpretation stronger than this: Jane uttered a sentence that determines the intension

(1) $\langle$**not**, the empty set$\rangle$

– i.e., (very roughly) Jane uttered the negation of a sentence false in all worlds. Our report should be capable of the following interpretation: Jane uttered a sentence that determines the intension

(2) $\langle$**not**, $\langle$**is even, seven**$\rangle\rangle$.

In order for this to be the case, we have to be able to form a t-clause that names this intension. Cresswell does not give us the means to do this. What we have is the operator '$that_0$' and, for any categories $t_1, \ldots, t_n$, the operator $that(0/t_1, \ldots, t_n)t_1, \ldots, t_n$. Obviously, '$that_0$' won't do the trick. Neither will '$that_{(0/0)0}$'. We can use this to form

(3) $\langle that_{(0/0)0} \langle$**not**, $\langle$**is even, seven**$\rangle\rangle\rangle$.

But this names (1), not (2), since the 'that'-operator in question is sensitive only to the intension of '$\langle$**is even, seven**$\rangle$' as a whole, not to its structure – it is defined only for $\langle$**is even (seven)**$\rangle$, not for $\langle$**is even, seven**$\rangle$.

This is a problem of execution, since it can be corrected by sufficient complications in the syntax and semantics. A natural correction – the one Cresswell (1985, pp. 85–7) himself seems to intend and which I ascribe to him in the text – would inductively define a collection of 'that'-operators that would make a surface t-clause have one reading for each member of the family of intensions it determines. This is a slightly bothersome enterprise, since the definition has to capture just the structures that yield syntactically well formed sentences; or else, we make things like 'that Bob Mary smoke' well formed.

[This is the reading that treats the 'that' in (2) as being of the type (1/((0/00)00). See footnote 11 for an explanation.] This will be false, for Jane didn't utter a sentence that determines this intension. She uttered a sentence that determines

(4) ⟨and, M, R⟩.

And this is no more identical with (3) than ⟨1, 2, 3⟩ is identical with ⟨1, 3, 2⟩. None of the other intensions determined by 'M and R' is identical with (3) either.

It does no good to consider a reading that reads *more* structure into the t-clause. The same problem arises. The only reading of (2) on which it says something true is the reading on which its t–clause is a name of

(5) ⟨and(M,R)⟩.

[Here, the type of 'that' is (1/0).] This is the reading on which the t-clause names a wholly structureless intension.

But this is unfortunate, to say the least, for then the only reading of (2) on which it says something true is one that implies

(6) Jane said that Mick is sexy, and no rock star is sexy, and Mick is not a rock star.

The (unstructured) intension of the content sentence of (6) is the same as that of (2). But surely Jane did not say this.

Cresswell might point out that on his view there are readings of (6) not entailed by the reading of (2) true in the case we are discussing. This is correct, but it is not clear how this improves matters. I take it that the appeal to structured intensions is supposed to supply an account of attitude ascriptions that is more in accord with our intuitions than the account that makes them simply ascriptions of relations to structureless intensions. So it is surely fair to appeal to our intuitions, concerning what our sentences do and do not imply, in evaluating it. And surely we do have intuitions as to whether a normal use of (2) implies (6), or whether there is *some* sense in which the truth of (2) implies the truth of (6): Our intuitions are, I believe, that there is *no* sense in which the truth of (2) requires the truth of (6). Of course, perfectly analogous points can be made with respect to other attitude verbs. The point arises no matter what semantics we ascribe to them, as long as we follow the general pattern Cresswell suggests.

The point is not an isolated one. Similar arguments can be made with respect to ascriptions such as the following:

Jane said that M or R,

which seems to be equivalent to

Jane said that R or M.

Likewise,

Jane said that Mick ate a bun in the train at rush hour,

which seems equivalent to

Jane said that Mick ate a bun at rush hour in the train.

Or

Jane said that a happy, fat man was dead,

which would seem to be equivalent to

Jane said that a man who was dead was fat and happy.

For good measure, we can include

Jane said that a man who wore a hat visited her office

and

Jane said that a man who visited her office wore a hat.

This line of argument seems to show that attitude verbs display kinds of sensitivity (or insensitivity) to structure that Cresswell's theory does not account for. Insofar as it is the aim of Cresswell's theory to explain how it is that "attitude verbs can be sensitive in varying degrees to the structure of the sentences which follow them" (Cresswell 1985, p. 6), this seems to be a serious failure of the theory. Arguably, the most puzzling fact about attitude verbs and the structure of the sentences they look at is the fact that some verbs seem to be sensitive only to some logical transformations. For example, 'says' seems indifferent to permutation around 'and', but will not, in general, allow substitution of the form

Ba, and no B is A, and not Aa

for the logically equivalent form

Ba, and no B is A.

27

I am hard pressed to see any good reason for positing an ambiguity in t-terms beyond this fact. *If* this sort of phenomenon is to be explained in terms of an ambiguity, it is not the sort of ambiguity Cresswell invokes.

One problem with Cresswell's account, then, is that the ambiguity he posits doesn't give a satisfactory explanation of the phenomena it ought to explain. Another problem is that the ambiguity claim, at least in the strong version in which Cresswell makes it, is dubious. Consider

that Mick is sexy and Jane is repulsed.

On Cresswell's view, this is five ways ambiguous. What evidence is there, in the actual speech and intuitions of English speakers, that it is ambiguous at all, much less in Cresswell's five ways? Note that the ambiguity in question has a considerable effect on truth conditions and implication relations. No two of the readings are truth conditionally equivalent; the readings vary considerably in the sorts of inferences they sanction. If we think that truth conditions have something to do with semantic competence – a view to which Cresswell, who thinks that semantic competence is knowledge of truth conditions (see, e.g., Cresswell 1978), is committed – we should expect such a wide-ranging ambiguity to be reflected in the intuitions of speakers. It does not seem to be.

Because it posits these ambiguities, Cresswell's view seems vulnerable to versions of the argument reviewed in Section 1. Abbreviate as follows:

B: Barbers shave only those who don't shave themselves, and Jones the barber shaved all Lionel's attackers,
A: Anderson shaves himself,
C: Anderson didn't attack Lionel,
D: Jones didn't attack Lionel.

On Cresswell's view,

(a) Jane said that *B* and *A*

has a reading on which it entails (a reading of)

(b) Jane said that (*B* and *A*) and *C*,

and (a) has another reading on which, while it does not entail (b), it does entail

(c) Jane said that (*B* and *D*) and *A*.

28

I doubt that much support for the validity of such inferences is to be found in the intuitions of speakers.

3. THE STRUCTURE OF PROPOSITIONS

To reject Cresswell's view is not to reject the view that 'that'-clauses name structured intensions. But one might think that part of the argument against Cresswell could be turned against any view that had t-clauses naming structured intensions, or anything else that was sententially structured.

The argument at the end of Section 2 pointed to the fact that certain pairs of t-clauses, such as

(P) that Mick is awake and Jane is asleep,
   that Jane is asleep and Mick is awake

seem to be in some important respect equivalent. They certainly seem to be intersubstitutable after 'says'. The natural explanation for this is that the two terms name the same thing. It is even possible to argue directly to this conclusion, provided appeals to common philosophical intuitions are allowed: *that S* names whatever *the proposition that S* names; but surely the proposition that Mick is awake and Jane is asleep is the proposition that Jane is asleep and Mick is awake. But the two t-clauses displayed above can't name the same thing, if they name wholly structured intensions. Thus, the view that they do name wholly structured intensions is wrong.

One response to this argument is to say that the t-clauses of (P) name *sets* of structured intensions; indeed, they name the same set. This sort of response concedes the claim of propositional identity but tries to hold onto the spirit of the view that t-clauses name wholly structured intensions. If we adopted such a view, we would define an equivalence relation ϵ on structured intensions and say that a t-clause *that A* named the set of those intensions i such that i bears ϵ to the structured intension of A. If an intension i bears ϵ to j if (but not only if) $i = \langle \textbf{and, A, B} \rangle$ and $j = \langle \textbf{and, B, A} \rangle$, then the t-clauses in (P) name the same thing.

There is a problem with the equivalence-class approach, as well as with the objection that inspires it. Even ignoring quotational contexts, pairs of t-clauses related as are the members of (P) do not seem to be *everywhere* intersubstitutable *salva veritate*. In fact, there is a kind of argument, suggested by Cresswell's example, that seems

29

to show that no structurally distinct t-clauses are invariably inter-substitutable. Applied to (P) it goes thus: A student is learning German (or, better, is learning logic in German). There is a dialogue whose natural translation is something like this:

– Jethro, suppose it is true that Mick is awake and Jane is asleep. Will it also be true that Jane is asleep and Mick is awake?
– Hmmm. Yes, it will be true that Jane is asleep and Mick is awake.

One argues that, although (abbreviating in the obvious way)

(1) The student deduces that J and M

is true,

(2) The student deduces that M and J

is not (Cresswell 1985, pp. 77–80). One can imagine generalizing this argument for any pair of structurally distinct t-clauses.

Is such an argument successful? One might be tempted to argue that 'deduces' is quotational and that the surface form *a deduces that S* is true iff what *a* names deduces the sentence S. But since the sentence the student deduces is not 'Jane is asleep and Mick is awake', but 'Jane schlaft und Mick ist aufgewacht', it seems that this is not an apt response. And for the case of the pair (P), it seems that the intuition concerning the distribution of truth values to (1) and (2) is quite widely shared. So it would seem that, at least in the case of (P), the argument is successful in blocking the claim that the members of pairs of t-clauses like (P) can always be substituted for each other without changing truth value.

This provides a positive reason for denying that the proposition that J and M is the proposition that M and J, for it provides a reason for saying that you can do something to the first proposition (deduce it) without doing it to the second. If the argument generalizes, we have a positive reason for saying that any structural difference in the sentences in a t-clause marks a difference in what they name.

It might be said that the argument does not completely generalize, in that there are sentences A and B that determine distinct structured intensions but that are such that

The student deduced that A

and

The student deduced that B

30

are necessarily equivalent. Perhaps this might be urged for a pair such as

that an old, feeble man coughed

and

that a feeble, old man coughed.

Perhaps; perhaps not. Suppose the argument does not generalize to show that *any* t-clauses whose content sentences are structurally distinct fail to be intersubstitutable. Specifically, let us suppose for the sake of argument that the last-mentioned pair of t-clauses are intersubstitutable.

Still, why not take a difference in the PSMs of t-clauses' content sentences to suffice for a difference in what they name? [Here and below, 'PSM' is used in sense (a), as explained in Section 2.] We can say that the sort of phenomena discussed above – that 'says' is closed under 'conjunction permutation', whereas 'deduces' is not; that all verbs of attitude are closed under the 'adjectival permutation' displayed by the 'coughed' sentences – is explained by reference to the relations named by these verbs. The fact that, necessarily, one believes (hopes, etc.) a proposition p iff one believes (hopes, etc.) q doesn't *require* that $p = q$.

On this treatment, most putative facts about the "logic of assertion" – for example, the putative fact that

a said that A and B

entails

a said that B and A

as well as putative facts about the "logic" of other propositional attitude verbs, are not facts that we should expect to fall out of an account of the nature of propositions (viz., out of an account of the nature of what t-clauses name). Rather, most such facts, if they emerge in the course of an account of the semantics of attitude ascriptions at all, will emerge only in the accounts of the relations named by individual attitude verbs.

Such a view of the bearing of a t-clause's structure on the individuation of what it names seems the most reasonable one. We have seen that most structural differences between t-clauses apparently require a difference in what they name (assuming that an

31

ambiguity view like Cresswell's has been ruled out). And there aren't *that* many sorts of structural differences that call forth an intuition of propositional identity, anyway. All the examples that I can think of, of structurally dissimilar t-clauses whose content sentences are commonly thought to "say the same thing," seem to involve one of the following: conjunction permutation, disjunction permutation, permutation of adjectival or adverbial modifiers; movement of material into or out of a relative clause; permutation of arguments around "obviously" symmetric predicates (e.g., '=') or function signs ('+'). So it's not as if, given a verb such as 'believes' or 'says', there will be an indefinite, open-ended collection of t-clauses that are intersubstitutable after the verb, *salva veritate*.

Still, I expect that people will object that I'm cutting the propositions too finely. Let me briefly address two such objections. First, let me return to the intuition that (as I sometimes hear it put) this view must be wrong because to believe that A and B is to believe that B and A, and thus the objects of those beliefs, the proposition that A and B and the proposition that B and A, have to be identical.

I have already given a reason, having to do with deduction, for thinking that this intuition is incorrect. And construed as a demonstrative argument, the intuition really won't do. First of all, the premise seems a little question begging. It sounds as if it is simply the claim: that A and B is that B and A. Perhaps the argument is intended thus: Necessarily, for any x: x believes that A and B iff x believes that B and A. Thus, the proposition that A and B is the proposition that B and A.

But then the argument isn't valid. I agree that, of necessity, whoever believes (viz., has the relation named by 'believes' to) the proposition that A and B believes that B and A. This is an interesting fact about belief and the two propositions. It doesn't follow that the propositions are identical. To argue in this way is something like arguing thus: Necessarily, a number has the same cardinality as omega iff it has the same cardinality as omega + 1. So omega = omega + 1.

I have found that, even after you point out that the conclusion of this argument doesn't follow from its premise, people persist in giving it. So let me address what I take to be the underlying worry. This is that in some sense the belief that A and B must be the very

32

same belief as the belief that B and A. But it couldn't be, if beliefs are relations to propositions, and the propositions are distinct.

Now, the expression 'the belief that so and so' strikes me as ambiguous. One way of reading it is as 'what one believes, when one believes that so and so'. Another way of reading it is as 'the sort of state one is in, when one believes that so and so', with this capable of further disambiguation, depending upon the sort we are interested in.

Suppose we take 'the belief that A and B' in the first sense. As I observed above, I don't deny that what one believes, when (a) one believes that A and B, is any different from what one believes when (b) one believes that B and A. I claim that, necessarily, (a) obtains iff one is related to the proposition that A and B *and* to the proposition that B and A. The same goes for (b). So in this sense I don't deny that the beliefs are the same. I simply see relation to two things where others see relation to one thing.

Suppose we take 'the belief that A and B' in the sense of 'sort of state one is in when one believes that A and B', and suppose that the sort in question is psychological, in some broad sense. Then it in no way follows that the belief that A and B is different from the belief that B and A, given the distinctness of the propositions that A and B and that B and A. There is no reason at all that we might not characterize the same psychological state (in some broad sense of psychological state) by reference to a relation to different propositions. After all, we characterize the same number by referring to different sums, as in $2 + 4 = 1 + 5$; we may characterize the same physical state using different descriptions, and so on.

Another objection to the proposal is this. Note that certain free-standing 'wh'-phrases, like 'what I say' and 'what Jane thinks about John's behavior', could be said to be, or at least have the semantical properties of, singular terms. Sentences like

What I said was crazy; don't take it seriously,
What I said was that Bob is a donkeybottoms

strongly suggest such an account. If they are to be treated like singular terms, then presumably they are of the ilk of definite descriptions – 'what I say' would get regimented as 'the p such that I said p'. So the last sentence displayed above is regimented as an identity.

If this is correct, then seemingly indisputable judgments about what I said, when I uttered 'Bob is sad and Mary is happy', conflict with the treatment of t-clauses we are contemplating. If I uttered this, then surely it is true both that

What I said is that Bob is sad and Mary is happy

and that

What I said is that Mary is happy and Bob is sad.

If these are identities, then there is trouble brewing on the treatment I'm suggesting, since the t-clauses on that treatment name distinct structured intensions.

The problem with this objection is that it is not clear that the 'wh'-phrases really are functioning as terms in these examples. If asked about John's behavior, I might say that what I think about John's behavior is that it is rather immature. Arguably, this is true, just so long as I think it. This is so even though there are many other (contextually relevant) things I think about his behavior. If so, the 'wh'-phrase isn't functioning as a definite description; it is, instead, functioning like 'the brother of JFK' in 'Teddy Kennedy is the brother of JFK'. In this sentence, the phrase 'the brother of JFK' appears to be an *in*definite description. This seems a perfectly plausible thing to say about the behavior of 'what I think of John's behavior' in 'What I think of John's behavior is that it is immature'. I am inclined to think that much the same thing can be said about 'what I said'.

In Sections 1–3 I have tried to make a case for the view that, generally, the structure of a t-clause's content sentence is reflected in the individuation of propositions: In general, t-clauses whose PSMs differ name different things. In developing the argument for this view I have tacitly assumed that the way that this structure will be reflected in propositions is by literally being there; for a structured intension literally has the structure of its associated PSM.

Since I intend to hold onto this assumption, and since it might appear somewhat gratuitous, I should say something in its defense. Someone might observe that, even if the structure of a t-clause is reflected in the individuation of propositions, it doesn't follow that the propositions themselves have any structure at all. They might, for all that, turn out to be Twinkies – so long as, for example, no Twinkie named by *that A and B* is named by *that not A*.

I suppose. There are several questions we might ask about propositions. One is the question Under what conditions do two t-clauses name the same proposition? Another is, Are propositions entities sui generis, or are they constructions out of other entities, say syntactic structures and possible referents of linguistic items? The remarks about Twinkies are relevant to the second question. Here I am concerned mostly with the first. For the purposes of doing semantics, the best course, if we are convinced that certain aspects of sentential structure are reflected in the individuation of propositions, is to read those aspects right into the proposition itself.

Although I have defended the view that propositions reflect the structure of the sentences that express them, I don't mean to suggest that we will, or should, end up with a theory on which the structure of a proposition is invariably isomorphic to the surface structure of the t-clauses that name it. For example, it would not conflict with anything in the argument of the preceding sections if we were to embellish on the structure provided by a PSM for the purposes of semantics. For example, we *might* find it useful to read distinct structures into what is named by t-clauses of the forms *that aRa* and *that aRb* even though the PSMs of their content sentences will, in most syntactic theories, turn out to be the same. As mentioned in Section 2, we might find it useful or necessary, in order to get an adequate theory, to transform the structures of PSMs before using them to manufacture propositions. For example, we might want to do this in the case of idioms. Or it might be that in certain cases what structure we map a PSM onto will depend upon what lexical material is attached to the terminal nodes of the PSM.

These last remarks are relevant to an objection suggested by the following remarks of George Pitcher (1964):

It might seem obvious that . . . there must be one constituent of a proposition . . . corresponding to each main grammatical part of a sentence. . . . There is [however] a foreign language – I have just invented it – in which the proposition we express by saying 'the cat is on the mat' is expressed by the one-word sentence 'Catamat'. Are we to say that when a speaker of this new language says 'Catamat' he is expressing a proposition with only one constituent? But then how could that be the same proposition as the one we express by saying 'The cat is on the mat', since ours has three constituents? (p. 12)

As it stands, Pitcher's example is too underdeveloped to constitute much of a threat. Is this language one in which, for example,

'Dogamat' expresses the proposition that the dog is on the mat, 'Catapelt', that the cat is on the pelt, and so on? Then there probably are, in a nonarbitrary sense, three grammatical constituents of 'catamat', given that there are three grammatical constituents of 'the cat is on the mat'.

One might object that nonetheless it is certainly not *obvious* that, if sentences of different languages say (precisely) the same thing, then any semantically relevant reference made by one sentence is mirrored by such a reference in the other. This last condition seems to be required, on the view that the proposition a sentence expresses recapitulates, at a semantic level, the structure and constituency of the sentence. So it's not obvious that sentences of different languages that say precisely the same thing determine the same highly structured propositions.

If there were a large, varied body of fairly noncontroversial examples of this phenomenon – sentences intuitively saying the same thing but not making the same explicit references to individuals or properties – we would have a genuine objection to the view. If there were a limited number of examples, the most reasonable procedure would be to treat such examples either as being like idioms ('Henry kicked the bucket'), in that certain apparent references the sentence makes are not *semantically* relevant (i.e., not relevant to assessing what the sentence says), or as cases in which references are made, but made by expressions that occur at a level of logical syntax.

To my knowledge there are not all that many cases of sentences that clearly say the same thing but apparently involve different references. And the clear cases that do exist seem most plausibly treated in the manner of idioms. For example, consider reflexives in languages like French. A Frenchman who assertively utters 'Hespère se leve' says that Hesperus rises. It *looks* as if he makes two references to Venus in doing this, in order to say what he does by saying that the planet does a certain thing ("leving") to itself. It seems to me that the right thing to say about this case is that the appearance is, semantically, illusion and that 'se leve' is to be interpreted in these occurrences as a whole: Assign it whatever 'rises' is assigned in English. The upshot is that, at the level of logical form, the French and the English have the same structure, with expressions with the same semantic interpretations. There is nothing ad hoc about such a procedure in this case.

36

One might respond that it is not obvious from one example that we will always be able to assign comfortably the same structures to sentences that intuitively say the same thing. I grant that it is not obvious. But I don't see any reason to assume that we will not be able to do this. And, as I have tried to show, the idea that propositions are as structured as the sentences that express them has a good deal to recommend it.[12]

It seems correct to say, at a certain airy level of generality, that propositions mirror the structure of sentences that express them. We adopt this assumption for the balance of the book.

4. TWO SORTS OF SENTENTIALISM

A common story about attitudes and their ascription goes as follows: Ascriptions of propositional attitudes are relational. In an ascription *a believes that S* the clause *that S* functions as a term, the verb 'believes' as a relational predicate. The 'that'-clause names something that is in important ways structured like a sentence: It has constituents that correspond to terms and predicates, and it has a structure that to some extent apes that of the sentence in the t-clause.

Propositions – what t-clauses name – are objective, mind-independent entities. Their constituents are individuals and properties, or constructions from possible worlds (where such worlds are *not* creations of the mind), or some other nonpsychological sort of thing.

This doesn't mean that we can't have interesting psychological relations to propositions – after all, we believe them. But it's surely correct to think belief and the other attitudes, *qua* relations to a proposition, are relations that we have in virtue of some "more psychological" or "narrower" psychological state. Just as we assert the proposition that snow is white *by* uttering or writing a sentence, so we believe the proposition because we are in one or another psychological state. (This isn't to say that the state alone determines

12 In the final analysis, the claim that sentences that say the same thing determine the same structured intensions is an empirical, or quasi-empirical, hypothesis. It is not to be established by *a priori* argument; it might be refuted by the fact that it was not possible to construct a theory adequate to the data (such as our intuitions) that conformed to it. I have been trying to make the point that there does not seem to be evidence that makes it reasonable to reject the claim; earlier parts of this chapter give what I take to be positive evidence in its favor.

a proposition. In general, it is in virtue of being in a certain psychological state *and* in virtue of our contextual and historical situation that we believe a proposition.)

The story about attitudes and their ascription I am rehearsing holds that the psychological states underlying attitude ascriptions, those in virtue of which one gets related to a proposition, are themselves relational. In fact, they are relations to entities that are, in important ways, structured like sentences of natural language. In particular, these entities have constituents that correspond to terms and predicates, as well as a structure that in one way or another apes the structure of sentences.

Finally, the story concludes, the truth or falsity of an attitude ascription

a believes that *S*

depends upon a suitable relation between the semantic object of belief named by the t-clause and one of the psychological objects of belief of the individual named by *a*.

This story involves two sorts of sentialism. One is 'semantic sentialism' (SS), according to which t-clauses in attitude ascriptions name entities − semantic objects of belief − with the above-named sentential properties. The other is 'psychological sententialism' (PS), according to which belief and other propositional attitudes are mediated relations. They are relations mediated by relations to entities − psychological objects of belief − that resemble sentences in the ways mentioned above. Sections 1−3 have been devoted to a defense of only one sort of sentialism. Thus far, we have said nothing about PS.

Psychological sentialism has seemed wildly implausible to many. Perhaps the most common objection to PS involves the presumed existence of tacit beliefs. These are beliefs we are supposed to have, but which it is implausible to think are "stored as sentences." Putative examples are syntactic and mathematical beliefs (1 is a number, '1' is a word, 2 is a number, '2' is a word, . . .) and common beliefs that, although obvious, are rarely formulated explicitly. Examples of the latter might be the beliefs that dogs are not wombats and that few if any wombats have been an object of adoration of teenage Americans.

More generally, PS has been said to be objectionable because there is reason to think that many of the representations underlying belief ascription – perceptual states, imagistic memories, maplike representations, representations of how to perform an action (like tying a shoe) – are nonsentential.

I think that semantic sententialism has suffered from a sort of guilt by association with PS. So it is important to point out that the two views needn't hang together. I also think that PS is somewhat less implausible than is commonly supposed. But more of that later. Let me first address the relation between PS and SS.

Let us suppose for the moment that PS is not at all close to the truth. How would that impugn SS? One might be tempted to argue as follows: Semantic sententialism is the doctrine that 'believes' names a relation to a sentence-like entity. 'Believes' names belief. So SS is the doctrine that belief is a relation to a sentence-like entity. To say that PS is not at all close to the truth is to say that belief is not a relation to a sentence-like entity. So if PS is not at all close to the truth, SS is not either. This is a bad argument. It trades on an unfortunate, if unavoidable, ambiguity in the expression 'belief'. By 'belief' we can mean either (a) the relation that a correct semantics for English assigns to the verb 'believes', or (b) the psychological state or states that underlie ascriptions of belief. These need not be identical.

We might find it useful to characterize the psychological states in terms of a relation to a sentence-like entity. This might be the case if, for example, we found it useful (1) to characterize deduction, or other attitudes such as saying, in terms of a relation to a sentence-like entity, and (2) to say that deduction and belief were relations to the same sort of entity. The argument of Section 3, in part, made the point that we do in fact find (1) useful. And we do, presumably, find (2) useful as well. At least we do seem to characterize deduction and belief as relations to the same sort of thing, as in 'He deduced that I don't care, and then came to believe it'.

From the fact that we find it useful to *characterize* the psychological state in terms of a relation to a sentence-like entity, it does not follow that it *is* such a relation. To borrow an analogy from Grandy (1986), we describe what a map tells us by using sentences; this doesn't mean that maps do their stuff by having sentences on them. Returning to the argument above, SS is the doctrine that the semantic relation belief is a relation to a sentence-like entity. If you like, it is the doctrine that we characterize the psychological relation in terms of a relation to a sentence-like entity. The supposition that

PS is false doesn't contradict this, since PS is a doctrine about psychological states or relations, not semantic ones. As noted, one can be sentential about one of these relations without being sentential about the other.

Thus, the claim that we have a large number of tacit beliefs, or the claim that a good number of the states underlying true belief ascriptions are not relations to sentence-like entities, does not undermine SS. However, these claims do seem to undermine the simple story that a true belief ascription is true in virtue of a suitable relation between what a t-clause names and a sentence-like psychological object of belief. After all, if the claims about tacit belief and so on are correct, then the psychological states corresponding to true ascriptions of tacit beliefs don't involve sentence-like objects to begin with.

I believe that this simple story is substantially correct, and so I want to say something in defense of PS. So far I have gotten along with a vague characterization of PS. It's time to say more about the doctrine I mean to defend. There are many views like PS in which attitudes are relations to sentences, which I do *not* want to defend. For example, I am thoroughly agnostic as to whether our beliefs are sentences that play a computational role in our psychology, a role that makes the analogy between the mind and a computer an apt one. The psychological sentialism I espouse is silent on whether such a picture of our mental life is appropriate. Nor do I wish to defend any of the alarming forms of nativism that philosophers like Jerry Fodor have tied to the hypothesis that attitudes are sentential.

The sentialism I want to defend is a view about the relation between states of belief and their content. It makes the picture of belief as a relation to a sentence an apt picture.[13] It is a relatively modest, though not wholly innocuous, view. Broadly speaking, it is what I take to be implicit in claims like this: In order for something to count as the belief that Reagan is a Republican, it has to have a part or an aspect that represents Reagan, and a part (aspect) that represents the property of being a Republican. More generally, for something to be a system of beliefs, it must have something anal-

13 I should say, "It makes the picture of belief, desire, and the other attitudes . . . ." This makes for awkward writing, so I suppress reference to other attitudes.

ogous to the representational substructure present in the natural languages we speak. That is, just as a sentence that says that Reagan is a Republican contains a part ('Reagan', or 'the president', or 'that bozo over there') that represents Reagan; so does a state that counts as the belief that Reagan is a Republican.

Psychological sentamentalism is thus a doctrine about the way in which a psychological state that determines a belief is related to the content of the belief determined. It holds the following:

1. Such states possess a constituent structure.
2. For each believer, there is a principled and projectable way of assigning values to the constituents of these states. In particular, there is a way of singling out some constituents as analogues of terms and predicates; the constituents thus singled out can be assigned, in a principled and projectable way, individuals, properties, and relations as values, as things that these parts represent. (In general, such assignments of values can be made only relative to the believer's contextual or historical situation.)
3. There is also for each individual a principled and projectable way of getting from the overall structure of such states, and the assignments mentioned above, to an assignment to each of the states of what it represents. Thus, some analogue of a Tarskian assignment of truth conditions to sentences is possible in the assignment of content to belief states.
4. Whether two of an individual's belief states represent the same thing depends in part on the constituent structure mentioned in 1 and 2. In particular, a necessary condition for the identity of what two such states represent is that the "terms" and "predicates" they have as constituents represent the same things.

Since this probably doesn't sound as if it lives up to its advance billing (I did call it modest), let me point out some of the things the view does *not* commit one to. For one thing, there is no reason that the constituents of the belief states that PS invokes have to be very much like the words of a natural language. For example, there is no reason that belief states couldn't involve things like perceptual images, with their parts or aspects playing, in some cases, the roles of terms or predicates. (This is part of the reason I try to speak of parts *or aspects* of a given state.)

For another, the view doesn't imply that thought requires the possession of a public language, or even a rudimentary ability to communicate with others. Psychological sentamentalism does require that if Fido believes that I have a bone, then he is in a state,

41

parts or aspects of which represent me and being a bone. It doesn't require that he be able to tell Rex about this. The view is simply neutral on the question Do dumb brutes have beliefs?

Nor is PS committed to a sort of atomism about representation that many philosophers find offensive. Here is Stalnaker's (1984) description of the offending view:

> It holds that the most basic kind of representation relation – the kind from which all other representational relations derive – is a relation between linguistic atoms – the semantically simple expressions – and elements of the world. The name–object relation and the predicate–property relations come first; the sentence–proposition relation is derivative. One may contrast this kind of account with one that tries to explain basic semantic representation on the level of sentences and propositions, and then to explain the representational properties of simpler expressions in terms of their role in determining the representational properties of the sentences in which they are parts. (p. 34)

Psychological sententialism commits us to there being a certain sort of relation between the "mental sentence," which is a belief, and what it represents. It requires that there be a correspondence between the representation and what it represents, one that is captured by the kind of assignment adumbrated in clauses 1–4. This doesn't require that the assignment of content to the parts of the mental sentence be conceptually or otherwise prior to the assignment of content to the state.

Perhaps this will be clearer if we think about the relation between a natural language sentence and what it says. Consider the following views:

(i) It is only by reference to the behavior of an expression in uses of a wide variety of sentences that we can arrive at the proper assignment of a semantic value for the expression.

(ii) What sentences say is to be individuated in terms of structured entities whose constituents are the values of the terms and predicates that occur within the sentences.[14]

View (i) is something like holism (as opposed to atomism) with respect to the content of natural language sentences; (ii) is something like semantic sententialism. It is obvious, I think, that these views

14 I am again simplifying to achieve readability. Typically, expressions and sentences take different values on different uses, as words like 'I' and 'now' and the sentences containing them attest. This doesn't affect the point.

are not mutually exclusive.[15] There is not even any particular tension between them; one can comfortably hold both. Psychological sentientialism requires that an analogue of (ii) be true in the case of beliefs and desires. It doesn't rule out that an analogue of (i) be true as well. There is no more incompatibility or tension in one case than in the other.

A related point worth noting is that it's perfectly consistent with PS to say, for example, that what makes a belief conjunctive is that it involves a certain functionally characterizable relation among states (which are themselves beliefs). In fact, PS allows that the assignment of a value to such a relation, which makes the relation realize conjunction, may be an assignment we could make only by reference to the function of the relation in the totality of one's behavioral economy.

In short, PS doesn't claim that "subject–predicate representation" or "atomistic representation" is conceptually prior to "sentence–proposition representation." It simply claims that the former sort of representation is to be found in any system of states that qualify as beliefs and that any accurate assignment of content to beliefs will respect its presence in certain ways. I go on at some length about this because a good part of my strategy for defending PS consists in pointing out that this view doesn't have the horrible consequences that some philosophers have alleged it, or some of its close relatives, have. I think it is important to point out that it doesn't deprive Fido of a mental life, nor does it commit us to rejecting functionalism, nor to embracing an obnoxious atomism about representation.

I want to say something about the status of PS. It may sound as if PS is a substantive empirical hypothesis about the mind, one of the sort that a philosopher (at least a philosopher like myself, who has no pretensions toward sophistication in empirical psychological theory) has no business advancing. I don't think this is true, anymore than it is true that certain versions of functionalism (be they right or wrong) are the sort of hypotheses that philosophers have no business espousing. I shall explain.

Some phenomena can be described in a number of ways – if you like, at a number of levels. The idea that this is so surfaces at several

---

15 Stalnaker himself (1984, chap. 2) seems prepared to admit this claim. See his discussion of the "theory of interpretation."

places, one of them being the philosophy of psychology. Some hold that mental phenomena are accurately describable at (a) a level of folk psychology, (b) a level of empirical psychology, and (c) a level of neurophysiology.

If this is true, it might well be that the sort of structures or laws that hold at one level do not have analogues at other levels. For example, it might be true that we more or less instantiate a theory one gets from some regimentation of folk truisms about belief, desire, and so forth. If so, we are describable at level (a).[16] It might

16 I do not think that folk truisms like those of the form of

(a) If x believes that (if A then B) and x wishes that B and . . . , then x will try to make it the case that A

have completions that turn them into true, exceptionless generalizations, much less completions that make them into true causal principles. The idea that folk psychology truly describes us ought to be understood as the idea that principles like

(a') Believing that (if A then B) and wishing that B *disposes one* to bring it about that A

or

(a'') Believing that (if A then B) and wishing that B *tends to* make one try to bring it about that A

is true. (Obviously, these are abbreviated and need more qualification in their antecedents.)

To say this, by the way, is not to say that such principles are rough statements of causal laws. It seems to me that (a') or (a'') might be true and therefore available to explain action without encoding or approximating, in any interesting sense, some causal law. Not all explanation proceeds by invoking causal laws.

In invoking the idea that we might be truly describable by folk psychology (FP), neither do I mean to endorse the idea that the vague collection of rough truisms and rules of thumb that constitutes FP defines attitude verbs, say via one or another Ramsification of FP. (Lewis 1970 and Loar 1981 suggest that FP does so define its theoretical terms.) I quite agree with Schiffer (Schiffer 1987, chap. 2) that FP is far too weak to so this. (Stalnaker 1984 contains arguments that bear on the question of whether folk psychology is strong enough to define 'believes', 'desires', and so on. See the example of Albert, Mary, and the cello in chap. 1.)

It is not even clear that principles like (a') and (a'') are necessary truths. Suppose the 'tends' of (a'') is more or less statistical. Might not there be a world in which, as a matter of fact, beliefs and desires practically never lead to actions? If so, then (a''), so interpreted, would be false at such a world.

The most plausible thing to say about folk psychology, I think, is *simply* this: Most of FP's tenets are actually true – or at least approximately true. Period. This provides a weak test for semantic theories about attitude verbs: They should be consistent with the idea that most of FP's tenets are approximately true. It does not provide one with a basis for empirical psychology or with a recipe for

also be that good empirical psychology theory will not have a place for states that obey analogues of folk psychology's belief + desire = action schemata. This might be true, for instance, if the best psychological theory we could develop did not invoke analogues of the relations named by the natural language 'believes' and 'desires'.

Of course, if this turned out to be true, it wouldn't follow that the states and laws posited at level (a) were somehow unreal or phony. There is no reason that, given some topic – say human behavior – there can be only one way to theorize accurately about the topic. And to argue that folk psychology, if not part of the best empirical psychological theory, is a false theory is to risk committing ourselves to the view that such things as political and economic relations are also unreal or phony.

Now, there is such a thing as folk psychology, a somewhat inchoately articulated, but generally accepted theory of the mental. And so there undeniably are the three levels of description mentioned earlier, even if there is less than full agreement about whether the level (a) is even approximately accurate and what its relations to the other levels, if it is accurate, might turn out to be.

In asking about the status of PS, one is asking (in part) a question about where it is supposed to fit in the three levels of description. I claim that it's part of level (a). So I am committing myself to the claim that it's part of our commonsense conception of the mental. So PS, although it is an empirical hypothesis, isn't the sort of empirical hypothesis that philosophers have no business uncovering or, to a certain extent, defending; for part of the philosopher's business is investigating the coherence and tenability of our everyday conceptions of philosophically interesting phenomena, like the mind or meaning.

Note that there are really two questions to ask about PS. First, one may ask whether it is indeed a part of the commonsense conception of mind, be that conception accurate or not. Second, one may ask, supposing that folk psychology (minus PS, if PS be part of it) is more or less correct, whether folk psychology plus PS itself is correct.

---

finding the meaning of 'believes'. It simply gives one a very weak constraint on a semantic theory about attitude verbs.

I think that there is good evidence for an affirmative answer to the first question. First, there *is* a strong, widespread intuition that beliefs have the sort of subrepresentation property that PS claims they have – that is, that something is the belief that... *a*... only if it contains a component that represents *a*. It is just very hard to imagine what would justify calling a state a belief that Reagan was a fool, if it didn't involve something that could be said to represent Reagan.

Second, the fact that SS is true is, I think, extremely good evidence for the claim that PS is an important part of the way we think about belief. In a sense, SS is the view that we *characterize* certain psychological states as relations to sententially structured entities. Psychological sententialism is the view that such a characterization is completely appropriate, since these states *are* relations to sententially structured entities. It is quite reasonable to think that there will be a match between what we think beliefs are like and the way in which we characterize them. So it is quite reasonable to think that, if SS is true, PS is an integral part of our everyday conception of the mental.

Let me repeat that I don't offer this as evidence for the view that PS is actually true. It is evidence that PS is so firmly entrenched in our commonsense view of the mental that it is an integral part of any theory that deserves the name of folk psychology. I take it that, if this is true, then it is reasonable to suppose that the truth of PS is presupposed by the semantics of verbs like 'believes' and 'desires'.

My defense of the claim that PS *is* actually true (*modulo* the claim that the rest of folk psychology is substantially correct) is, as I observed earlier, by and large negative: I have tried (and will presently again try) to show that absurd consequences don't flow from the supposition that it is true, the complaints of many philosophers notwithstanding.

I am aware that this is only a partial defense of the truth of PS. My excuse is that, for the purposes of this book, that is all that is required. The issue I am primarily concerned with is the semantics of verbs like 'believes' and of their companion t-clauses. Psychological sententialism is of interest here because, if something like the simple story rehearsed at the beginning of this section is correct, the truth of PS is presupposed by those semantics.

So it is incumbent on me to show not so much that PS must be

46

true, but that it isn't (obviously) false and that the idea that it is true isn't obviously at variance with our practices of ascribing beliefs and other attitudes. In this context, then, the sort of partial defense of PS that I am giving will suffice.

As observed earlier, perhaps the most common objection to PS is that, since we have a large number of tacit beliefs, it can't be correct. So I will conclude my partial defense of PS by defending it against this objection. (I will not address worries about the putatively nonsentential nature of the representations underlying many true belief ascriptions. I think that the sort of line exploited in defense of the simple story against the argument from tacit beliefs could be used to defend the simple story against such worries. But I won't argue for that here.) I will argue that, although many of the putative examples philosophers give of tacit beliefs are examples of beliefs, they aren't tacit beliefs. It is perfectly reasonable to hold that, in any interesting sense of 'tacit belief', there aren't any.

5. TACIT BELIEFS

According to PS, to have a belief is to bear a relation to a sentence or sentence-like entity; let us use the term 'acceptance' for this relation.[17] How should one characterize the notion of tacit belief? One might propose something along the lines of the schema

x's belief that S is a tacit belief iff (a) x believes that S and (b) x does not accept the sentence 'S'.

If accepting S is to have a "real" relation to S, as opposed to a proxy of S, this won't do. Suppose Hans believes that 2 and 2 is 4, and does so in virtue of his explicitly and audibly tokening a sentence that expresses this belief: 'Zwei und zwei ist vier'. Then his belief shouldn't turn out to be tacit. But on the above definition it would seem to, for it would be true that Hans believes that 2 and 2 is 4; but Hans, who speaks no English, presumably bears no psychologically interesting relation to the sentence '2 and 2 is 4', and so does not accept it.

17 'Acceptance' is being used technically here; the relation shouldn't be confused with other relations with names spelled the same. Likewise, the word 'token' is given a stipulative sense below, at the beginning of the 'ugly' example, and is used with this stipulative sense throughout the section.

The problem is that the "language" of the psychological objects of belief (POBs) need not be the same as the language used to ascribe belief. We can get around this if we assume that in a weak sense the languages have the same semantics: That is, the structured intensions of POBs include the structured intensions of natural language sentences. Then we might say that

x's belief that S is a tacit belief iff (a) x believes that S and (b) x does not accept any sentence that determines the same structured intension as 'S'.[18]

It seems that the story reviewed at the beginning of Section 4 must either acknowledge a very large number of tacit beliefs or deny the truth of a very large number of obviously true ascriptions. Suppose, for example, that I "think to myself," in the way that I think to myself, when I read and think correct what I read, the sentence

(1) Mick is fat and ugly.

Let's use *token* for this relation to a sentence. However we are to explain acceptance, it is clear that tokening should suffice for acceptance, and so in tokening (1), I accept it. (This tacitly assumes that the, or a, language of POBs is English. I simply smuggle this assumption into the discussion. I don't think that it affects anything in this context.)

In virtue of my accepting (1), it is true that I believe that Mick is fat and ugly. But it is surely also true, given that I accept (1), that I believe that Mick is ugly, that something (and someone) is fat and ugly, and that something is either fat or ugly. But I have not tokened any of these other sentences. So it

18 The existence of tacit beliefs so defined is not *strictly* incompatible either with PS or with what I called above the simple story, the claim that both SS and PS are true and that the semantics of 'believes' can be explained in terms of suitable relations between what a t-clause names and a psychological object of belief. The simple story doesn't require for the truth of

x believes that T

that x accept a sentence with the *same* intension as T's.

I have defined tacit belief as I have because it seems the most apt definition of the notion. I don't capitalize on the bare fact, that the simple story and the existence of tacit beliefs thus defined are compatible, in my defense. As I observe later, other definitions of the notion of the tacit belief are possible; I argue that the most obvious one is not of very much interest, from the perspective of philosophy of mind or of psychological theory.

would seem that I don't accept any of them. Therefore, all of these beliefs – that Mick is ugly, that someone is fat and ugly, and so on – must be tacit.

This argument calls for some discussion. An advocate of the simple story should not accept it. He should point out that the argument passes rather quickly from 'didn't token S' to 'didn't accept S'. Given a sentence S, there will be on any plausible version of PS a number of states, states distinct from natural perspectives in psychological or physiological theory, that will count as states of accepting S. Nothing in PS prevents us from saying that a normal adult who tokens a sentence of the form

(2) a is F and G

thereby accepts not only the sentence tokened, but also the corresponding sentences of the forms of

(3) a is G,
(4) Something is F and G.

Furthermore, it may well be that the overall psychological organization of an individual determines whether his being in a particular state counts as his accepting a sentence. For example, an individual with sufficient logical prowess who tokens a sentence of the form of (2) may thereby accept one of the form of

(5) Something is either F or G.

But this need not hold true for every adult.

In criticizing our first characterization of tacit belief, I suggested that, however the notion of acceptance was to be fleshed out, it was to be a "genuine" relation to a sentence. It was not to be an indirect, psychologically uninteresting relation, like the relation you bear to the German sentence

Wenn du dieses nicht lesen kann, bist du ein Esel,

in virtue of uttering an English sentence that translates it; nor was it to turn out to be a relation in some other way disingenuous. Some might think that in suggesting that by tokening a sentence of the form of (2) one thereby comes to accept sentences of the forms of (3)–(5), I have made acceptance a disingenuous, or at least psychologically uninteresting, relation.

A crude way of expressing the worry is as follows: Look, you surely don't think that when you token (1) there is, somewhere in your head, something that tokens all the obvious consequences of (1). So there can't *really* be tokens of the sentences 'Mick is ugly' and so forth in your head in the case under discussion. This means that acceptance is some mediated, disjunctive relation, like 'having tokened or being disposed to token or...'. But to admit this is to take a good deal of the interest out of psychological sententialism. After all, PS is the view that beliefs are sentences in the head. What this move does is make PS a view that beliefs are sentences that might have been in the head if circumstances had been right.

I said it was a crude way of expressing the worry. Our crude conversant is working with a particularly crude model of what it is to "have a sentence in a head." He thinks that any state that should count as having a sentence in the head, and thus any state that should count as acceptance, must be pretty much like the state we called tokening. Put otherwise, he thinks that the only psychologically interesting sense in which a sentence could be in one's head would be a sort of inner speech.

Perhaps an advocate of PS should say the following about sentences and acceptance: A sentence is to be thought of as being determined, in part, by a set of constituents. For a natural language sentence, the constituents are terms, predicates, and other items of various grammatical categories. Let us stipulatively call the constituents of the mental sentences PS postulates *concepts*. To token a sentence, of a natural or other language, is to have its constituents in various relations. And to accept a sentence, in the sense in which the term is used in PS, is, analogously, to have its constituents related in certain ways. To accept 'Mick is ugly', for example, is to have certain concepts – those corresponding to 'Mick' and 'is ugly', let's suppose – and to relate them in certain ways.

There is more than one way to realize a sentence of a natural language. For example, you can write, 'Something is ugly', or you can utter it. Why shouldn't the same be true of acceptance? An advocate of PS might plausibly say that, when a normal adult speaker of English tokens the sentence 'Mick is fat and ugly', he comes to bear a number of different sets of psychologically real and interesting relations to the concepts that make up not only the "mental sentence" 'Mick is fat and ugly', but also the mental sentences 'Mick is ugly' and 'Something is fat and ugly'. As evidence for this, an advocate of PS can point to the fact that, once one tokens the sentence, one acquires a host of properties, including (but not exhausted by) dispositions to assent to the natural language analogues of the mental sentences.

From certain perspectives in psychological theory, the relations one bears to the concepts involved in 'Something is ugly', when one tokens the sentence, are very different relations from those that one bears to these concepts when one tokens, say, 'Mick is fat and ugly'. But this does *not* imply that it would be bad psychology to type these relations together as different ways of accepting the sentence 'Something is ugly'. The case is not unlike that of typing together certain vocalizations and inscriptions as realizations of the same sentence. The psychological sententialist will argue that there are (or that we should expect to find) positive reasons for such groupings – for example, similarity of behaviorial effects.

At the least, this is a natural and reasonable psychological hypothesis, and anyone who wishes to deny it owes us an extended argument. So far as I know, objections to psychological sententialism in the literature do not give such an argument. Either they are compatible with the view that in the case under consideration the beliefs in question are not tacit, or they apparently work with a very crude view of what acceptance is, a view that equates it with tokening.

The upshot is that, by itself, the objection we crudely expressed above doesn't give an advocate of PS very much to worry about. Any normal adult who tokens 'Mick is fat and ugly' is surely related to concepts corresponding to 'Mick' and 'is ugly' in such a way that it is *not* bad psychology to say that he bears a relation to a mental correlate of 'Mick is ugly' of the same sort as one who tokens (a mental correlate of) that sentence. It is not bad psychology, that is, to say that he bears the same belief-making relation to this sentence as a tokener thereof. Anyone who says otherwise owes us a detailed argument.[19]

19 There are a number of objections to the notion of a concept as it is used in PS that must eventually be met. For example, the line of defense of PS in the text requires the defender of PS to say something like the following: For any person u who can believe that something is ugly, there are concepts c and c' such that c corresponds to 'is ugly', c' corresponds to existential quantification, and whenever u accepts 'Something is ugly', he relates these concepts in an appropriate way. Since acceptance is not simply tokening, this requires PS to say that there

Let me summarize the points about PS that I have so far made. (a) In order to be psychologically real, acceptance need not be very much like inner speech. (b) We may expect that, for any sentence S, there will be a number of psychological states that would constitute accepting S. (c) Something that would naturally be described from some perspectives as a state involving a single sentence (e.g., tokening 'Mick is fat and ugly') may be one that constitutes the acceptance of a number of sentences. (d) Whether being in a particular state constitutes accepting a sentence can be expected to vary across individuals, depending upon such factors as intelligence and collateral knowledge.

Let's turn to somewhat meatier examples of tacit beliefs. Here are two passages that seem to support the claim that we have a rather large number of tacit beliefs:

> In addition to all the relatively *difficult* facts I have mastered, such as that New York is larger than Boston and salt is sodium chloride, there are all the easy ones we tend to overlook: New York is not on the moon, or in Venezuela; salt is not sugar, or green, or oily; salt is good on potatoes, on eggs; tweed coats are not made of salt; a grain of salt is smaller than an elephant.... Surely I can think of more than a thousand things I know or believe about salt, and salt is ... one of thousands upon thousands of things I can do this with. Then there is my knowledge of arithmetic: two plus two is four, twenty plus twenty is forty.... My beliefs are apparently infinite, which means that their storage, however miniaturized, will take up more room than there is in the brain. (Dennett 1975, p. 45)

> "It would not be counterintuitive to assert that Bertrand Russell believed (indeed knew) that Big Ben was larger than Frege's earlobe, even if, as is almost certainly the case, Russell would have had to infer the belief from other beliefs were the question ever to have arisen" [from S. Stich].... I

will be any number of states – like tokening 'Mick is ugly' – that on some levels of description have nothing to do with any concept of quantification but that are such that being in them more or less automatically results in putting the concept of existential quantification into a new relation. And this can seem somewhat bizarre. How many things, a critic might ask, do you think happen when you say to yourself 'Mick is ugly'?

I think it is perfectly plausible to say that many things happen. Only a picture of concept arrangement which makes it like Leggo manipulation makes this implausible. Most sophisticated versions of functionalism, for example, are perfectly compatible with the idea that a "single input" can result in a system going into a large number of new states. Of course, there are *many* worries about the notion of a concept as it is mobilized later, some of them significantly more serious than the one just mentioned. It is beyond my brief to do anything more here than acknowledge the fact that my defense of PS simply assumes the coherence of the notion.

don't think it is plausible to say that all such apparent beliefs are only potential beliefs, for they may play an actual psychological role in the believer's actions and reasoning even if the believer never entertains the propositions. . . . We should also accept the [claim] that Russell, and even we people with more ordinary minds, may have an infinite number of independent beliefs. (Stalnaker 1984, p. 68)

These passages raise a number of issues. A good place to begin is the claim that we have an infinite number of beliefs. We may ask both whether there is good reason to suppose this to be so and whether, if true, the claim shows that PS is mistaken.

Consider Dennett's allusion to sequences of mathematical beliefs. Surely it is either here or in the field of syntactic beliefs ('a' is an expression; ' 'a' ' is an expression; . . .) that the most likely argument for an infinite number of beliefs is to be found. But exactly what claim is Dennett making? It is clear that there are infinite sequences of sentences that express pairwise distinct possible beliefs, large initial segments of which any of us can rattle off. We can even give rules that, if followed correctly, enable one in principle to generate successively each member of such sequences.

But this doesn't show that we believe what each sentence in such a sequence expresses. There is a clear difference between antecedently having a belief that so and so and being so situated that, should so and so occur to one, one would immediately see that it was true and come to believe it. It is just this fact that scotches dispositionalist analysis of belief, as is so nicely shown by the example in Audi (1982) of a man who doesn't realize that he is talking too loudly, but would assent to 'you are talking too loudly' and believe that he was if someone were to mention it.

The appropriate thing to say about the mathematical sequences seems to be that, after a certain point in the sequence, it is just false that the sentences express one's beliefs, though one would (ignoring practical limitations on attention, memory, etc.) come to believe what any such sentence said if one were to hear and reflect on the sentence. Certainly, there is no fact about my behavior that can't be satisfactorily explained by such an assumption. So there seems to be no compelling evidence against the assumption.

It ought to be observed that the existence of infinitely many distinct beliefs wouldn't clearly refute interesting versions of PS anyway. We had occasion above to observe that, on any reasonable version of PS, being in a state that, from some perspectives in

53

psychological or physiological theory, is a unitary state may make it the case that one accepts a number of sentences. So the existence of infinitely many beliefs refutes a version of PS only if that version of PS explains acceptance in such a way that a finite number of states couldn't determine the acceptance of infinitely many sentences. Since reasonable versions of PS will begin by divorcing themselves from the "acceptance = something like having it written down in a notebook" model, it is not clear why they must explain acceptance in this way.

There are subtle issues here. For example, in the sequence of possible beliefs – that 1 is a number, that 2 is a number, . . . – are there infinitely many distinct concepts? If so, doesn't *that* require the brain to have infinite storage? If not, what does PS mean by concepts? I don't intend to pursue these issues, since I have already argued that nothing is gained by positing infinitely many beliefs. But those who think there are infinitely many beliefs, and that this gives us a reason for rejecting sentential views of belief, ought carefully to consider why it is that they think this.

Let us turn to the other examples in the above passages. When it is alleged that a particular belief is tacit, one must ask two questions: Is an ascription of the belief true? If so, is the ascription underlain by the acceptance of a sentence with the appropriate properties? To answer the second question with respect to the putative belief that salt is not oily or Stich's earlobe belief would require taking a view on the exact nature of acceptance. I don't intend to do this. Rather, I want to suggest that a reasonable position might be one in which some of these beliefs turn out on a PS view to be actual, nontacit beliefs, whereas others turn out to be potential, but nonactual beliefs. That is, I want to suggest that a reasonable position for the psychological sententialist to take is that, in the sense in which I have characterized tacit beliefs, there turn out not to be any.

I have remarked that there are a number of ways for a sentence to be accepted. It does not seem unreasonable to suppose that many of the beliefs about salt that Dennett mentions might be genuine beliefs we have in virtue of accepting the relevant sentences but that the way in which we accept these sentences is not by tokening them in the sense of tokening adumbrated earlier.

Suppose, as many have suggested, that our knowledge is stored, at least in part, in a way that can be represented by interrelated

54

networks of concepts. To steal an example from Minsky (1987, p. 91), some of our knowledge about physical objects might be organized as represented by the following trees:

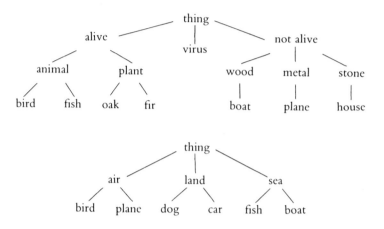

If your knowledge about the world is in part arranged in this way, then you need never have tokened

(A) Boats are things that are not alive that are found in the sea.

But a theory of acceptance which had you accepting such a sentence would not be an unreasonable theory. It does not seem any more unreasonable, or any worse a piece of psychology, to say this than to say that, when you token 'Mick is fat and ugly', you come to be related to 'Mick is ugly' in a way similar to the way you are related to 'Mick is ugly' when you token it. The cases seem more or less parallel. At least, I can see no reason to reject a theory that says this.

There is an objection to this line of argument we need to consider. Let us grant, assume, or pretend the following: Minsky's theory is more or less correct; having memory organized along the above sort of lines counts as a case of accepting but not tokening a sentence; words of English are the concepts that are constituents of mental sentences. Given this, the objector observes, it is still quite gratuitous to identify any of the sentences accepted, when one's memory is organized along the above lines, with the sentence accepted when one tokens (A). Why not say that (A) is not accepted in this case, although

(B) If a thing is such that, if it is not alive, then it is not in the sea, then it is not a boat

is?

This is a fair enough question. I think a fair enough response is that this is an empirical matter to be decided by the answers to questions like, Does a person who tokens (B) have a similar psychological makeup to one who has his memory organized along the above lines? The answer to the question may also vary across individuals. Perhaps it will be true of Pierre, the great logician, that having memory organized as above disposes him to do such things as infer the sentence 'x is not a boat' from 'If x is not alive, then it is not in the sea'. If so, then perhaps in virtue of having memory organized in this way, Pierre accepts both (A) and (B). But this need not be true of the lummox who has never mastered contraposition.

Presumably, whether or not we should say that a person accepts a sentence in a case like this will depend on a number of factors. One mark of whether we should say this will be, as Stalnaker observes, what sort of role the networks in question play in an individual's actual behavior and reasoning. From this perspective, it might be reasonable to say that, after a certain point, a sentence that someone would automatically assent to – say 'Frege's left earlobe was smaller than Big Ben' – was not a sentence he antecedently accepted, and so not one that established a belief. So perhaps this sort of case would be more appropriately assimilated to the case of merely potential beliefs about numbers and expressions.

Of course, even given a decently explicit theory, there may be cases in which it is difficult or even impossible to decide whether a certain sentence is accepted. This suggests that, on the sort of psychological sentialism I have been outlining, it may sometimes be indeterminate as to whether someone has a belief. I take it that this is no defect of such a view. Some claims are indeterminate, after all.

Let me say explicitly what I have and have not been trying to do in this section. I have been trying only to show that one popular line of objection to psychological sentialism and what I called the simple story about the semantics of 'believes' is far less conclusive than is often supposed. I have tried only to make it plausible that a coherent version of psychological sentialism should end up saying that there are no tacit beliefs. And, of course, the point

56

I have been arguing for depends on the characterization of tacit belief I have been using.

One *can* characterize the notion of tacit belief in such a way that no reasonable version of psychological sententialism could deny its existence. For example, one could say that any true belief ascription, which is not true in virtue of the ascribee's tokening of a sentence that determines the same intension as the ascription's content sentence, marks a tacit belief. One can define tacit belief in this way. But it is not clear that this sort of definition marks a theoretically interesting distinction between putative beliefs. At least, I think, this is the upshot of our discussion of the 'Mick is fat and ugly' case.

Some will object that I have said very little about the notion of acceptance. True, but given the limited goals of this section, more is not necessary. I have been trying to show that a certain sort of argument against PS does not undermine it. This can be done, I think, without giving a detailed account of the psychological processes that underlie belief ascription, which is what a detailed account of acceptance would be. As a philosopher, I have thought it best to refrain from psychological speculation. Armchair philosophy is bad enough.

The version of sententialism I have defended is very weak. It is sufficient, I hope, to validate the simple story rehearsed in Section 4 about the semantics of 'believes'. This story seems to me to be, in its essentials, on the right track. Of course, as it stands, it is very vague. It simply requires that the truth of an attitude ascription – in particular, the truth of an ascription of belief or desire – be a function of some relation between a semantic and a psychological object of belief. So far, I haven't suggested what this relation might be. That is the task of the rest of this book.

2

Some cognitive
theories of content

My taste is for keeping open house for all sorts of conditions of entities, just so long as when they come in they help with the housework.

H. P. Grice

Propositions are the sorts of things named by 'that'-clauses (t-clauses). What would a concisely stated theory about propositions be like? It might begin by saying something about how the simplest expressions in a t-clause contribute to the proposition it names. Usually, a theory does this by explaining how to assign certain things – let's call them 'contents' – to such expressions. Next it gives a recipe for getting from the contents of the expressions in a t-clause, and the clause's syntax, to the proposition named.[1]

Chapter 1 said a good deal that was relevant to the second part of such a theory, but not much that was relevant to the first.[2] The conclusions of Chapter 1 strongly suggest that to the question

How do we get from a sentence and the contents of its simple expressions to a proposition?

we should give an answer that goes roughly

Replace the simple expressions with their contents.

1 I remind the reader that I tend to suppress mention of such facts as that assignments may have to be made relative to a context or a use of an expression. Some theories take a fairly holistic view of the assignment of content. For example, the theory of Boër and Lycan discussed in Section 4 of this chapter assigns conceptual roles to whole sentences, and not directly to their parts. I ignore this complication in these introductory, largely motivational remarks.
2 True, we often spoke as if contents were constructions from possible worlds. But this was because the theories we picked as examples were ones that made use of such constructions as contents.

It's time to turn to the question

What are the contents of simple expressions?

Much of the debate over propositions has revolved around this question. It has generated a distressing number of proposals about content. Among other things, the content of a use of the name 'John' has been identified with each of the following: its referent; the, or some favored, way in which the user thinks about the referent; the functional, or conceptual, or computational role of 'John' in the user's (or someone else's) psychology; the word 'John' itself (sometimes the type, sometimes a particular token); one or another possible-worlds intension associated with the use; a causal or informational chain linking the use of the word with its referent; and various pairs or even trios of the above sorts of things. Philosophers seem to discover a new theory of content almost as often as physicists discover a new fundamental particle.

There's some order in the chaos. Most answers to the question What does the expression 'John' contribute to the proposition that John is happy? seem to be versions of one, or combinations of several, of the following views:

1. *The broadly referential view*. Contents are workaday, broadly referential semantic values of expressions, such as objects and properties. On most such views, the content of an expression is what it contributes to determining truth conditions outside of attitude ascriptions.
2. *The cognitive view*. The content of an expression is not exhausted by its broadly referential properties. Intrinsic to an expression's content is one or another of its cognitive or psychological roles for speakers.
3. *The linguistic view*. The content of an expression has as a part, or is to be individuated in terms of, the expression itself.

Examples of pure versions of each view are probably familiar. Russellians embrace versions of the referential view. Fregeans advocate versions of the cognitive view. Quine and some others have flirted with the linguistic view, because they rejected the ontological or other commitments of the first two views.

I am unhappy with each of these views, at least as they are usually developed. In this and the next two chapters, I explain some of the reasons for my unhappiness, as well as present a theory of content that I think correct.

This chapter is devoted to cognitive theories of content and to the views of the semantics of attitude verbs accompanying such

59

theories.[3] I start with these theories because the view that some such theory is correct seems to be the dominant one. The argument of this chapter is for the most part a negative one. Frege's view of content and attitude ascription seems to me to be mistaken. So do its modern descendants.

At the heart of the theories I discuss here are the following theses: A proposition is something that can be individuated only in terms of some notion like that of *cognitive role* or *a way of thinking* of something. Furthermore, the proposition a t-clause names is associated with the latter's content sentence in a nonarbitrary way. What makes an attitude ascription, say

(1) Barbara believes that Anne is married,

true is that the proposition the t-clause names is identical with, or at least is very similar in content to, one to which Barbara bears an interesting psychological (or quasi-psychological) relation. In short, these views assume that attitude ascription involves a *match of nonreferential cognitive content* between what the t-clause names and some object of attitude of the person under discussion.

This is what I think is mistaken. The cognitive role or way of thinking that is associated with an expression varies from person to person. Because of this, no way of working out this proposal is at all faithful to the way in which we in fact ascribe attitudes. The problem with Frege's theory is not that the notion of sense is obscure or that sense can't determine reference. The problem is that it can't be made to fit with the way in which we talk about the beliefs and desires of others. It gets the facts about attitude ascription wrong. Something analogous is true of other cognitive theories.

Though I think these views to be mistaken, I do *not* conclude that something like the cognitive role of 'Anne is married' for Barbara is completely irrelevant to the truth of ascriptions like (1). In succeeding chapters I give a theory in which it turns out that something reminiscent of the cognitive role of the sentence is, or at least can be, relevant to the truth of the ascription. But the theory I finally arrive at doesn't make use of anything like a match of nonreferential, cognitive content in giving the truth conditions of (1). It doesn't assume that we can make interesting comparisons across persons of a sentence's nonreferential, cognitive content. It

3 In order to avoid prolixity, I often speak of a particular theory of content instead of the theory of content paired with a view about the semantics of attitude verbs.

doesn't individuate the content of an expression like 'Anne' in cognitive terms. The theory I end up giving really isn't very much like those I discuss in this chapter.

There are too many cognitive theories of content to argue against all comers. So I concentrate on two representatives. Sections 1–3 are concerned with Fregean theories of content. Section 4 takes up a theory proposed by Stephen Boër and Bill Lycan. This theory is something of a compromise between referential theories of content and cognitive ones. It holds (roughly speaking) that the content of a t-clause is sometimes something like a Russellian proposition and sometimes a conceptual role, the role of the content sentence in a person's psychology. I argue that the theory fails for reasons related to the reason Fregean theories fail. I end the chapter by drawing a few morals about the relation between the way a sentence functions when someone uses it in thought and the way it functions when we use it to talk about what someone thinks.

1. A PROBLEM FOR FREGEANISM

Frege's view of the semantics of attitude ascriptions is perennially popular, and understandably so.[4] According to Frege, 'that'-clauses in sentences like

(1) Barbara believes that Anne is married

pick out *thoughts*, where a Fregean thought is quite literally a way of thinking of something. For example, the thought that Anne is married – that is, the thought that I express when I say, 'Anne is married' – is the result of combining a way of thinking of Anne, the one I associate with 'Anne', with a way of thinking of marriage. *Sense* was Frege's term for a way of thinking of something; a thought is something that is (or could be) the sense of a declarative sentence.[5]

4 The classic statement of Frege's views on attitude ascription is "On Sense and Reference." Its standard English translation is in Geach and Black (1952). Also worth reading for an introduction to Frege's thoughts is "The Thought," translated in Geach (1977).
5 In this informal exposition, I ignore some subtle, and not so subtle, points about Frege's views. For example, Frege insisted that senses were objective, mind-independent entities. My cavalier use of 'ways of thinking' as a gloss for 'senses', though it apes Frege's words, is liable to mislead the uninitiated.

   Another issue I downplay in the text is this: The sense of a proper name is a way of thinking of what the name refers to; it presents the name's referent, to

Of course, there are many ways of thinking of Anne – as the young woman in the corner, as the lawyer who made Liggett & Meyer settle out of court, and so on. Strictly speaking, then, there are many Fregean thoughts that Anne is married. But this, it might be said, is exactly what we should expect and want from a theory about thoughts and the sentences that ascribe them: Whoever thought that we and the Chinese think *exactly* the same thing when we think that Mao was a communist?

Because there are different ways of thinking about the same thing, and because different names of one thing can have different senses associated with them, Frege's view seems superior to natural developments of referential theories of content. Consider, for example, a Russellian view that makes the content of a proper name its bearer, and that of a predicate a property or relation. Most views of this sort identify the proposition expressed by the sentence 'Twain is Clemens' with something consisting of the relation of identity, the man Twain, and the man Clemens. Thinking of sentences and propositions as we did in Chapter 1, we might say that such a view identifies the proposition expressed by the sentence

(2) ⟨'is', ⟨'Twain', 'Clemens'⟩⟩

with what we get if we replace its expressions with their Russellian interpretations:

(3) ⟨Identity, ⟨Twain, Clemens⟩⟩.

use Frege's jargon. But what do the senses of other expressions, in particular predicates and sentences, present? Frege's answer was, a bit roughly, this: A sentence's sense presents its truth value; a predicate's sense is a way of thinking of its extension. (Frege scholars will forgive my turning courses of values into sets.) Most modern Fregeans have given up these two aspects of Frege's view. For example, McGinn (1983) and Forbes (1989) present Fregean views on which predicate senses present properties (in something like a Russellian sense thereof) and on which sentence senses present states of affairs, entities rather like Russellian propositions. (The reader is cautioned to consult these authors for a precise statement of their views.) Below, I assume that the Fregean adopts such neo-Fregean views about the reference of sentences and predicates; nothing in the argument turns on this assumption.

Like almost everyone else who does semantics, I bandy the word 'property' about without much explanation of what I intend by it. ("More or less what Russell meant" is surely not much explanation.) I expect properties to be adequately represented for the purposes of semantics in terms of their possible-worlds intensions. I assume that they are "desensitized." That is, they can be individuated without reference to ways of thinking of extensions. So, for example, the properties of being water and being H_2O are identical, as are the properties of being an eye doctor and being an ophthalmologist.

Now, (3) is also the proposition the Russellian says is expressed by 'Twain is Twain': If we interpret the sentence

(4) ⟨'is', ⟨'Twain', 'Twain'⟩⟩

in Russellian fashion, we again wind up with (3). Twain is, after all, Clemens. Since the propositions are the same, a Russellian view that sees 'believes' as naming a relation to a proposition has to say that whoever believes that Twain is Twain believes that Twain is Clemens.[6]

This strikes many as a *reductio* of the Russellian view. One important motivation for Frege's view is to avoid just this result. A person needn't associate the same senses with 'Twain' and 'Clemens'. Perhaps Barbara associates a sense like *the most famous resident of Hartford* with the first name and one like *the author of Huck Finn* with the second. If so, the thought she expresses with 'Twain is Twain' will be different from that she expresses with 'Twain is Clemens'. If, in saying 'Barbara believes that Twain is Twain' or 'Barbara believes that Twain is Clemens', we're ascribing these thoughts to her, the truth of one ascription doesn't require the truth of the other.

For Frege, senses are the contents of expressions – they are the contributions expressions make to determining what a t-clause names. They are also the cognitive values of expressions for their users. This means two things. First, it means that understanding an expression consists, in good part, of having or grasping a sense for the expression. Second, it means that we are supposed to appeal to senses in explaining the differing epistemological attitudes – finding informative, surprising, and so on – we have toward sentences, as well as the different epistemological properties – being informative, being a priori, and so on – the sentences have. The attitudes to the sentences are reflections of the attitudes we have toward the sentences' senses, for senses are the objects of attitudes like belief, desire, assertion, and deduction. The properties of the sentences, on Frege's view, are inherited from the thoughts they express.

Frege also supposed that the sense of an expression determines what it refers to. A sense provides a condition, or a set of properties, or something along these lines, something that can determine a

---

6 The same sort of problem arises for views that take contents to be intensions semantically associated with expressions and accept the conventional wisdom that names are rigid designators of their bearers.

reference. An expression, Frege said, refers to whatever its sense uniquely determines.

Frege has been vigorously and I think correctly criticized for this last supposition. The details of these criticisms, especially those of Kripke, Kaplan, and Putnam, are well known and widely accepted. I will not repeat them in detail. I will sketch one, in order to give the reader unfamiliar with Frege's views a feel for them.[7]

The most natural model for the sense of a proper name is one in which it is a concept the user associates with the name. The concept itself can be thought of as being given by one or more descriptions the user associates with the name. Frege himself encourages this view of senses. He suggests that for some of us the sense of 'Aristotle' is that of 'the pupil of Plato and the teacher of Alexander the Great'; for others it is given by 'the teacher of Alexander the Great who was born in Stagira' (Frege 1892, p. 58).

Now, it can hardly be denied that most uses of most proper names of the famous refer to the people we would naturally take those uses to refer to. Mundane uses of 'Einstein' pick out the formulator of the special and general theories of relativity; mundane uses of 'Botticelli' pick out Botticelli. This is true even of uses of the names by individuals who would misdescribe the referents of the name or would be unable to construct a description of the referent altogether. The man who persistently describes Einstein as the inventor of the atomic bomb still refers to Einstein when he says 'Einstein could have solved this problem'; the man who can tell you, of Frege, only that he was some German philosopher may still refer to Frege with 'Frege'. But then, given the picture of sense mentioned above, in which the sense of a name for an individual is identified with a descriptive condition he associates with the name, the sense of the names in such cases doesn't determine their reference. Einstein didn't invent the atomic bomb; in the 'Frege' case, the speaker apparently doesn't associate a *definite* description with the name, and so associates nothing with it that determines a unique individual. So the idea that sense determines reference, as sensible as it might at first sound, seems to be a mistake.

This aspect of Frege's view of sense can be excised from his treatment of attitude ascriptions. The easiest way to excise it is to

---

7 Kripke's criticisms are to be found in Kripke (1980); Kaplan's in Kaplan (1977). See also Putnam (1975). Salmon (1981) contains a helpful discussion of these criticisms. The example in the text is due to Kripke.

surrender the idea that a sense determines a reference in an interesting way. We can suppose that something else makes a word refer, and just build the reference of a name into its sense. If we do this, we will think of a Fregean sense as being a pair of things, what Frege might have identified as a sense, along with a referent.[8]

On this view, the first part of the sense of 'Aristotle' *may* be something like a concept that determines Aristotle and Aristotle alone. But it *need* not be. The sense of 'Aristotle' need not even "contain" information that is true of Aristotle. We might as well allow that the conceptual part of a sense doesn't have to correspond to a definite description. It could even be something that would be best captured by a partial or indefinite description, like 'a Latin poet'. Or it could contain, or consist in, an image or an ability to recognize someone, for that matter. This is something of a departure from Frege, to be sure. But it is a departure that makes his overall view of the semantics of attitude ascription more plausible.

We can excise the view that sense determines reference from Frege's views without really affecting what he had to say about sentences like 'Barbara believes that Anne is married'. But it is not easy to see how to excise the claim that the sense of an expression varies intersubjectively. On practically any reasonable way of understanding the notion of sense as a way of thinking of an object, we would expect it to be quite often the case that different people associate different senses with the same proper name, as in the example given by Frege of the various senses of 'Aristotle'. And presumably different people may associate different senses with the same predicate, while using it to refer to the same property.

Of course, there is nothing in Frege's view that would *prevent* different people from associating the same sense with a name or a predicate. It is just that, given the fact that our concepts tend to differ, as does our education, culture, and general *Weltanschauung*, it will be a common occurrence that the senses we associate with our words differ, even though their reference does not.[9]

This presents a problem for Frege's view of attitude ascription. Recall that for Frege the t-clause in

---

8 McGinn (1983) can be seen as adopting this strategy.
9 This point is distinct from the now familiar one that sentences containing demonstratives and indexicals must vary in sense from use to use. Since presumably any proper name might suffer from intersubjective variations in sense, even eternal sentences such as '2 + 2 = 4' may vary in sense from person to person.

(5) Barabara believes that Anne is married

names a thought; the sentence as a whole says that Barbara believes this thought. But there isn't on Frege's view such a thing as *the* thought that Anne is married. So a Fregean theory has to make some choices about what sense is named by the t-clause in a sentence like (5). Is it the sense the speaker would express with 'Anne is married'? Is it the sense Barabara would express with the sentence, or yet some other sense? This is a serious problem for Fregeanism, taken as a doctrine about the semantics of natural language.[10] Let us examine the three most obvious solutions to it.

First, perhaps the most obvious solution is that in (5) 'that Anne is married' names the sense of 'Anne is married' for the person we are talking about, Barabara. More generally, in an ascription

a V's that *S*,

the t-clause names the sense that *a* associates with *S*. (Qualifications must be made for demonstratives and indexicals, as in 'Barbara thinks that I'm here'. Let's ignore this nicety.)

This will not do. Nebuchadnezzar associated no sense whatsoever with 'Hesperus is not Phosphorus'. So on this proposal, 'that Hesperus is not Phosphorus' names nothing in

(6) Nebuchadnezzar believed that Hesperus is not Phosphorus.

So the ascription is not true. This is not good.

Second, and no better, is the proposal that in an attitude ascription a t-clause names its sense for the person making the ascription. At least this is no better given that the relations named by propositional attitude verbs are the relations we would naturally think them to name. I suppose we have some handle on what these relations are; call the relation we would naturally take 'believes' to name Big-B Belief. If 'believes' names Big-B Belief and, in (6), the t-clause names my sense for 'Hesperus is not Phosphorus', (6) is still probably not true; for Nebuchadnezzar probably did not grasp precisely the sense that I associate with this sentence. On a more pedestrian

---

10 Kripke (1979) mentions this problem. He considers only the second solution of this section. The only Fregean I am aware of who has given the problem extended consideration is Forbes (1987a and ms. 1). His solution in these works is that discussed in Section 3. He has recently backed away from this solution and has abandoned the match of content picture that traditional Fregeanism presupposes. Some of the criticisms of Fregeanism in this and the next two sections are developed at greater length in Richard (1988).

level, if your sense for 'Aristotle' has a different conceptual content than mine, as it did for the two men in Frege's example, I will most likely not speak truly if I try to ascribe to you a belief about Aristotle.

Third, a solution the Fregean might explore involves saying that proper names are special, in that they do something like "always take wide scope" in attitude contexts. On this proposal, (6) would be equivalent to something like

(7) $(\exists x)(\exists y)(D(x, \text{Hesperus}) \& D(y, \text{Phosphorus}) \&$ Nebuchadnezzar believed that $^s x$ is not $y^s)$

where '$D(x, y)$' names the relation a sense bears to its reference – it may be read 'x is a sense that determines y' – and the s's are "sense quotes," an analogue to corner quotes.[11]

There are certain advantages to this treatment of proper names in attitude ascriptions. For example, given a standard Fregean treatment of *de re* attitude ascriptions – ascriptions of the form suggested by

(8) a believes, with respect to b, that she is F

– the wide-scope treatment of names facilitates a Fregean explanation of the validity of the inference from something of the form of

(9) a believes that b is F

to (8), when b is a proper name. By 'a standard Fregean account of *de re* ascriptions', I intend ones that regiment sentences of the form suggested by (8) by ones of the form suggested by

(10) $(\exists x)(P(x, b) \& a$ believes $^s x$ is $F^s)$,

where '$P(x, y)$' indicates a relation that entails that named by '$D(x, y)$', but is perhaps more restrictive. Call such a relation 'presentation'. If the Fregean feels that the sense of a name always presents its bearer, he may then give names a wide-scope treatment in attitude ascriptions, regimenting sentences whose form is suggested by

---

11 The idea behind sense quotes is suggested as follows: Suppose that 'x' is a variable that has been assigned the sense of some proper name t. Then $^s x$ is tired^s names the sense of the sentence t *is tired*. I believe that David Kaplan invented this device.

(11) a believes that $A(t_1, \ldots, t_n)$

(where the t_i's are precisely the proper names in the t-clause) by sentences whose form is suggested by

(12) $(\exists x_1) \ldots (\exists x_n)(P(x_1, t_1) \& \ldots \& P(x_n, t_n) \& a$ believes $^s A(x_1, \ldots, x_n)^s)$.

This automatically validates inferences such as that from (9) to (8).

My primary objection to this is that it robs Fregeanism of most of its interest as a doctrine about the semantics of English. First, there is a clear sense in which this "Fregean solution" is not really Fregean, for it gives up the idea that the t-clauses of most attitude ascriptions *refer* to senses. To construe (6) as (7) is to give up the idea that there is some sense p, such that 'that Hesperus is not Phosphorus', as it occurs in (6), refers to p.

Second, on this account of attitude ascriptions, much substitution of coreferential proper names in attitude ascriptions preserves truth. For example, the inference – John believes that Twain wrote *Huck Finn*; Twain is Clemens; thus, John believes that Clemens wrote *Huck Finn* – would be perfectly valid on this account. This wipes out what was supposed to be the primary virtue of Frege's view over referential accounts. Finally, the Fregean can hardly stop with the exportation of names. Presumably, much the same treatment must be extended to predicate expressions, since the senses of these will vary intersubjectively. We end up exporting pretty much all of the nonlogical vocabulary in the t-clauses of attitude ascriptions. From the perspective of the truth conditions the theory ascribes to sentences, this makes a Fregean theory of content appear to be little more than a baroque version of one or another referential theory.

2. AN OBVIOUS SOLUTION RECONSIDERED

Perhaps we were too hasty in rejecting the first solution. We might think that a sentence such as 'Hesperus rises in the morning' has associated with it *some* function – call it f – from individuals to senses. Function f takes me to my sense for the sentence, Willy Brandt to his sense for some German equivalent thereof, Nebuchadnezzar to the sense of some Babylonian equivalent. To say that x believes that Hesperus rises in the morning is to say that x believes the value of f applied to himself.

Of course, we need to be told just how this function operates when there are multiple equivalents of a sentence for a particular individual. We need to know what the function does with an individual who has beliefs that would naturally be ascribed with a sentence, no equivalent of which he understands. Ideally, we would like an assignment of values to the simple expressions that might appear in a 'that'-clause which would determine, for an arbitrary t-clause, just what function it named. But these, you might say, are just the details. The general idea is sound enough.

I disagree. This idea won't provide a satisfactory solution to the Fregean's problem. I will develop two objections to this view. The first is that it gets wrong the truth conditions of iterated attitude ascriptions – ones with more than one attitude verb, such as

Jane believes that Barbara believes that Anne is married

and

Anne wishes that Stevie wondered whether she loved him.

Developing this objection requires a mildly complex argument. The reader who has no patience for technicalities might want to skip to Part B of the section, where the second objection – that the view renders certain obviously valid arguments invalid – is presented.

A. Iterations

Let us consider certain turgid details, in particular how the Fregean will treat multiple embeddings such as

(1) Jane believes that Barbara believes that Anne is married.

(I often abbreviate this sentence as the extended-first-orderese '*jBbBMa*'. I analogously abbreviate its constituent expressions as '*j*', '*bMa*', etc. Each '*B*' should be understood as having absorbed a term-forming 'that'.) We are considering an approach on which *that S* in *Jane believes that S* names the sense for Jane of a sentence equivalent to *S*. It will simplify matters if we suppose that this equivalent is just the sentence *S*. (None of the criticisms below turn on this.)

On Frege's own version of Fregeanism, what a t-clause names is a function of what the expressions in the t-clause name when they occur therein. Frege said that 'that Anne is married' names the sense of 'Anne is married' because, in the t-clause, 'Anne' names its sense and 'is married' names its sense; the clause as a whole names the result of putting these together. The idea that the reference of a t-clause, just like the reference of any other complex name, is determined by the semantics of its parts is an extremely reasonable view. One would hope and expect that on the present view we would be able to characterize what a t-clause names in such a way.

Presumably, we would do this by assigning functions to the expressions that might appear in such a clause that would conspire to make the t-clause as a whole name the right sense. For example, we might assign to 'Anne' a function taking each person to his sense for 'Anne', and assign to 'is married' a function taking each person to his sense for that expression. In 'Jane believes that Anne is married', we then apply these functions to the subject of the ascription, Jane, getting her senses for the words. Combining these, we get Jane's thought that Anne is married, which the t-clause names in this context. Things procede analogously with 'Barbara believes that Anne is married'. The functions are now applied to Barbara, with the result that the t-clause in this instance names Barbara's sense for 'Anne is married'.

With this much machinery in place, we may speak of the expressions in a t-clause naming the requisite senses, the senses that are the values of the functions assigned to them. So we speak of 'Anne' as naming Jane's sense for 'Anne' in 'Jane believes that Anne is married', and naming Barbara's sense for 'Anne' in 'Barbara believes that Anne is married'. All this makes it reasonable to suppose that 'Barbara' in (1) names its sense for Jane; likewise for the second occurrence of 'believes'. But what does '*Ma*' name? There seem to be three possibilities:

(a) the sense Jane associates with '*Ma*',
(b) the sense Barbara associates with it,
(c) what Frege called an indirect sense.

The last is a sense that presents a sense.[12] On option (c), '*Ma*' in

---

12 According to Frege, when a sentence appears after a verb like 'believes', it refers to its usual sense, and it expresses something Frege calls its indirect sense. Given certain of Frege's assumptions (the sense of an occurrence of an expression determines its reference; a sense can determine at most one reference; a sentence's usual reference isn't a sense), it follows that a sentence's indirect sense is distinct from its usual one.

Frege doesn't tell us anything substantial about indirect senses. The literature

(1) names a way of thinking of one of the many thoughts that Anne is married. Presumably, it names a way of thinking either of the sense Jane associates with '*Ma*' or of one of the senses Barbara associates with it.

None of (a)–(c) has very happy results. Consider option (a). According to the natural version of this story, no matter how many verbs of propositional attitude intervene between *e* and *e'* in an ascription of the form

e V's that ... *e'* ...

(V a verb of propositional attitude), *e'* refers therein to its sense for the referent of *e*. (Of course, talk about the sense of *e'* for the referent of *e* must be just a *façon de parler*, given the Nebuchadnezzar objection in Section 1. Such talk is harmless enough, provided we realize that it must eventually be replaced with a definition of the function that maps an embedded sentence to its embedded referent.)

The problem with this suggestion is as follows: Just as sense can vary intersubjectively, so, it would seem, one person may associate different senses with two expressions whereas another associates the same sense with those expressions. For example, Barbara might associate different senses with 'Hesperus is Hesperus' and 'Hesperus is Phosphorus', whereas Anne associates the same sense with both sentences. Let us suppose that this is so and that Anne's sense for both sentences is the same as the sense Barbara associates with 'Hesperus is Hesperus'.

Suppose that Barbara can say truly

(2) I believe that Hesperus is Hesperus; I don't believe that Hesperus is Phosphorus.

Anne ought to be able to report this accurately by saying

is full of discussion about whether Frege ought to have invoked such things, whether he was committed to an infinite hierarchy of indirect senses for any expression, and so on. Perhaps the best discussion of these issues is Parsons (1981). I have benefited from Parsons's work in coming to see what a Fregean could, can't, or must say about multiple embeddings – not that Parsons is responsible for the turgid argument in the text.

If doubly embedded expressions name indirect senses, we will have to assign a family of functions to each expression *e* in order to characterize what is named by a t-clause. Expression *e* will be assigned one function, *f*1, which takes an individual to his customary sense for *e*; another, *f*2, taking an individual to his indirect sense therefore; and perhaps others, should we need more than one level of indirect sense. Singly embedded, *e* will name *f*1(*e*); doubly embedded, *f*2(*e*); and so on. I suppress this complication in the text.

71

(3) Barbara believes that Hesperus is Hesperus; Barbara doesn't believe that Hesperus is Phosphorus.

And on this account she can, for in (3) the embedded sentences refer to Barbara's, not Anne's, senses for those sentences.

So far, all is well. But it seems that not only can Anne truly say that Barabara believes that Hesperus is Hesperus, she could come to know that Barabara believes this. And if she can know this, she can say that she knows it, in a straightforward way, by saying

(4) I know that Barbara believes that Hesperus is Hesperus.

And it is here that the problem arises. For 'Hesperus is Hesperus' in (4), on the proposal we are considering, refers to *Anne's* sense for this sentence. So its reference in (4) is the same as the reference of 'Hesperus is Phosphorus' in a use of

(5) I know that Barabara believes that Hesperus is Phosphorus

by Anne. If (4) is thus true, then, by Frege's own principle that a difference in truth value requires a difference in reference, Anne's use of (5) must be true, too. But if Anne's uses of (3) and (5) would be true, so would her use of

(6) Barbara doesn't believe that Hesperus is Phosphorus, but I know that Barbara believes that Hesperus is Phosphorus.

This is not acceptable. Since the assumptions powering this argument seem quite reasonable, not to mention Fregean in spirit, it is best that we pursue other ways of working out the details.

On the last strategy, a t-clause changed its reference with each new embedding. Let us consider strategy (b), on which multiple embedding does not affect the reference of a t-clause or its constituents. One might say that an embedded sentence always refers to the sense it has for the subject of the "closest" verb of propositional attitude. On this strategy, 'Anne' in

(1) Jane believes that Barbara believes that Anne is married

would refer to its sense for Barbara, not for Jane.[13]
Here is what is wrong with this. Suppose that Barabara thinks

---

13 Actually, this will not quite work as it stands. It requires 'Robbie is sleeping', in the true ascription 'Virginia believes that Santa knows that Robbie is sleeping', to refer to Santa's sense for 'Robbie is sleeping'. Since this exists no more than does Santa, the ascription to Virginia would be false because of reference failure. This can be remedied by making the functions associated with expressions (the

of Anne as the mother of Emily. Suppose that in fact her senses for 'Anne' and 'the mother of Emily' are the same. This would make it the case that the senses she associates with 'Anne is married' and 'the mother of Emily is married' are the same. Now compare sentence (1) with

(7) Jane believes that Barabara believes that the mother of Emily is married.

The situation here is much the same as it was before with the sentences

(4′) Anne knows that Barbara believes that Hesperus is Hesperus,
(5′) Anne knows that Barbara believes that Hesperus is Phosphorus.

On option (a), (4′) and (5′) had to agree in truth value, because 'Hesperus is Hesperus' had to name in (4′) what 'Hesperus is Phosphorus' named in (5′). They named their senses for Anne, the *overall* subject of the sentences, and Anne associated the same sense with each of them. On option (b), (1) and (7) must agree in truth value, because 'Anne is married' in (1) and 'the mother of Emily is married' in (7) have to name the same thing, the one sense that Barbara, the *closest* subject for these expressions, associates with them.

This is just as bad as what happened with option (a). It is clear that (1) could be true without (7) being true. Jane need never have heard of Emily for (1) to be true. But if she has never heard of Emily, then surely (7) would not be true.

This leaves us with option (c). On this option, we say that in (1) 'Ma' names a sense of – a way of thinking of – one of the thoughts that Anne is married. Suppose it names a sense of Barbara's way of thinking that Anne is married. Then we have the following problem: Just as we infer from

(8) Barbara believes that Anne is married

that

ones that give us an expression's embedded reference) operate on the senses, instead of the references, of the closest verb of propositional attitude. (Somewhat ad hoc strictures are then required on the functions to ensure the validity of the inference pattern

a believes that *S*,
a = *b*,
Hence, *b* believes that *S*.)

The resulting treatment is more complicated, but no more satisfactory, than that discussed in the text.

(9) Anne is such that Barbara believes that she is married,

thereby ascribing a *de re* belief about Anne to Barbara, so we can validly infer from (1) that

(10) Anne is such that Jane believes that Barbara believes that she is married,

thereby ascribing a *de re* belief about Anne to Jane. Such inferences ought to be valid. They are not on this option.

Recall the discussion of *de re* ascriptions in Section 1 of this chapter. The inference from (1) to (10) would be regimented by a Fregean as follows:

(1') *jBbBMa*.

Thus,

(10') $\exists s(P(s, a) \& jB^sbBMs^s)$.

But this is invalid, since '*a*', as it occurs in (1'), does not name a sense that presents Anne, but a sense of a sense that presents Anne. Inferring (10') from (1') is something like inferring 'There's a name of Anne that I used yesterday' from 'I used a name of a name of Anne yesterday'. Exactly the same problem arises if we suppose that '*Ma*', as it occurs in (1'), names a sense of Jane's sense for 'Anne'.

There are other problems with option (c) as well. For example, if we say that an embedded expression names a sense of its sense for the subject of the closest verb of attitude – for example, that 'Anne' in (1) names a sense of Barbara's sense for 'Anne' – we have a very difficult time making sense out of ascriptions such as

(11) Jane believes that someone believes that Anne is married

when 'someone' takes a narrow scope. Either the subject of the second 'believes' in (11) is 'someone' (and what sense does *he* associate with 'Anne'?), or it is a bound variable (and the same problem arises).

If we have embedded sentences naming senses of senses of expressions for the *overall* subject of the ascription, other problems arise. For example, if 'Anne is married' in

(1) Jane believes that Barabara believes that Anne is married

names a sense of *Jane's* sense for 'Anne is married', (1) seems to say that Jane thinks that Barabara believes the thought that *Jane*

74

thinks, when she thinks, 'Anne is married'. But on Fregean terms, this shouldn't be the case: Jane might *truly* believe that Barbara believes that Anne is married, without its being the case that Barbara believes whatever thought Jane thinks when the latter thinks, 'Anne is married'.

We began this section supposing that a way could be found to avoid the obvious objection to the view, that *that S* names its sense for *a* in *a believes that S*. We discussed what one would say on such a view about multiply embedded sentences. There seemed to be three possibilities: They refer to their senses for the overall subject of the ascription; they refer to their senses for the closest subject; they name senses that present what they refer to on one of the first two possibilities. In each case, the account we arrived at was unacceptable. Since there seems to be no other plausible choice for the referent of such sentences, I conclude that this view cannot give an acceptable account of multiple embeddings. This seems an adequate reason for rejecting it.

B. Flaccidity

There is another serious problem with the proposal we are considering: It makes t-clauses flaccid in an unacceptable way. On this view, what a t-clause like 'that Billy is riding a moped' names depends upon its linguistic environment, and not just on such features as the time and location of the speaker, what she is demonstrating, the causal chains between names and individuals, and so on. Such a clause will typically switch reference as it moves from 'Rusty believes that' to 'Emily believes that'.

It seems clear that t-clauses in English do not behave in this way. Arguments of the following form are obviously valid:

Rusty believes that Billy is riding a moped.
Emily believes everything Rusty believes.
Hence, Emily believes that Billy is riding a moped.

are obviously valid. They would not be on the proposal under consideration. It would seem that this proposal is committed to treating the argument as being of the following form:

rBa.
$(p)(rBp \rightarrow eBp)$.
Hence, eBa.

75

But since *a* is flaccid in the way observed above, this turns out to be no more valid than the inference 'Rusty spit on his own dog; Stevie spit on everything Rusty did; hence, Stevie spit on his own dog'.

This objection assumes that the quantifier in the second premise of the argument is objectual. If the quantifier were substitutional, the argument would be valid, even though the t-clause is flaccid in the way noted.[14] Could a determined Fregean evade this objection by insisting that quantification over senses is substitutional, not objectual?

There is something quite disingenuous about such a response. Surely a hallmark of Fregeanism is its commitment to the claim that *there is* (objectual quantifier) something identical with the thought that snow is white, or at least that, for each person who can think that snow is white, *there is* (objectual) something that is the sense that person thinks when he thinks that snow is white. Since the Fregean is committed to objectual quantification over senses in any case – just to explain his position – why would he

14 In the usual, objectual interpretation of a quantifier, one assumes a domain of objects over which the quantifiers range – the domain is the sum, as far as the quantifiers are concerned, of what there is. One characterizes a relation between members of the domain and sentences with free variables, like '*x* is a duck', of satisfaction or truth making. The idea behind the relation is suggested as follows: A thing from the domain makes '*x* is a duck' true just in case it is a duck. On an objectual treatment, an existential quantification like '$(\exists x)(x$ is a duck)' ('Something is a duck') is true just in case something in the domain makes '*x* is a duck' true.

In a substitutional interpretation of a quantifier, one trades in talk of domains of objects and satisfaction of open sentences for talk about a class of expressions – the quantifier's substitution class – and the truth of substitution instances constructed from the substitution class. The following is a very rough example: Suppose we had a quantifier 'Σ' that behaved syntactically like the objectual existential quantifier '$\exists$'. We want to interpret it substitutionally. We would specify a substitution class for the quantifier, say, the set of names of the language. Then we would say that a sentence '$\Sigma x(\ldots x \ldots)$' was true iff for some term α in the substitution class '$(\ldots \alpha \ldots)$' was true. For example, if the substitution class consisted of the names 'Mickey', 'Goofy', 'Donald', the sentence '$\Sigma x(x$ is a duck)' would be true just in case at least one of 'Mickey is a duck', 'Goofy is a duck', 'Donald is a duck' was true.

Note that not only do we need to be told what the substitution class of a substitutional quantifier is, but we need some antecedent account of the truth conditions of the substitution instances, if we are to give an account of truth conditions in which some quantifiers are treated substitutionally. (The best introduction to substitutional quantification is Kripke 1976.)

reject the claim that quantification in English over the objects of attitudes is itself objectual?

There are other problems with this maneuver. We can introduce one such problem by reminding ourselves of some of the subtleties involved in substitutional interpretations of the quantifiers. Consider the sentence

If there is always someone who is the mayor, then there is someone who is the mayor and is such that it is always true that he is mayor.

It is natural to suppose that the form of this sentence is indicated by

$$A(\exists x(x = \text{the mayor})) \rightarrow \exists x(x = \text{the mayor \& } A(x = \text{the mayor})).$$

Here 'A' is the tense operator 'It is always the case that'.

I take it that the sentence is not a logical truth. Thus, if we were to interpret the existential quantifier substitutionally, we would have to be careful to specify that its substitution class was limited to terms that are "temporally rigid." In particular, we would want to bar the term 'the mayor' from the quantifier's substitution class. Otherwise, on any natural tense logic, we make the sentence valid.

The general point is that, in treating a natural language quantifier substitutionally, one must be careful in specifying its substitution class if one is to get truth conditions and entailment relations right. Not only are we generally forced to introduce new expressions to form the substitution class (in order to get the quantifier to "range" over all the things intuitively in the quantifer's "domain"), but we must also carefully circumscribe the substitution class to ensure that its members are appropriately rigid with respect to the class of operators with which the quantifier can interact.

Now, it seems that most t-clauses of English are temporally flaccid, in the sense that they pick out different propositions relative to different times. Frege himself was quite explicit about this (see, e.g., Frege 1918.) Because of this, a substitutional interpretation of propositional quantification does not square well with the seeming invalidity of arguments such as the following:

Emily believed that Billy was riding a moped.
Emily still believes all she once did.
Hence, Emily believes that Billy is riding a moped.

I assume that the form of this argument is given by

$P(eB(\text{that}(\exists x)(Mx \ \& \ Rbx)))$.
$(p)(P(eBp) \rightarrow eBp)$.
Hence, $eB(\text{that}(\exists x)(Mx \ \& \ Rbx))$.

Here the 'P' is the past-tense operator, and '$(\exists x)(Mx \ \& \ Rbx)$' is a representation of 'Billy is riding a moped'. *No matter what* semantics we ascribe to the past-tense operator, this comes out valid on a substitutional interpretation of the universal quantifier, as long as 'that $(\exists x)(Mx \ \& \ Rbx)$' is in the substitution class of the quantifier. Since the argument is invalid, we must exclude the t-clause in question from the quantifier's substitution class.

Once this clause is excluded from the substitution class, the Fregean who goes substitutional no longer has an explanation of why the original problem argument is valid; for the claim that the propositional quantifier was substitutional explained the validity of the original argument only on the assumption that sentences like the one just mentioned were a part of the quantifier's substitution class. Of course, this also suggests that practically no English t-clause will be a member of the substitution class of the propositional quantifier. One wonders what, then, would be the quantifier's substitution class.

We have seen two good reasons to resist the idea that the Fregean can treat 'everything' in 'Emily believes everything Rusty believes' substitutionally. So the original objection to the idea that, in *a believes that S, that S* names its sense (or the sense of one of its equivalents) for *a*, stands. So does the first objection made in this section. This way of doing things doesn't seem to work.

3. SENSE AND SIMILARITY

Perhaps the Fregean should jettison the idea that a belief ascription ascribes Big-B Belief in what its 'that'-clause names. Instead, the Fregean might assign another relation to the verb 'believes', the relative product of some relation R and Belief. If he did this and was clever in selecting R, he might be able to revive the second solution of Section 1, allowing t-clauses to name the sense their users associate with them. An ascription *a believes that S*, used by an individual *u*, would be true iff *a* Big-B Believes a thought that bears R to the thought that *u* expresses with S.

I cannot pretend to consider every plausible candidate for R. I will instead discuss what seem the most likely candidates, relations of similarity. On such views, a use of *a believes that S* says that *a* believes a thought that is similar to the one the speaker expresses with *S*.[15] I attempt to keep the argument as general as possible: My goal is to show that serious problems arise, no matter how we construe similarity of sense.

Similarity accounts are not liable to the objection raised toward the end of Section 2. Such accounts will ascribe to the problem argument of that section the form ascribed to it there:

rBa.
$(p)(rBp \rightarrow eBp)$.
Hence, *eBa.*

But now, as long as we evaluate premises and conclusion relative to the same context, the term '*a*' cannot switch reference from premise to conclusion. So there is no context in which all of the premises of the argument are true and the conclusion isn't. The argument is valid.

Similarity proposals would appear to face a dilemma. Let us suppose that the sense of a term presents an individual; that of a predicate, a property. Then we can define a notion of referential similarity for thoughts. Speaking very crudely, "atomic thoughts" are referentially similar if their constituent senses present the same things (taken in the appropriate order, of course); conjunctive thoughts are referentially similar if the thoughts of which they are conjunctions are referentially similar; and so on.[16] For example, the

15 Forbes (1987a and ms. 1) develops this approach. All of the criticisms developed here seem applicable to his view. Forbes has tried to avoid counterintuitive consequences, like that involving what is later dubbed the echo principle, by postulating an ambiguity in belief ascriptions involving names, between a "wide-scope" reading such as that discussed in Section 1 and the reading that is the subject of this section. I discuss the sort of strategy in Section 5; see also Richard (1988).

16 It would be difficult to give a full-scale definition of such a notion without introducing a notion of logical complexity for thoughts. Frege might have resisted such a notion. In fact, Frege would have resisted the conclusions of Chapter 1. For example, he would have said that the sense of '*Fa*' was the result of applying the sense of '*F*', which he thought to be a function, to the sense of '*a*'; he would *not* have taken this result to be a set, but a "unity." (See Hodes 1982).

We are accepting the conclusions of Chapter 1; thus, we won't take time to argue with Frege. In any case, many modern Fregeans would not be troubled by the idea that thoughts can have logical complexity; most would agree that thoughts need to be referentially similar in order to be identical or similar in the sense relevant to this discussion.

The text should be understood in such a way that to say that a sense *s* presents

79

thought Mo expresses with 'Elizabeth is tipsy' is referentially similar to that Curly expresses with 'Beth is tipsy', provided that the terms refer to the same individual and the predicates pick out the same property, even if Mo and Curly's conceptions of Elizabeth and tipsyness differ considerably.

Call the kind of similarity appealed to in the truth definition of belief ascriptions *overall* similarity. It is plausible to think that referential similarity is necessary for thoughts to be similar overall. Either referential similarity of thoughts is sufficient for overall similarity or it isn't. If it is, then a similarity proposal reduces to the exportation solution of Section 1, which makes the notion of sense semantically otiose. But if it isn't, then we seem to lose a principle that we might call the echo principle: If both you and I use a sentence *S* in such a way that its constituents, when we use it, refer to the same things, then, if you can express a belief using *S*, I can use *S* to ascribe that belief to you. It would seem to be the truth of such a principle that justifies my saying, 'Barbara thinks that Anne is married', having heard Barbara say, 'Anne is married', and thinking her sincere; it underlies the feeling that Emily's part in the following dialogue couldn't be false:

Rusty: Anne is married.
Emily: If Rusty just said something that he believes, then he believes that Anne is married.

If referential similarity doesn't suffice for overall similarity, then presumably there will be cases of exchanges like the above, in which Rusty's thought is not similar overall to the one Emily expresses with 'Anne is married', and so Emily is wrong on a similarity account.

Natural accounts of sense and of overall similarity suggest that it would be common for referentially similar thoughts to fail to be similar overall, even when the thoughts are expressed by different uses of one sentence. Suppose that a sense is composed of a conceptual content (which might be expressed by means of a definite or indefinite description) and a part that determines the reference – perhaps the referent itself, or a causal "tail" that determines the

x is to say something stronger than that it simply is a concept of x. Thoughts like those expressed by me with 'Twain is dead' and 'Clemens is dead' are supposed to be referentially similar, although neither is supposed to be referentially similar to that I express with 'The author of *Huck Finn* is dead'.

reference. It would be natural to suppose that similarity was to be determined by the conceptual part of a sense (with the proviso that senses whose tails lead to different individuals aren't similar). Then senses of terms, one thinks, would often fail to be similar overall: To think of Aristotle as the most famous student of Plato would not be similar overall to thinking of him as the principal teacher of Alexander; to think of Cicero as a Latin poet would not be similar to thinking of him as some famous speaker, maybe an Italian.[17]

This sort of problem is quite general. Consider a monolingual French speaker, F, and a monolingual English speaker, E, and their respective senses, for 'London' and 'Londres'. It would be grotesque to suppose that our sense for 'London' was not similar overall to both of these senses, for surely we can successfully ascribe to F and E their mundane beliefs about London's pulchritude, unemployment rate, and so on using 'London'. If E has a belief he can express with 'London is not pretty', we can ascribe it to him with that sentence; if F has a belief she can express with 'Londres est jolie', we can ascribe it to her with 'London is pretty'.

The Fregean may be tempted here by the grotesque. He may insist that the thought that F expresses with 'Londres est jolie' can be stunningly different from our own. F may, for example, think that London is a tiny town where no one speaks English, and so on. Do we really want to say, the Fregean may ask, that F thinks what we do when we think that London is pretty? If not, the Fregean presses, then surely there is merit to the claim that we cannot truly say that F thinks that London is pretty.

Three points should be made here. First, in such a case, we would without hesitation say 'F believes that London is pretty'. We might allow that F thinks of London somewhat differently than we do. But we do not infer that F fails to think that London is pretty. Second, it is worth pointing out that such a case is *naturally* described as a case in which F thinks that London is tiny, that London has few English speakers, and so on. We feel no embarrassment over this; it would never occur to a normal speaker to deny the truth of

---

17 The reader will notice that I have shifted from talk of the similarity of thoughts to the similarity of senses of terms. This is mostly for the sake of expository convenience. I do assume that a similarity account of the semantics of belief ascriptions would countenance talk of similarity of the senses of terms and that such similarity would be relevant to the similarity of thoughts of which the term senses were constituents.

such a claim. The position we are discussing would deny the truth of such claims, even while making them. (Note that in the preceding paragraph, in order to formulate the Fregean's objection, we had to make just these claims.)

Finally, the strategy seems particularly unacceptable in the case of ascriptions of assertion. The Fregean would say that these, just like ascriptions of belief, are ascriptions of relations to senses. It is difficult to see any merit at all in a view that insists that, because F has a different conception of London than we do, we are unable to truthfully say that F said that London was not pretty, when F assertively utters, 'Londres n'est pas jolie'.

That we can *obviously* ascribe beliefs to the monolingual F with 'London' in this way seems to constitute compelling evidence against the account we are considering. At least it does in the company of the reasonable principle that, if a rather large collection of sentences are obviously true, a semantic theory should not make their truth at best unobvious; for it is not obvious that others have senses of London and of other objects that are similar overall to our own. Indeed, on reflection, it seems rather obvious that many do not.

Another problem for similarity proposals arises once it is acknowledged that one person might associate the same sense with distinct expressions, whereas others might associate referentially similar but distinct senses with the expressions. Suppose that A and B use 'Hesperus' and 'Phosphorus' as names for Venus, and that A associates one sense with them, B two quite different senses. It might be that A's sense for the two terms was the sense that B associated with 'Hesperus'.

This leads to sad results. For example, since A associates the same sense with 'Hesperus' and 'Phosphorus', she will associate the same senses with 'Hesperus is Hesperus' and 'Hesperus is Phosphorus'. So A can say truly, 'Whoever believes that Hesperus is Hesperus believes that Hesperus is Phosphorus': The sense named in the consequent is the same, after all, as the one named in the antecedent. And assuming that identity suffices for overall similarity, A will be able to truly say, 'B believes that Hesperus is Phosphorus', given merely that A can truly say, 'B believes that Hesperus is Hesperus'.

Let me make a somewhat more general point, one that applies not only to the current suggestion, but to most Fregean views about attitude ascription. Fregean theories about attitude ascription are motivated by appeals to our intuitions about whether someone could, for example, believe that Hesperus is Hesperus, without believing that Hesperus is Phosphorus, or that Cicero orated, without thinking Tully did. If you reflect on the last objection, I think you will come to see that, even supposing that these intuitions are perfectly correct, they do not suffice to motivate a theory like Frege's. Indeed, they actually seem to *undermine* such a theory.

Whether we can say of B 'He thinks that Hesperus is Hesperus, but not that Hesperus is Phosphorus' does *not* seem to depend upon whether the senses of the relevant sentences are the same or similar for B and for us. Certainly there is nothing in our day-to-day practice of attitude ascription that could be construed as looking for evidence, for sameness or similarity of sense, as a basis for our ascriptions. We just listen or look: If B utters 'Tully is tubby' and we think him sincere, we will say, 'He thinks Tully is tubby'. What does similarity of sense have to do with it?

This strongly suggests that, whatever we are doing when we ascribe attitudes, it isn't very much like what Frege thought we were doing. If senses are relevant to attitude ascriptions, they are relevant in a somewhat indirect and unobvious way. The upshot is that traditional Fregeanism is just on the wrong track when it comes to the semantics of attitude ascriptions.

I have argued that the Fregean is unable to supply an adequate answer to the question What does a t-clause in an attitude ascription name? once he takes his own view, that senses vary intersubjectively, seriously. Senses seem to be bad choices for the contents of expressions. I will close this section by considering two Fregean responses to the arguments of this and the previous sections.

First, there is Graeme Forbes's (1987b) suggestion for defending similarity accounts against the sorts of objections we have just considered: We should, he suggests, "use our intuitions about which ascriptions are right and which wrong to constrain the similarity relation, i.e., we employ the methodology of Lewis 1979" (p. 209).

The strategy Forbes has in mind is used by Lewis to defend a similarity analysis of counterfactuals. Lewis observes that there is an "extreme shiftiness and context dependence of" criteria of similarity. Because of this, Lewis (1979) suggests, the thing to do is not to start by deciding, once and for all, what we think about similarity of worlds, so that we can afterwards use these decisions to test [the analysis]. . . . Rather, we must use what we know about the truth and falsity of counterfactuals to see if we can find some sort of similarity – not necessarily the first one that springs to mind – that combines with [the analysis] to yield the proper truth conditions. . . . In looking for a combination that will stand up to the test, we must use what we know about counterfactuals to find out about the appropriate similarity relation – not the other way around. (p. 43)

How will Forbes apply this strategy? Presumably by looking at a wide range of more or less paradigmatic, successful ascriptions of attitude. From these, we are to extract a set of criteria (and perhaps some way of weighing them) that explain how overall similarity is to be construed.

What uses of attitude ascriptions are paradigmatic? Many have thought that the uses in ordinary explanations of behavior are par-adigmatic – that is, the sorts of uses suggested by 'He's waving because he wants to get Ann's attention' or 'He hit me because he thought that I had insulted his wife'. I think it is fair to say that Forbes's strategy can succeed only if we can extract from the corpus of successful behavior-explanatory ascriptions a suitable set of cri-teria for similarity. Of course, such criteria have to make most of these ascriptions true on a similarity account. And the criteria had better go considerably beyond this: Thoughts are overall similar only if they are referentially similar. Otherwise, sense becomes, semantically, otiose.

It is dubious that such criteria will be forthcoming. Suppose that Randi is waving, and you ask me why. I will tell you, 'He's waving because he wants to get Ann's atttention'. Whether this is a suc-cessful explanation doesn't seem to have very much to do with whether Randi and I think of Ann in similar ways. Perhaps I think of her as my best former student, whereas he thinks of her as his wife to be. This seems pretty much irrelevant to whether or not I have given a correct explanation of his behavior.

Suppose, for the sake of argument, that Fregean thoughts are the objects of attitudes like belief and desire. Then it would seem that, normally, so long as there is *some* sense x that presents Ann to Randi under which he wishes, ^{s}The attention of x is gotten^s, and he thinks, ^{s}If there is waving, the attention of x is gotten^s, and these wishes and desires are part of what moves Randi to wave, I have correctly explained Randi's behavior. So even if we buy in on a Fregean account of what it is that we think and wish, identity or similarity of sense doesn't seem to have very much to do with whether our explanations of action are successful or true. This suggests that Forbes's strategy can't get off the ground. There is every reason to think that there will be a fairly wide and *unsystematic* variation between the senses of the ascriber's sentences and the senses actually believed or desired in the cases in which behavior-explanatory ascriptions are successful.

Another response to the argument of the past few sections is this: What you have shown is that sense must by and large be constant across speakers. Frege's intuitions on *this* point were just wrong. But once one corrects Frege on this issue, none of the criticisms of the past sections are at all telling.

One wonders what someone who makes this response could possibly have in mind. Surely it is intrinsic to *Frege's* notion of sense – the notion of a way of thinking of a thing – that it will vary as do culture and education. It's all very well to concede that sense must be constant across speakers, if anything like Frege's theory is to succeed. But simply to concede this, with no hint of what an alternative theory of sense might be like, is quite idle.

Now there is one sort of theory that invokes a notion *somewhat* like Frege's notion of sense and holds that that which is invoked is more or less constant across speakers. I have in mind certain versions of what has come to be called "conceptual role semantics." It is to a consideration of some of these theories that we now turn.

4. CONCEPTUAL ROLE

It is often suggested that a sentence's conceptual role (CR) is relevant to its behavior in attitude ascriptions. In this section, we will look at a theory of attitude ascriptions which makes use of the notion of CR, that of Boër and Lycan (1986). Some preliminary comments on the notion of CR are in order.

A number of notions fall under the rubric 'conceptual role'. For the most part, when people talk about the CRs of sentences, they have one of the following in mind:

1. *Inferential role.* Two sentences have the same inferential role for an individual just in case the individual is disposed (or otherwise inclined, programmed, or whatever) to make the same inferences

to and from the sentences. Such a notion is discussed in Harman (1973, 1982).

2. *Linguistic role.* We might extend the notion of inferential role so that it includes the evidential and behavioral aspects of a sentence for an individual, arriving at a notion that we might call linguistic role. Relevant to overall linguistic role are also evidential relations – both those between sentences and sentences and those between sentences and experiences – and motivational relations between sentences and behavior. Sellars originally emphasized the importance of this notion (see, e.g., Sellars 1954).

3. *Computational role.* On some views of mental processes like belief, they involve computational relations to sentences. If we accept such views, we may speak of a sentence's computational role. Analogously, versions of functionalism that are committed to the view that the "input" and "output" of certain mental states are sentences may allow a useful notion of functional role. Various writers, Lycan (1982) for example, have examined uses to which this notion might be put.

4. *Probabilistic role.* Given a speaker of a language, it seems possible in principle to assign subjective conditional probability functions to the language's sentences. The functions give the probability the speaker assigns to a sentence, given the truth of other sentences in the language. Such assignments capture important facts about the psychological role of the sentence for the individual, ones related to the facts underlying the other notions of conceptual role. Field (1977) works out such a notion in considerable detail and discusses its role in semantics.

Ignoring doubts one might have about the third notion (because of doubts about the sort of psychological theory it presupposes), there is no denying that there is such a thing as the conceptual role of a sentence, in any of these senses of 'conceptual role'. The notion of CR can do useful work in theories in the philosophy of mind. It may even be useful in empirical psychological theories. It does not follow that the CR of a sentence has very much to do with the semantics of attitude ascriptions.

In fact, since the CR of a sentence appears to be extremely idiosyncratic, it is not easy to see how an appeal to CR could get around the sort of arguments given in the past sections. This is perhaps clearest for a notion of CR like Field's. For someone like me, who accepts 'Kaplan is the author of *Demonstratives*', the subjective probability functions determined by 'Kaplan is tired' and 'the author of *Demonstratives* is tired' are identical (or almost so). For someone who doesn't accept the identity, they are quite different. So any attempt to make a 'that'-clause like 'that Kaplan is tired' name its CR (on this construal of CR) or its CR paired with its truth conditions will certainly fall afoul of versions of the arguments we have given against Fregean theories.[18]

Some advocates of CR in semantics have felt differently. For example, Boër and Lycan have a view of CR on which it is supposed to be true that the CRs of English sentences are more or less constant across English speakers. They also hold that, for example, exchanging one name of a person for another name of that person generally changes the sentence's CR. For most of us, the CR of 'Tully is bald' is distinct from that of 'Cicero is bald', even though we know that the names are coreferential.

It is reasonable to think that, if there is such a notion of CR to be had, it can do semantic work; for CR so construed is not idiosyncratic in the way that, for example, probabilistic role is. This, and the fact that Boër and Lycan's theory is arguably the best worked out example of a CR semantics for attitude ascriptions, is sufficient motivation for examining their theory.

Let's begin by summarizing the overall structure of Boër and Lycan's views on attitude ascription. Following Davidson, Boër and Lycan suggest that the surface grammar of attitude ascriptions is somewhat deceptive. Although

(1) Odile believes that snow is white

seems to be only one sentence, it is really two. Sentence (1) is aptly represented as

(2) Odile believes that. → snow is white.

Here the arrow represents a demonstration. The rough idea is that, when we utter (1), we are saying Odile is related to a certain thing. We do so by pointing out the (sort of) thing she is related to: The reason we say 'snow is white' when we utter (1), on this view, is to give ourselves something to point at.

Boër and Lycan say that (1) is a case of what Quine calls deferred

18 This is no criticism of Field, who is pessimistic about finding any semantically useful notion of interspeaker identity of meaning beyond identity of reference. See, e.g., Field (1977, pp. 398–9).

87

reference – we refer directly to one thing in order to refer indirectly to another. (Quine's example is of pointing to the gas gauge and saying, 'It's empty', thereby referring to the tank.) In the case of (1), we use 'that' to refer indirectly to a set of sentences, those that play the same kind of role for Odile as 'snow is white' does for us. Sentence (1) says something like Odile believes-true one of *those* sentences, where *those* sentences are the ones that play a snow-is-white role for Odile. (Boër and Lycan subscribe to a rather strong version of psychological sententialism.)

The sort of role that is relevant depends upon the speaker's interests. In some contexts, semantical role (SR) is relevant; in others, CR is. A sentence's SR is explained in more or less Russellian terms. For example, Fa and Gb have the same SR just in case a and b are terms that pick out the same thing, and F and G are predicates that determine the same property in a more or less Russellian sense of 'property'. We will discuss the assignment of CR in detail below. For the moment, we can say that Boër and Lycan's notion of CR makes it something like a fusion of the notions of linguistic and computational role.

In any case, 'that' in (1) ends up picking out the class of sentences which play for Odile the same contextually salient role as does 'snow is white' for the speaker. What a sentence of the form of (1) does, on Boër and Lycan's account, is roughly this: It says that Odile believes-true a sentence that has, for her, the same (contextually salient) role as does 'snow is white' for the speaker.[19]

Here is an example of how this works. Suppose Odile observes Twain enter and says, 'Clemens is here'. She would not say, 'Twain's here', for she knows Twain as 'Clemens'. In fact, she

---

19 Some technical niceties: Actually, the 'that'-terms name certain functions. The basic idea is that the 'that' in (1) names, in a context c, the function that takes an individual u to the set of formulas which have the same M-role for u as does 'snow is white' for the speaker of the context. Here, M is whatever sort of role is salient in context c. For example, if semantical role is salient, then in a use of

Odile says that Lille is dangerous

by me, 'that' names a function which takes Odile to the set of sentences whose SR for her is the same as the SR of 'Lille is dangerous' for me. 'Says' is assigned a function which operates on an individual and such a function: $Says(u, f)$ gives us truth iff u assertively uttered one of the members of $f(u)$. Similar assignments are made to verbs such as 'believes' and 'knows'. Even this involves some slight simplifications of Boër and Lycan's account. They don't affect the argument.

would be behaving differently if she accepted 'Twain is here', having always wanted to meet Twain.

I want to know if Odile realizes that Twain, my rival for her affections, has come. So I ask Mutt, 'Does Odile realize that Twain's here? Mutt knows that she saw him walk in. So Mutt says,

(3) Odile realizes that Twain is here.

This is a perfectly acceptable report, and would naturally be taken to be true, even though Odile would deny 'Twain is here'. Boër and Lycan can say that (3) is true, since it was SR, not CR, that was salient in the context of Mutt's utterance. For Odile did "realize-true" a sentence ('Clemens is here') that has (for her) the same SR as 'Twain is here' had for Mutt, the speaker.

Across the room, you want to know if Odile realizes that Twain, who she has always wanted to meet, is here. So you ask Jeff, 'Does Odile realize that *Twain* is here?' Jeff knows that she rejects 'Twain is here' and so says (at the same time Mutt speaks),

(4) Odile doesn't realize that Twain is here.

Again, the report is perfectly acceptable and would be taken to be true by a party to the conversation apprised of all the relevant facts – what sentences Odile accepts, her dispositions to behavior, and so on.

Part of the point of Boër and Lycan's account is to allow them to say that Jeff's report is true, too, even though it appears to contradict Mutt's. They would say that, in this sort of situation, CR is salient. If the CR of 'Twain is here' for Jeff is different from the CR for Odile of any sentence she realizes-true, (4) will be true; for if CR is at issue, then (4) says (roughly) that Odile realizes no sentence with the CR for her of 'Twain is here' for Jeff.

Examples like this are, I believe, of some importance; any adequate theory of attitude ascriptions has to deal with them somehow. What we have here is a sentence, (3), with no obvious indexical or ambiguous elements (save the verb tense, which is irrelevant). It seems to have, at one time, different truth values – it's "true for Mutt" and "false for Jeff." A little less controversially, someone in Mutt's context, apprised of all the relevant facts, would not object to Mutt's utterance. Such a person, even if he were asked, 'Is it *strictly speaking* true that Odile believes that Twain is here?' would say that it was. In this sense, Mutt's utterance is completely acceptable. Likewise for Jeff's.

Acceptability in this (quasi-technical) sense doesn't *entail* truth. But it is natural to begin by assuming that acceptable uses of sentences are by and large true ones. Boër and Lycan give an account that, if it works, would seem to allow us, by and large, to assign truth to acceptable attitude ascriptions and falsity to the rest. This would be a significant virtue of their theory.

If it works. In order to determine whether it does work, we need to look more closely at Boër and Lycan's (1986) notion of CR. Their initial gloss of the notion runs thus:

> Very roughly, a sentence S plays for a speaker x the same conceptual role that a sentence S' plays for a speaker y just in case x and y mobilize S and S', respectively, in closely similar ways in practical and theoretical reasoning (i.e., the pattern of "moves" associated with S in x's public or internal language game is functionally equivalent to that associated with S' in y's language game). (p. 53)

They go on to say that sameness of CR is marked by sameness of "motivational, evidential, and inferential feature[s]," as well as parallel "causes, inferential properties, and behavioral effects" (pp. 53–4). The notion of CR is supposed to be "narrow" or "autonomous." This means at least that CR and SR vary independently, with neither determining the other. In Putnam's Twin Earth cases, a sentence has the same CR for different speakers, but divergent SRs; sentences like 'Tully is tubby' and 'Cicero is tubby' are ones which, for most of us, have differing CRs without a difference in SR.

So far, it is rather difficult to see how Boër and Lycan could say that CR is more or less constant across speakers. What we said about the subjective probability functions determined by 'Cicero is bald' and 'Tully is bald' – that they would vary across speakers, especially between speakers who do and ones who don't accept 'Tully is Cicero' – would seem to be equally true of the notion of CR we just outlined. A speaker who accepts the identity will make quite different inferences from 'Cicero is bald' than one who doesn't. The same sort of thing is true of motivational and evidential factors associated with the sentence.

In a section that suggests how their theory applies to puzzle cases, Boër and Lycan address this problem. They consider the case of Jones, who believes-true the sentence 'Cicero was bald', but not 'Tully was bald'. Does Jones believe that Tully was bald? "One

. . . feels that there should be no *unequivocal* answer . . . the question has a strong 'yes and no' feel to it" (Boër and Lycan 1986, p. 78).

Boër and Lycan suggest that

(5) Jones believes that Cicero was bald

can be true in a situation, even though

(6) Jones believes that Tully was bald

is not, as long as it is CR, not SR, that is salient in the context. In those situations, the answer to the question is no, because the question amounts to: Does Jones believe something with the CR for him of 'Tully was bald' for us? If SR is at issue, though, both ascriptions will be true, since the SRs of the two sentences, for Jones and for us, are the same. So if Jones believes-true 'Cicero was bald', he believes-true something that has for him the SR that 'Tully was bald' has for us. But if CR is at issue, the 'Cicero' sentence will typically be true even though the other isn't.

Note that (5) can be true while (6) is false only if the speaker is focusing on CR *and* the CR of 'Cicero was bald' for the speaker is the same as it is for Jones. So if, as Boër and Lycan suggest and most speakers of English believe, most of us could correctly say of a man like Jones 'He thinks that Cicero was bald, though he doesn't think Tully was', the CR of 'Cicero was bald' must be the same for most speakers of English. A similar argument shows that the CR of 'Tully is bald' must be constant across English speakers. Of course, the conceptual roles of the two sentences must also be distinct.

Here is how Boër and Lycan address the problem we raised earlier: that for most of us, the CRs of the two sentences would appear to be the same. Conceptual role, they say,

is a matter of what pattern of moves is assigned to a . . . formula by the rules of a particular language game. . . . The rules of the game "assign" patterns of permissible and obligatory moves at the outset, in abstraction from any particular playing of the game; i.e., the rules determine the *intrinsic* combinatory powers of the pieces. . . . *Cicero is Tully* was never an axiom or meaning postulate of our language game, nor has it become such (any more than "All and only creatures with kidneys are creatures with hearts," to which we also assent.) . . . In saying that Jones believes-true a sentence [with the same conceptual role for him as 'Cicero was bald and Tully wasn't' for us] we are saying that Jones believes-true something whose *intrinsic* combinatory powers [match that sentence's]. . . . The only utterers who cannot truly affirm ['Jones believes that Cicero is bald'] while denying

['Jones believes that Tully is bald'] are those for whom "Cicero" and "Tully" are *definitionally* related. (p. 81)

What differentiates the CR of 'Cicero is bald' and 'Tully is bald' then? Boër and Lycan suggest that it is intrinsic to our language game that it contain axioms of the form

N is named 'N'

for each name N (p. 82). This gives distinct names distinct intrinsic combinatory powers:

Cicero is named 'Cicero'

will be a theorem (a free move?) in our language game;

Tully is named 'Cicero'

will not be. So the inferential powers of sentences containing the two names differ intrinsically.

Since the notion of CR has here undergone some refinement, we need to reconsider carefully the question When do expressions have the same CR for different speakers? We should first reemphasize that Boër and Lycan's approach will be successful only if they are able to answer this question in such a way that it turns out that the CRs of sentences are more or less constant across speakers of the same language.

This is because it is only if the notion is thus constant that the theory will be able to treat like cases in like ways. There isn't any relevant difference between your saying, 'Jones thinks that Cicero is bald, but he doesn't think Tully is', my saying this, and a gentleman in Left Overshoe, Nebraska, saying it. Either all of us can say this truly, or none of us can. So either all of us have the same CR for 'Cicero is bald' as Jones does, or the theory is a failure. And since cases that seem perfectly parallel to Jones's can be constructed using the names of the mundane, it had better be that the CR of sentences like 'George Smith is tired' (Smith being my neighbor) are more or less constant across the relevant subpopulation of English speakers.

After introducing the notion of *intrinsic* functional role, Boër and Lycan do not return to the question When is the conceptual role of X for x the same as that of Y for y? This is unfortunate, since it is somewhat opaque as to what aspects of inferential, evidential, and motivational role are supposed to be intrinsic to a sentence or its constituents.

Actually, this is not wholly opaque in the case of some "observational" predicates and sentence-forming operators. Connections with certain (narrowly individuated) experiences will be intrinsic to the predicates ('red' and experiences of red); what is characterized by introduction and elimination rules will be intrinsic to broadly logical operators. But it is somewhat difficult to see what could be intrinsic to proper names.

This is the case I will concentrate on for the balance of this section. I will argue that the idea that we can meaningfully compare the CRs of sentences containing proper names across individuals is quite dubious if we try to explain CR in the way in which Boër and Lycan propose. I will also argue that Boër and Lycan's theory simply does not have acceptable results in the very sort of case – the Jones/'Cicero'/'Tully', astronomer/'Hesperus'/'Phosphorus', and Pierre/'London'/'Londres' cases – they themselves discuss.

The notion of CR as applied to proper names can be developed in one of two ways.[20] Either it is a relatively thin notion, with relatively few "rules" and "axioms" relevant to intra- and interpersonal identity of CR, or it is relatively fat. In the former case, we would expect only (a) orthographic rules, such as the

N is named 'N'

rules, or (b) relatively simple "axioms," such as

Kaplan is a man,
Lille is a French city,

to enter into such determinations. The latter axioms might be characterized as sortal axioms, in a broad sense: They characterize, in some basic sense, what sort of thing the name names. It is plausible to think that such axioms are required for possession of the name: You haven't mastered 'Lille' if, for example, you think that Lille is a basketball player; indeed, you probably haven't mastered it if you don't know that it's a city.

We might expect some exceptions, of course. Names introduced

---

20 The attentive reader will note that I henceforth slip into talking about the CR of subsentential expressions, as well as the CR of sentences. Those who find such atomization of the notion of CR offensive can take this talk as a convenient shorthand for roundabout talk about the CRs of sentences in which the expressions occur.

by explicit definition might have richer CRs. The same would be true of names with a special connection to theories – for example, names with roles in a theory like the roles of 'force', 'mass', and 'acceleration' in physical theory.

The fatter notion of CR would extend the thin one by allowing some extra axioms into the intrinsic category. Perhaps they might be ones like that suggested by

Kaplan once looked like this: $-|-$
$$\overset{\text{o}}{\underset{(\ \ )}{-|-}}$$

or

Kaplan writes about ethics.

(Since CR and SR are independent, the axioms needn't encode accurate information.) Being *intrinsic*, we would presumably want such axioms to be limited to some small set acquired around the time that the name is acquired. Obviously, such a fat notion of CR will make it vary widely among speakers. Even if it turned out that most of us had similar axioms for the names of the famous and infamous – something that one doubts – it certainly would not be true that most of our axiom sets for the names of the mundane are the same if they are so constructed. We typically acquire the names of the mundane in different ways, and at different times and places. So such a theory will not be adequate; it will certainly fall prey to the arguments of earlier sections. We had best concentrate on the thin notion of CR.

We need to answer, on a thin theory of CR, the question When is the CR of X for x the same as that of Y for y? We may assume that the question has been answered for the case when $x = y$. In the intraindividual case, CR will presumably slavishly follow orthography, because of the "N is named 'N'" rules, as well as analogous rules for predicates. (Of course, there will be exceptions for definitional equivalents.)

For the case in which x is not y, it would seem the answer ought to be: when and only when x and y have or can apply the same axioms to X and Y, respectively. (I construe 'axioms' here in such a way that they encode motivational and evidential factors. The Kaplan-looked-like-this axiom above is an example.) When is this the case? Suppose that the rules that x applies to the name N are of the forms

N is human,
N is named '*N*'.

There would seem to be two answers to the question When does *y* apply the same rules to the name *M*? The first option is that he does, provided he applies to *M* rules of the form of

M is human,
M is named '*M*'.

The second option is that he does, provided that he applies to *M* rules of the form of

M is human,
M is named '*N*'.

The second option makes the orthography of a term essential to interpersonal comparisons of conceptual role; the first option does not. Since it's natural to think that a simple difference in spelling can't mark a difference, between you and me, in CR, it's natural to think that the first option provides the right kind of answer to our question.

If the first option is the correct answer, the game is up. It makes it true, for example, that the CR of 'Cicero' for me is the same as the CR of 'Tully' for almost every speaker of English except myself; for on the thin theory we are pursuing, the CR of 'Cicero' for me is determined by something like the rules

Cicero is human,
Cicero is named 'Cicero'.

On the first option the conceptual role of 'Tully' for you is the same as that of 'Cicero' for me if the rules relevant to your use of 'Tully' are those obtained from my rules by a systematic substitution of 'Tully' for 'Cicero' therein:

Tully is human,
Tully is named 'Tully'.

On a thin theory we would expect that these are the very rules that are relevant to the conceptual role of 'Tully' for most speakers.

Indeed, the first option seems to make the conceptual role of 'David Kaplan' for me the same as the conceptual role of 'John Perry' for you. The fact that the terms differ in reference is wholly irrelevant to the question of whether they share CR. And the rules that govern 'John Perry' for you – we may suppose they are

John Perry is a philosopher,
John Perry is named 'John Perry'

– are obtained from the rules governing 'David Kaplan' for me,

David Kaplan is a philosopher,
David Kaplan is named 'David Kaplan',

by substituting 'John Perry' for 'David Kaplan'. (It also turns out, on this alternative, that the relation, x has the same conceptual role for me as does y for you, isn't an equivalence relation.)

At this point the reader may be inclined to protest that there should be more built into the notion of CR, even on a thin construal. For example, the rule

Cicero was an orator

should be built into the CR of 'Cicero', at least for those who know he's an orator. Something similar should be true of 'Kaplan' and 'Perry'.

There are two responses to this protest. First, remember that we are trying to take the idea of *intrinsic* CR seriously. Why should this last rule be intrinsic in Boër and Lycan's sense? It can't be just because we learned that Cicero was an orator when we acquired the name, for if this were the case, then other information, idiosyncratic to our acquisition of the name, would also enter into CR, making the CR of a sentence vary across individuals. The point of pursuing a thin notion is to prevent this.

Furthermore, suppose we accede to the claim that something about the role (and not just the "sort") associated with a name should be built into its CR – so we get a job, or a nationality, or some such role built into CR. We still would seem to end up with the sort of (strange) identifications of CR noted above. For example, it would still seem that the names of twentieth-century philosophers should all have the same CR and the names of nineteenth-century American novelists (Sam Clemens, Mark Twain) should all have the same CR when we compare CR across individuals.

There is a sense in which someone who explains interpersonal identification of CR using the first option above is simply saying that, when it comes to proper names, such comparisons of CR don't make much sense. This is because there is no *intrinsic* difference (in Boër and Lycan's sense) between the way 'Kaplan' functions

in my behavioral economy and the way any number of terms –
'Perry', for instance – function in yours.

If we ignore for the moment the theoretical pressure on Boër
and Lycan to distinguish, for example, the CR of 'Cicero' for me
from the CR of 'Tully' for almost everyone else, we see that there
is a great deal to be said for this answer. The fact that the spelling
of two terms differs between idiolects certainly seems irrelevant to
the question of whether the CR of one term in one idiolect is the
same as the CR of another term *in another idiolect*. For one thing,
if spelling counts, then it would seem as if it were impossible,
except in the case of the introduction of a term by definition, for
orthographically distinct terms X and Y to have the same functional
roles for distinct x and y, respectively. This certainly seems wrong.

Boër and Lycan might insist that orthography counts. If enough
axioms about quotation are axiomatic, then it will be a theorem of
my language game that

$\exists x$(Cicero is named x, and x begins with a 'c').

But it won't be a theorem of your language game that

$\exists x$(Tully is named x, and x begins with a 'c')

unless you acquired 'Tully' (or 'Cicero') as a definitional equivalent
of 'Cicero' (or 'Tully'). Surely this much of a difference should
make a difference.

If we think back upon the original characterizations of CR that
Boër and Lycan give – those in which it appears to be a notion
from psychological theory or from the philosophy of psychology
– this doesn't seem very convincing. Suppose Lawrence speaks a
dialect of English that spells certain numerals differently:

andaone, andatwo, three, four, five, . . .

Then it would be a theorem of Lawrence's language game that

$\exists x$(andaone is named x, and x begins with 'a')

while the corresponding

$\exists x$(one is named x, and x begins with 'a')

wouldn't be a theorem of ours. We would not want to say that
this marked an important difference between the functional roles
of 'one < five' and 'andaone < five' for us and Lawrence. So spelling doesn't count here. In general, in any normal comparison of

something like the CR of one sentence for me with that of some other sentence for you, we would abstract from such things as orthography. We would feel that the difference they made *inter*personally was irrelevant (which is not to say that it is *intra*personally irrelevant).

The upshot, I believe, is that the notion of CR, in anything like its normal sense, cannot do the work Boër and Lycan wish it to do. It is their notion, of course, and they are free to cut it off from its psychological roots. So let us pursue what happens when they answer our question about interpersonal identity of CR using the second option. The question that immediately arises is, What are we to say about the CRs of the sentences of aliens, like the French and the Babylonians? Surely the case of Jones/'Cicero'/'Tully' is one whose treatment should parallel the treatment of the case of the ancient astronomer/'Hesperus'/'Phosphorus'. So Boër and Lycan need to be able to identify the CRs of Babylonian sentences with those of the English sentences that have become their canonical translations.

But it is difficult to see how Boër and Lycan can consistently do this. On the basis of the above discussion, it appears that they must appeal to a difference in orthography between my term 'Tully' and your term 'Cicero' in order to explain why it is that the CR of the one for me was different from the CR of the other for you. We saw that they were able to point to differences in "theorems in the language game" that the differences in orthography required. (Of course, we argued that these differences were really irrelevant.)

Now, precisely the same sorts of differences in orthography and theorems arise when we compare the CR of, say, 'Cologne' for me and 'Köln' for the German Bodo. For example, again assuming that the apparatus of quotation is intrinsic in the requisite sense, it will be a theorem of my language game that

$\exists x \exists y$(Cologne is named x, and y applies to a thing iff it is a cassion, and x and y both begin with 'c').

(This simply reflects the fact that 'Cologne' and 'cassion' both begin with 'c'.) But there isn't a corresponding theorem in Bodo's language game. Natural translations of this into German will not be theorems, since 'Cologne' translates as 'Köln', and 'cassion' translates as 'Munitionswagen'.

It is difficult to see why such orthographic differences, and the corresponding differences in theorems, should make a difference in the case of two speakers of English, but not in the case of a comparison between an English speaker and a German speaker. So it is difficult to see how, even ignoring the problems of comparisons of CR among English speakers on the thin notion of CR, this notion can be used by BL to develop a satisfactory theory.

So the notion of CR must be both pared down – we must get rid of the appeal to orthography in the individuation of CR across individuals – and plumped up – we must find something that is common across speakers, even across speakers of different languages, to anchor identifications of CR. Surely the prospects for finding something to do the latter job are quite dim, at least if the resulting theory is to be at all responsive to our intuitions concerning the truth and falsity of attitude ascriptions. Let us wax rhetorical: What could such an entity be? Consider yourself, me, and our friend from East Overshoe. We learned the name 'Kaplan' in different ways. We have very different beliefs about him; we are inclined to make different inferences from sentences in which his name appears. It is simply not plausible that there is some common, intrinsic core to our uses of 'Jones is talking to Kaplan' that, on the one hand, serves to justify an identification of its CR for all of us and, on the other, is meaty enough to distinguish the CR it plays for me from the CR that 'Jones is talking to Perry' plays for you.

Even if we suppose that interpersonal identifications of CR (including ones among speakers of different languages) are unproblematic, there is a serious objection to Boër and Lycan's account: It seems unable to treat similarly cases that should be treated in the same way.

Remember what Boër and Lycan say about the case of Jones: that the question Does he think that Tully is bald? has a "strong 'yes or no' feel to it." It has the answer 'yes' in some contexts, 'no' in others. This is not an implausible response to the question. I will assume for the balance of the section that it is this that we must say about such cases if we propose to explain what is puzzling about them by appealing to CR.

Suppose that Jones should begin to wonder whether "Tully is bald."[21] After some research, he comes to believe "Tully is bald."

---

21 Here and later, I use double quotation marks after attitude verbs in the following way: *a V's "S"* is used to say that *a* is in a state in which he could express the attitude associated with *V* by using *S*, and is disposed to do so. For example,

Suppose this happens on Tuesday. It is clear that we ought to say the same thing about the question: Was it only on Tuesday that Jones came to think Tully bald? as we do in the original case about the question: Does Jones think Tully is bald?

Let us assume that the notion of CR can be explained in such a way that this works out. This requires that, for most English-speaking x, the CR of 'Tully is bald' for x is the same as it is for Jones. It would seem that this is the only way in which we can be assured that most English speakers can truly say, in the appropriate contexts, 'Jones came only on Tuesday to believe that Tully is bald', for this is true in no context in which SR is salient. And it will be true in a context in which CR is salient only if the CR of 'Tully is bald' for the speaker is the same as the CR for Jones of some sentence that only on Tuesday does he come to believe true. It is difficult to see what this could be, save 'Tully is bald'.

This solution cannot be extended to cases that seem to be perfectly parallel. In particular, it cannot be extended to cases like that of Kripke's Pierre.[22] Suppose that Pierre believed "London is large" since the time he became proficient in English, but he does not realize "Londres est grande." It is only after reading a book in French that he realizes "Londres est grande."

Suppose that the date of the reading is July 14. Is it true that only on July 14 does Pierre realize that London is large? The question has a strong yes and no feel about it. There will be contexts in which we would naturally say that this is true, and those in which we would naturally say it is false.

So it should be that most of us could truly say in certain contexts, 'Only on July 14 did Pierre realize that London was large'. If this

---

'Pierre believes "Londres est jolie" ' is short for 'Pierre can express a belief by saying "Londres est jolie," and is disposed to do so'.

22 Pierre is a logician raised in France speaking no English. He there comes to accept the French 'Londres est jolie' and acts like any Frenchman who has a belief thereby expressible. He comes to London in mysterious circumstances, not knowing that he is in the place the French call 'Londres'. Learning English directly, without translation into French, it never dawns on him that he is in 'Londres'. He comes to think that the city he is in is particularly ugly, and thus accepts, and acts like someone who believes what is said by, 'London is not pretty'. See Kripke (1979) for a discussion.

Boër and Lycan, it should be observed, explicitly claim that their theory applies to the case of Pierre. The section in which the Jones case is discussed is entitled "Kripke's Puzzle about Belief"; Pierre is replaced by Jones for the sake of brevity.

is not true, then the theory does not treat like cases – Jones/'Tully'/
'Cicero', Pierre/'London'/'Londres' – in a like way.

This puts impossible demands on the theory. We have

E: London is large.
F: Londres est grande.

Either the CR of F for Pierre is the same as that of E for us or it
isn't. If the latter, we are done; in no context will it be true that
he learns only on July 14 that London is large.

Suppose that the CRs are the same. Then the CR of E for Pierre
cannot be the same as the CR of E for us, on pain of falsifying the
claim that the belief emerges only on July 14. This is somewhat
surprising, to say the least. But it is not just this that is objectionable.
Surely if the CR of E for us is distinct from the CR of E for Pierre,
this will also be true of the CR of other English sentences involving
'London'. No explanation of the difference, save that 'London'
plays different roles in Pierre's and our behavioral economies, seems
credible; but this can be expected to carry over to any sentence in
which 'London' occurs.

There will be any number of things about London that Pierre
"believes in French" and that he "learns in English" in the course
of learning English. For example, Pierre always believed, "Londres
a des grands parcs." We may expect that it comes as something of
a shock to Pierre to discover that "as ugly as London is, it has some
large parks." Suppose he discovers this on Guy Fawkes Day.

Did Pierre discover only on Guy Fawkes Day that London has
large parks? The question is perfectly parallel to all the earlier questions. A theory should not treat it any differently than any of the
other questions. Of course, Boër and Lycan's theory must treat it
differently. We have seen that the theory is forced to say that 'London has some large parks' has a different CR for Pierre than it has
for us, if it is not to give some other question a nonstandard treatment. Boër and Lycan must thus say that in no sense did Pierre
learn this only on Guy Fawkes Day.

Boër and Lycan's theory doesn't give a satisfactory account of
attitude ascriptions. If we suppose that the notion of CR is a notion from psychology, as Boër and Lycan lead us to believe, it
seems impossible to justify the sort of interpersonal identifications of CR they want to make. If we cut the notion off from

its psychological roots and "go orthographic," it seems impossible to make the right kinds of identifications and distinctions of CR across speakers of different languages. And no other method of defining *intrinsic* CR offers much hope of making these identifications in the way Boër and Lycan's theory demands. Finally, as we just saw, even if it were possible to make such identifications, the theory would seem committed to a rather unsystematic way of dealing with cases, treating in quite different ways cases that seem perfectly parallel.

We have seen that there is little reason to believe that other accounts of CR will provide us with anything that fares much better as a constituent in the content of sentences. For CRs, as for Fregean senses, the right conclusion to draw seems to be this: If they are relevant to the semantics of attitude ascriptions, their relevance is not all that obvious.

5. CONCLUSION

Here is a picture of both the function of 'that'-clauses and of the nature of attitude ascriptions. Associated with my uses of a particular sentence – say, 'Twain is dead' – is a certain sort of state. It is mental in an important respect: It can't be individuated (solely) in terms of truth-conditional content. It must be individuated, at least in part, in terms of some cognitive notion, such as sense or conceptual role. And this sort of state is public in an important sense: Other people, ones different from myself in background and culture, can be in a state of the very same, or of a very similar, sort.

Furthermore, when I say, 'So and so believes that Twain is dead', and thereby say something true, the t-clause helps pick out the associated state. It does this by naming something that is, or characterizes, the cognitive content of the state: a sense, a CR, or some other cognitive critter. In any case, my sentence is true provided that so and so is in the state thus picked out, or at least in one very similar to it. On this picture, the truth of an attitude ascription depends upon a match of cognitive content between what a t-clause names and some psychological state of the ascription's subject.

Something like this picture stands behind most of the views we have discussed in the past few sections. As will become clear in Chapter 3, I think there is an element of truth in this picture. But as I hope the discussion of this chapter has convinced you, there is also something fundamentally wrong with it.

It seems to me that the basic problem with this picture is the idea that there must be some interesting match of nonreferential, cognitive content between my uses of S and one of your states, in order for *You think that S* to be true. Reasons for thinking this to be wrong emerged several times in this chapter. One place was the end of Section 3. We observed that it was clearly *irrelevant*, both to the truth and to the behavior-explanatory power of my uses of

(1) Randi wants Ann to smile,
(2) Randi believes that if there is waving, Ann will smile

whether Randi and I think of Ann (or smiling, or waving) in cognitively similar ways. Randi, for instance, could think that Ann was a *boy*. But if he thinks, 'If there's waving, then that one [Ann] will smile,' and he wants 'that one [Ann] smiles', then, at least in normal circumstances, what I say will be true. And if Randi acts on these thoughts and wishes, my sentences will be as behavior-explanatory as such ascriptions ever are.

Our discussion of CR pointed to a related problem with this picture. As we saw, many notions of cognitive content or CR don't even allow us to make interesting comparisons of CRs of sentences across individuals. If we can't do this, then, of course, the above picture of attitude ascription has to be scrapped. And even when we can make such comparisons, it often seems that the fact that a name has the same CR for you and me is something of an accident, and irrelevant to attitude ascription.

A Fregean, or other theorist who takes content as something cognitive, may try to put a happy face on all of this. I grant, the Fregean may say, that (1) and (2) may explain behavior without a straightforward match of content between 'Ann smiles' (or other sentences used in the ascriptions) and some state of Randi's. But this can be explained by an appropriate regimentation of these sentences. Perhaps we should read the joint use of (1) and (2) as coming to

(3) There are senses x, y, and z such that x presents Ann, y presents the state of affairs of there being waving, and z presents the property of smiling, and Randi wants $^s z(x)^s$, and Randi believes ^{s}if y, then $z(x)^s$.[23]

23 The ^{s} are the sense quotes of Section 1. Note that it won't do here to use two quantifiers, one for each ascription. If we use two quantifiers, the ascriptions

103

So you see, the Fregean concludes, everything is perfectly Fregean here.

Let's recall the original point: The case of Randi is the *typical* case. It seems that, more often than not, we should expect that the senses on which people are acting, when we explain their behavior, are going to diverge rather widely from the senses of our sentences. Certainly, from an epistemological point of view, this is almost always the case. For all we usually know or care to find out, there just isn't an interesting match of nonreferential content between our sentences and the states of others when we successfully ascribe attitudes to them. This is true in cases in which we're not interested in explaining behavior as well. Who knows *what* sense Jones, who accepts 'Cicero orated' but not 'Tully orated', associates with the terms 'Cicero' and 'Tully' and the predicate 'orated'? Certainly we quickly arrive at a judgment about such cases, without any information that would help us decide whether Jones's way of thinking of Tully and ours are similar or different.

The happy-face strategy gets around this point by conceding it. Whenever we interpret attitude ascriptions using this strategy, the sense that the ascriber associates with S in his use of *He believes that S* is *irrelevant* to the truth of the ascription. And insofar as our ignorance, or indifference, to the cognitive values of expressions of others triggers the happy-face interpretation of ascriptions, it seems that this strategy winds up being little more than a sophisticated version of the exportation solution discussed at the end of Section 1. You will recall that our complaint against that was not so much that it was wrong as that it seemed little more than a baroque version of the Russellianism that the Fregean so vehemently rejects.

An unregenerate Fregean might admit that the match of content picture that stands behind traditional Fregeanism and various modern variants thereof won't work. Unregenerate, he insists that, *still*, surely Hammurabi believed that Hesperus was Hesperus but not that Hesperus was Phosphorus. That this is true, he insists, *must*

could be true if Randi used one sense, or way of thinking, of Ann in the belief, a different one in the desire. If we use distinct quantifiers, the truth of the ascription is about as compelling a piece of evidence, for the claim that Randi is inclined to wave, as the joint truth of '$\exists x(x$ is cookie)' and '$\exists x(x$ isn't a cookie)' is for the claim that there is something that is and is not a cookie.

have *something* to do with the differing ways that Hammurabi represented Venus to himself.

I haven't denied any of this. I have just argued that Frege's and allied explanations of how this comes to be are wrong. In the next chapter, I will try to get the explanation right.

3

Ascribing attitudes

Let us now try to answer the much discussed question as to how a sentence reporting belief is to be analyzed and, in particular, whether such a sentence is about a proposition or a sentence or something else. It seems to me that we may, in a certain sense, say that (i) [John believes that *D*] is about the sentence '*D*', but also, in a certain other sense, that (i) is about the proposition that *D*.

Rudolph Carnap, *Meaning and Necessity*

Consider Mutt and Jeff, who agree on what sentences Odile accepts. They agree about her dispositions to behavior. They agree on just about everything that seems relevant to the question Does Odile believe that Twain is dead?

They don't agree on the answer. When Mutt was asked, it was because someone wanted to know whether Odile would list Twain under dead Americans. Mutt knew she accepted 'Twain is dead' and thus said yes. Jeff was asked by someone who couldn't understand why Odile, who is pointing to Twain's picture, wants to meet him. Doesn't she realize that Twain is dead? Jeff knew she rejected 'He's dead'. He answered that, no, Odile didn't believe that Twain was dead.

What are we to make of this? Observe that Mutt and Jeff's utterances are acceptable in the quasi-technical sense of Chapter 2: A party to Mutt's conversation, who knew the relevant facts, would accept his utterance as correct. The same is true of Jeff's utterance. As we observed in the preceding chapter, acceptability is good evidence for truth. By and large, when what we say would be said to be true by someone in a position to know if it is true, what we say is true.

In this and the next chapter, I develop an account of attitude

106

ascriptions that honors this sort of evidence. It allows us to say of Mutt and Jeff that they're both right. Not because

(1) Odile believes that Twain is dead

is syntactically ambiguous. Not because there is a semantic ambiguity in the sentence. At least (1) is not semantically ambiguous in the way that, say,

(2) John dropped Susan

is.

I propose that 'believes' and other verbs of propositional attitude are indexical. The truth of (1) varies across Mutt and Jeff's contexts. There is not a change in reference in expressions other than 'believes', nor any change in Odile. And in some important sense, 'believes' remains constant in meaning. If we accept all this, then we will say that 'believes' is an indexical.

What varies across contexts that is relevant to the interpretation of 'believes'? I think that it's what counts as an acceptable translation of the sentences Odile accepts, in a broad sense of 'sentence'. What varies is what functions are acceptable translation or correlation functions. Sentence (1) is true in a context just in case its content sentence is an acceptable representation of some sentence Odile accepts. In some contexts, there are no substantive restrictions on translation at work: If Odile accepts *a is dead* for some name *a* of Twain, that makes (1) true, since 'Twain is dead' there translates any such sentence. In other contexts, there are substantive restrictions at work. In Jeff's context, it seems required that Odile accept *I am pointing at a* before 'Twain' can translate *a*; in Mutt's, it seems, 'Twain' translates 'Twain' and 'Twain' alone.

The most apt way of working out the details of this view makes the content of an expression – what it contributes to the propositions 'that'-clauses (t-clauses) name – a combination of the expression itself and its referential value. In a superficial sense, then, the account of content I will give is a compromise between a broadly referential account and a linguistic one.

I nonetheless consider my view close kin to recent Russellian views of attitude ascriptions. The Russellian position, on which, for example, it's *impossible* to know that Twain is Twain without knowing that Twain is Clemens, strikes some as so absurd as not to merit consideration. I think Russellianism is wrong, but hardly absurd. In fact, a strong case for the view can be made. In Section 1, I sketch this case, in part because its strengh is underappreciated. I also think that, if you look at the evidence and motivation for Russellianism and then compare it with my account, you will end up choosing my account. I honor Russellianism in order to undermine it.

In Section 2, I give an initial sketch of my view of attitude ascription, as well as compare it with the sort of cognitive accounts discussed in Chapter 2. The claim that attitude ascription involves translation will remind cognoscenti of Church's objections to Carnap's and other translational accounts of such sentences. Once I've sketched the view, I turn in Section 3 to consider how it fares in the face of Church's objections. There, I also discuss some objections to the effect that the view individuates propositions too finely. Section 4 applies the view to a number of puzzle cases, including Kripke's Pierre/London and Peter/Paderewski cases.

A full exposition of the view is somewhat lengthy; I have thought it best to break it up into two chapters. I have tried to keep this chapter fairly accessible. For the most part, it attends only to attitude ascriptions with very simple t-clauses, like 'Hammurabi believes that Hesperus isn't Phosphorus'. Some subtle issues – for example, a full discussion of "quantifying in" and the objectuality of the quantifiers, and differences between assigning truth conditions to sentence uses, as opposed to whole conversations – aren't discussed in much detail until Chapter 4. The present chapter completely ignores issues having to do with time and tense, allowing a considerable simplification of exposition. If this makes for a slightly more lengthy exposition than is absolutely necessary, it also, I hope, makes for one that can be taken in on a first reading. Having said what I won't now do, I now proceed not to do it.

1. RUSSELLIANISM

Russellian propositions, you will recall, may have individuals, properties, and relations as parts. Frege thought it absurd to say that a mountain, a doctor, or a philosopher could literally be a part of what one thinks or says; Russell and contemporary Russellians do not. Thus, Russell wrote to Frege: "I believe that . . . Mont Blanc itself is a component part of what is actually asserted in the proposition 'Mont Blanc is more than 4000 metres high'. . . . [What we assert] is . . . a certain complex . . . in which Mont Blanc is itself a . . . part."

Russell's views about propositions and their relations to the sentences that express them changed quite often during his career.[1] For our purposes, a Russellian view is one of the following sort:

1. It takes propositions to be structured entities, with a proposition's constituents and structure corresponding to those of sentences that express it in the manner discussed in Chapter 1.
2. It accepts the view about content suggested by Russell's remarks to Frege. On this view, the content of an ordinary proper name, like 'Mont Blanc' or 'Mark Twain', is simply its referent. Or, at least, the content of a name is simply a function of what it refers to; thus, coreferential names don't differ in content. Russellians take a similar view of the content of uses of demonstratives and indexical terms: Their contents, too, are simply a function of what they refer to.
3. The view assigns contents to other expressions in a broadly Russellian manner – properties and relations (or perhaps Russell's propositional

---

1 The passage from Russell is in Frege (1980, p. 169). When he wrote it (1904), Russell apparently still held that the propositions expressed by uses of sentences containing ordinary proper names like 'Mont Blanc' contain the referents of those names as constituents.

As is well known, Russell soon surrendered this view. He came to hold that most of the time proper names function as "disguised definite descriptions." Perhaps the most accessible statement of this view is in Russell (1912, chap. 5). Among other things, to say that a proper name n in a use of a sentence $S(n)$ by x is functioning as a disguised definite description is to say that there is some description the F such that x's use of $S(n)$ expresses the proposition that would have been expressed by a use of $S(the F)$ by x. [This glosses over subtleties concerning the scope of the description, as well as ones concerning the details of the counterfactual use of $S(the F)$.]

On this view, the propositions expressed with sentences containing ordinary proper names usually don't have the referents of the names as constituents. If, in uttering 'Mont Blanc is over four thousand meters high', I use 'Mont Blanc' as an abbreviation of 'the highest peak in the Alps', then the proposition I express is the proposition that the highest peak of the Alps is over four thousand meters high. Given Russell's theory of descriptions, this proposition does not contain Mont Blanc as a constituent. Rather, it contains various properties and relations, such as *being a mountain, being in, being as high as*, etc.

In adopting this view, Russell did not give up the idea that there are propositions with individuals as constituents. Rather, he came to think that most of us are unable to *grasp*, and therefore express, these propositions. Only if one had the epistemologically intimate relation of acquaintance to the constituents of a proposition was one in a position to grasp it. Again, see Russell (1912, chap. 5).

Contemporary Russellians emphatically do *not* hold that ordinary proper names are disguised definite descriptions. A good deal of the impetus to contemporary Russellianism came from the realization that this aspect of Russell's views about proper names was untenable. See, e.g., Donnellan (1972) and Kripke (1980).

109

functions) to predicates, logical operations or relations to logical operators, and so on.

4. The view takes verbs of attitude like 'believes' to name two-place relations between individuals and Russellian propositions, with an attitude ascription being an ascription of a relation to the proposition named by its t-clause.

Many philosophers have defended one or another version of Russellianism. It has been especially popular recently: In the past dozen years or so, Keith Donnellan, David Kaplan, Ruth Marcus, John Perry, Nathan Salmon, Scott Soames, and my (former) self have all defended versions of Russellianism.[2] Even Russell, at one point in his career, was a Russellian.

1 and 2 commit the Russellian to saying that replacing a name with a coreferential one generally doesn't affect what proposition a sentence determines. (Here and below, I often use 'name' and 'proper name' as short for 'proper name, demonstrative, or indexical'.)[3] If the proposition expressed by the sentence 'Twain is dead' – as we have been thinking of it, the sentence

(1) ⟨'is dead', 'Twain'⟩

– is gotten by replacing expressions with their contents, then if the content of a proper name is what it refers to, sentence (1) determines the proposition[4]

(2) ⟨the property of being dead, Twain⟩.

And this is the very proposition the sentence 'Clemens is dead' determines, for replacing expressions with Russellian referents in

(3) ⟨'is dead', 'Clemens'⟩

again yields (2).

Given this, 4 commits the Russellian to the claim that pairs of sentences like

---

2 See Donnellan (1974); Salmon (1986); Soames (1987a, b); Richard (1983, 1987a, b); Kaplan (1977); Marcus (1962); and Perry (1977). Russell (1903) is, in some ways, the classic statement of a Russellian view of propositions.

3 I remind the reader of my official neutrality about the semantics of definite descriptions. 'Names' as used in the text does not encompass such descriptions. I do not commit myself one way or another to whether on some occasions a description contributes its denotation to what is said by a sentence in which it occurs.

4 Remember that for the most part this chapter ignores the fact that sentences like (1) would usually be taken to express different propositions at different times.

(4) Odile believes that Twain is dead,
(5) Odile believes that Clemens is dead

can't differ in truth value: The t-clauses are two names of one proposition.[5] To a Russellian, supposing that (4) is true and (5) is false is a bit like supposing that Odile kissed Twain but she didn't kiss Clemens. On such a view, almost any substitution of one name (demonstrative, indexical) for another after 'believes that' preserves truth, so long as both terms name the same thing.

Many philosophers seem to think this view to be patently absurd. They feel it is *obvious* that, say, Lois Lane might not realize that Clark Kent can fly, though she realizes that Superman can fly. The Russellian denies that it is even *possible* that Lois realize one but not the other!

I think the view is wrong, but it is hardly absurd. In fact, I see Russellianism as the only coherent alternative to the view I will begin outlining in the next section. The purpose of this section is not to criticize Russellianism, but to explain it. Rather than refute the view, I propose to undermine it by giving an account that, on Russellian terms, is more successful than is Russellianism.

Why would anyone be a Russellian? I think there are three con-

---

5 Of course, I assume we are talking about uses of (4) and (5) in which 'Twain' and 'Clemens' refer to the same thing. In the text, I say that on the Russellian view it is *impossible* that someone believe that Twain is dead without believing that Clemens is dead. Strictly speaking, this depends upon whether the Russellian says that (4) and (5) themselves express one proposition.

Now, the Russellian usually says that (4) and (5) express the same proposition. Whether they do depends on whether t-clauses behave like proper names of propositions or as definite descriptions thereof. In the first case, (4) and (5) each express the Russellian proposition ⟨belief, ⟨Odile, q⟩⟩, where q is the proposition that Twain is dead. If 'that Twain is dead' and 'that Clemens is dead' are treated as definite descriptions of q, however, it is at least possible that (4) and (5) express different propositions – it depends on exactly what descriptions the t-clauses are assimilated to.

If we assimilated 'that Twain is dead' to 'the proposition expressed by this use of "Twain is dead," ' for example, and treated the other t-clause analogously, we would assign different propositions to (4) and (5). This wouldn't change the fact that (relevant) uses of (4) and (5) agree in truth value, since the Russellian proposition expressed by 'Twain is dead' is the Russellian proposition expressed by 'Clemens is dead'. However, assimilating t-clauses to descriptions might allow pairs of iterated attitude ascriptions such as

Odile believes that Tyler believes that all doctors are doctors,
Odile believes that Tyler believes that all doctors are physicians

to diverge in truth value. I know of no Russellian who has adopted the strategy of assimilating t-clauses to definite descriptions.

111

siderations that have pushed philosophers of late toward Russellianism. In reviewing them, I will concentrate on the way in which a Russellian justifies the view that names, demonstratives, and indexicals that refer to the same thing make the same contribution to a proposition.

First of all, considerations about reference and truth have led many philosophers to take Russellianism seriously. Remember that propositions are traditionally considered to be the bearers of truth and falsity, necessity and possibility, as well as the objects of the attitudes. Not only does Odile believe that Twain is dead, but it is true that Twain is dead. Even though Ralph believes that Venus is Mars, what he believes is impossible.

If we ignore for the moment the role of propositions as objects of the attitudes and concentrate on the other role, it seems clear that the contents of proper names, indexicals, and demonstratives are *best* analyzed so that coreferential names make exactly the same contribution to a proposition. This is part of the upshot of Kripke's arguments that proper names are rigid designators and Kaplan's arguments that demonstratives and indexicals are devices of direct reference. In giving these arguments, Kripke and Kaplan have suggested reasons for thinking it would be a *mistake* to try to represent the content of a name as something other than simply the name's referent (or simply a constant function that takes a world to the name's referent).

For example, Kaplan (1977) observes that the content of 'he' in a use of

He [we point at Paul] is happy

is usually thought to be something that determines an individual at different worlds. The proposition expressed by the use of the sentence is true at a world w iff the individual determined by the content of 'he' at w is happy at w. Given this assumption, the content of 'he' doesn't seem to be anything like a Fregean sense or a cluster of properties, which an individual must satisfy in order to be the referent of 'he' at the world. As Kaplan points out, if we point at Paul and say 'He's happy', what we say wouldn't be true at another world simply because someone there who looked and acted like Paul was happy. It wouldn't be true just because someone there who satisfied our most favored description of Paul was happy. After all, what we said was that *he*, that is, Paul, was happy. For that to

112

be true, at a world, it is necessary and sufficient that Paul, the very person we point at, be there and be happy.

There thus seems to be, as Kaplan puts it, a sense in which demonstratives and indexicals refer directly to their bearers: They don't refer via the mediation of a Fregean sense, or a cluster of properties (corresponding to a description), or some other sort of descriptive condition. If the contribution of 'he' to the proposition is simply something that determines a reference in the way mentioned above, then the content of 'he,' and other such terms, seems to be nothing more or less than the individual named – or something like the constant function from worlds to the individual in question. And this is exactly how the Russellian analyzes the content of such a term.

Likewise, Kripke (1980) argues that the reference of a proper name isn't determined in the way that a Fregean, or someone who took a name to be a disguised description, would say it is. In concert with the idea that a name's content determines its reference at both actual and counterfactual worlds, this suggests that a name's content is not a sense, or a cluster of properties, or some condition. Its most apt representation seems to be just the name's referent (or the constant intension corresponding to the reference).

As I remarked in Chapter 2, these sorts of arguments (which are, of course, developed in much greater detail in the works mentioned above) are widely accepted. If we grant the force of Kripke and Kaplan's points about reference and ignore the fact that propositions are supposed to play the role of objects of the attitudes, it seems that the Russellian account of a name's content is exactly right.

Alone, these points don't justify the Russellian's account of attitude ascription, unless we are strongly committed to the idea that the content of a name must be "unitary" in some sense – unless, that is, we are committed to the idea that a content must be *only* a referent, or *only* a sense or cluster of properties. After all, it seems *a priori* possible that the content of a name turn out to be a somewhat miscellaneous collection of items – one, a referent or a constant intension; another, something like a Fregean sense, which comes into play only when attitudes are ascribed. Such a view, on which contents and therefore propositions turn out to be half-breeds, does seem somewhat inelegant. But if the choice is simply between such inelegance and the intuitions about truth of attitude ascriptions that the Russellian jettisons, the choice seems clear.

However, points related to the above speak more forcefully for Russellianism. Consider

It's possible that Paul is happy.

This is true only if the proposition, that Paul is happy, is possibly true. More generally, something of the form of

It's possible that *S*

is true iff the proposition expressed by *S* is possibly true.
   Now consider a claim such as

There's something that is not happy but could have been.

A natural, partial regimentation of this is

$\exists x(x$ is not happy & it is possible that x is happy$)$.

If we treat the quantifier here objectually, we will say that this sentence is true only if there is something *u* such that

It's possible that x is happy

is true when *u* is assigned to 'x'. And this, in light of the above, seems to commit us to saying that the quantified sentence is true only if there is something *u* such that the proposition expressed by 'x is happy', when *u* is assigned to x, is possible. Such talk certainly seems to commit us to Russellian propositions. If an open sentence expresses a proposition given *simply* an assignment of individuals to its free variables, such a proposition is presumably to be individuated simply in terms of individuals: The most natural candidate for the proposition expressed by

$\langle$'is happy', 'x'$\rangle$

relative to an assignment of, say, Paul to 'x' is the Russellian

$\langle$being happy, Paul$\rangle$.

In fact, variables under an assignment present particularly apt candidates for expressions with the sort of content that Russellians attribute to garden-variety names. After all, what could 'x', relative to an assignment of Paul to 'x', contribute to determining what is named by 'that x is dead', save Paul himself?
   So quantification into modal contexts gives us a reason for positing Russellian propositions; it gives us a reason for allowing that

the content of *some* terms is exhausted by their referents. Now, we can also apparently quantify into belief contexts, as in

There is someone who is such that (i) he isn't happy, (ii) he could have been happy, and (iii) David believes he is happy.

The natural quasi-regimentation of this is

$\exists x(x$ is not happy & it is possible that x is happy & David believes that x is happy).

If we assign a Russellian proposition to 'that x is happy' when it appears after 'it is possible', it seems perverse not to do so when it appears after 'David believes'. Furthermore, if we treat the two t-clauses differently, we will have a difficult time explaining why the above seems to imply 'David believes something that is contingently false'. The point is that Russellian propositions, once admitted as bearers of necessity and possibility, seem destined to wind up as objects of the attitudes, too.

Once the Russellian has gotten this far, he can argue in a number of ways that it is plausible to identify the proposition expressed by $\ldots x \ldots$, when X is assigned to 'x', with the proposition expressed by $\ldots t \ldots$, where t is a name of X. One observation he might make is that a proposition is the sort of thing one can *assert* using a (closed) sentence. What closed sentence would one use to assert the proposition expressed by 'x is happy' when Paul is assigned to 'x'? The natural answer is surely: Sentences such as '*He* [we point at Paul] is happy' or 'I [Paul speaks] am happy'. To concede this, of course, is to concede a good part of the Russellian position.

Or the Russellian may argue that the inference from

a believes that t is happy

to

$\exists x(x = t$ & a believes that x is happy)

is valid if t is a proper name, indexical, or demonstrative. It seems to follow, for example, from

David believes that Hesperus is rising

that

$\exists x(x =$ Hesperus & David believes that x is rising).

115

And this follows also from

David believes that Phosphorus is rising.

The simplest, most natural explanation of this is that the proposition that Hesperus is rising just *is* the proposition that is expressed by '*x* is rising' when we assign Hesperus to '*x*'. If so, then the same ought to be true of the proposition that Phosphorus is rising, since assigning Hesperus to '*x*' *is* assigning Phosphorus to '*x*'. And thus are we led to endorse the Russellian line on attitude ascriptions.

Of course, it is possible to resist such arguments. For example, you might posit two sorts of propositions. One sort is purely Russellian; the other is the kind of half-breed proposition mentioned earlier, in which the constituent of a proposition corresponding to a proper name is a pair of items – a Russellian referent and something like a Fregean sense. One might then say that, whenever one believes a half-breed proposition, one automatically believes the corresponding purely Russellian proposition. Given that sentences like '$\exists x$(David believes that *x* is happy)' ascribe belief in purely Russellian propositions, we have an explanation of the inference to this sentence from 'David believes that Hesperus is rising'. And the explanation doesn't imply that, if David believes that Hesperus is rising, then he believes that Phosphorus is, too.

Such responses are ad hoc. One can again say that, if the choice is between a somewhat inelegant theory and jettisoning our intuitions as does the Russellian, the choice is clear. Still, there is surely *something* to be said for the natural, elegant way in which the Russellian treats quantification into attitude ascriptions.[6]

There are other considerations that move people to become Russellians. Consider the way we ascribe attitudes. Ignoring for the moment certain special cases, like those involving Babylonians and Venus, it seems that we are generally indifferent to what name or indexical we use to report assertion or belief, so long as reference is preserved. Thus, if I point at Twain and say, 'He's happy', any of the following seem literally correct reports of what I say: MR said that Twain is happy, MR said that Clemens is happy, MR said

---

6 David Kaplan argues that quantification into modal and other contexts requires Russellian propositions in the introduction to Kaplan (1977). Salmon (1986) suggests that quantification into attitude ascriptions supports the Russellian line on attitude ascriptions. Some of the lines of argument in the text are developed in Salmon (1986).

that you (we are addressing Twain) are happy, MR said that I am happy (Twain is speaking). This certainly suggests that the terms are making exactly the same contribution to the proposition determined by the embedded sentences. (Donnellan 1974, 1979 and Soames 1987b make this point.)

Likewise, we can in general report the beliefs and assertions of speakers of foreign languages using any straightforward, name-to-name translation, so long as the translation preserves reference. For example, a Chinese who has a belief expressed by a sentence conventionally translated as 'Beijing is large' can have the belief ascribed to him either with 'He believes that Beijing is large' or with 'He believes that Peiking is large'. Again, the obvious explanation is that the names make the same contribution to the proposition named by a t-clause.

Some may observe that, even though it sometimes doesn't make any difference what name we use in ascribing an attitude, sometimes it does. In general, it might be said, when someone says that he doesn't believe that . . . *a* . . . (and understands what it is that he is denying), he is right. This is so even if *a* is a name, *b* is a coreferential name, and the person can truly say that he does believe that . . . *b* . . . . This is exactly what is going on in Hesperus/Phosphorus cases: Hammurabi can truly say that he believes that Hesperus rises in the evening; he can truly say that he *doesn't* believe that Phosphorus does.

It is not generally appreciated that this is open to serious dispute. A Russellian might claim that the way we reason about attitudes *commits* us to saying that, for instance, if a person can say

I believe that . . . *a* . . .

and *b* and *a* are coreferential names, demonstratives, or indexicals, then the person can also truly say

I believe that . . . *b* . . . .

In fact, I am responsible for an argument to this effect (Richard 1983).

Consider two people, A and B. A is talking to B on the phone. A is also watching B, across the way, talking in a phone booth. A doesn't know that the person to whom he is talking is the person he sees across the way. He sees the person across the way to be in

117

danger, but doesn't think that the person on the phone with him is in trouble. A would say to himself,

(6) I believe that she [he points across the way] is in danger.

He would dissent from

(7) I believe that you [he speaks into the phone] are in danger.

Let's suppose that (6), used by A, is true. The Russellian wants to show that (7), used by A, would be true, too. Observe that B can report the belief A expresses when A utters (6). Of course, B can't use A's exact words. But B can report A's belief by saying

(8) The person watching me believes that I'm in danger.

(I assume, for simplicity, that A and A alone watches B; nothing hangs on this.) If A's use of (6) is true, B's use of (8) is, too. Suppose that B utters (8) through the phone to A. That doesn't affect its truth. Now surely A can report what B says, when she uses (8) on the phone. To report what B says, A would most naturally say

(9) The person watching you believes that you are in danger.

If B's use of (8) is true, then so is A's use of (9). But it seems that (7) follows from (9) and

(10) I am the person watching you.

Since (9) and (10) would be true when spoken by A, so would (7). Q.E.D. It is plausible to think that, if the argument succeeds in this case, it would succeed for other pairs of first-person ascriptions that differ only by coreferential indexicals or demonstratives.

Soames (1987a) argues that this argument generalizes to proper names. If A says truly, 'I think that Twain is happy', Twain can say, 'A thinks that I'm happy'. It seems that it is generally true that third parties can then report what Twain says by saying, 'A thinks that Clemens is happy'. But if I can truly say, 'A thinks that Clemens is happy', surely A can say, 'I think that Clemens is happy'. (Since we will have reason to refer to such arguments later let's christen them 'context-hopping arguments'.)[7]

The upshot of all this is that there is support in the way we talk and reason about attitudes for the Russellian's claim that substi-

7 For further discussion of context-hopping arguments, see Section 4 and the appendix to this section.

tuting one name of a thing for another in a sentence doesn't change the proposition the sentence determines. The objection above – that someone who denies that he believes that so and so is almost invariably correct – should not by itself move one to reject Russellianism, for we seem to be committed to certain patterns of reasoning that belie this objection.

This isn't to deny that there is plenty of evidence in the way in which we talk and reason about attitudes for the claim that substitutions of one name of an object for another *do* affect propositional identity. For example, there are the resilient anti-Russellian intuitions of speakers about Hepserus/Phosphorus cases. Even the Russellian will admit that the evidence goes in two directions. The context-hopping argument and the rest give some, but not conclusive, evidence for the Russellian view.

I said earlier that there were three considerations that might incline one toward Russellianism. The third is the apparent failure of cognitive theories of content and attitude ascription to account for our practices of attitude ascription. Insofar as the primary rival to Russellian views of attitude ascription are such cognitive theories – and certainly many Russellians and Fregeans have seen the issue as one of standing either with the Russell of *Principles of Mathematics* or with the Frege of "On Sense and Reference" – this must be said to have some weight.

Because the anti-Russellian intuitions of speakers are so strong, no case for Russellianism can be considered complete before we have some explanation of why we have these intuitions. None of what we have mentioned thus far helps explain why almost everyone thinks that there are people who believe that Cicero was an orator, but not that Tully was; or the fact that everyone, even the most diehard Russellians, talk as if someone might have the one belief but not the other.

The standard Russellian line on this is that these intuitions are to be explained in terms of pragmatic implications. In saying that a pair of sentences like

(4) Odile believes that Twain is dead,
(5) Odile believes that Clemens is dead

can't differ in truth value, the Russellian offers an account of truth-conditional (or, as I will say, semantic) content. His is a suggestion about what sentences like (4) and (5) "strictly and literally say."

He grants that typical uses of (4) may get across something that typical uses of (5) do not. But this, he says, is a matter of their pragmatic implications, not their truth-conditional content.

The idea is to some extent parallel to the idea that, widespread intuitions of speakers to the contrary, uses of

(4′) Tonto jumped onto his horse and he rode into the sunset,
(5′) Tonto rode into the sunset and he jumped onto his horse

strictly and literally say the same thing: simply that a jumping occurred and a riding occurred. Here one suggests that there is a pragmatic, not semantic, implication of (4′) that the events occurred in a certain order: jumping, then riding. This is to say (among other things) that, although (4′) is often, perhaps typically, used to convey the idea that the events occurred in a certain order, and although (4′) typically does convey this to hearers, a use of (4′) would be a true use even if the order of events were riding, then jumping. (5′) has the same semantic content as (4′), but a somewhat different pragmatic implication. That this is so is strongly suggested by the fact that we can cancel such implications without absurdity, saying, for example,

(4″) Tonto jumped onto his horse and rode into the sunset. Not necessarily, however, in that order.

In the case of (4) and (5), one wants to know (a) what the implications in question are and (b) why we should suppose that they are pragmatic, and not semantic. Different Russellians give different accounts of the exact nature of the pragmatic implications of sentences like (4) and (5). I propose to outline a sort of generic Russellian account of what it is that such ascriptions pragmatically imply. What I have to say about it would apply, I think, to any of the proposals about such implications Russellians have made.

Although Russellians take attitudes like belief to be relations to Russellian propositions, they allow that such relations are *mediated* relations. For example, in *Demonstratives*, Kaplan (1977) uses the notion of believing a proposition under a particular character, or sentence meaning. Salmon (1986) invokes ways of apprehending Russellian propositions, ways that may involve, but needn't be exhausted by, the sentences we use to express them. Perry (1980) and Soames (1987a) speak of the different belief states that, for some proposition, may all be states in virtue of which one believes the proposition.

120

The intuition behind such views is that one has a proposition as an object of an attitude in virtue of being related to (or, in the belief state version, being in) some third entity that itself determines the proposition. (Strictly speaking, it is the third entity, along with one's contextual or historical situation, that determines the proposition.) On these views, one can believe the same proposition in many different ways. Or one may believe it one way and disbelieve it in another.

Since we are giving a generic account, let's simplify the picture somewhat and suppose that the mediators of attitudes are natural language sentences. In fact, let's be very crude about things and suppose that mediation is achieved by tokening, in some crude way, perhaps on a mental blackboard next to the pineal gland. Then, for example, we can observe that Odile may well have a token of

(11) Twain is dead

on her belief blackboard, without having a token of

(12) Clemens is dead

thereon. Jean may have a token of (12) on his board without having a token of (11) on it. In this case, although both Odile and Jean believe the Russellian proposition

(2) ⟨the property of being dead, Twain⟩,

they believe it under, or using, different mediators. Odile believes it under (11) and not (12), Jean using (12) and not (11).

Making the attitudes triadic in this way allows us to distinguish *what* someone believes, according to a Russellian (a Russellian proposition), from *how* she believes (a matter of what mediator(s) she uses). The Russellian says that the truth conditions of attitude ascriptions are only a matter of the what, not the how.

Of course, the how of belief is as important as the what. Whether Odile will faint, on hearing 'Clemens lives', is really more a function of the how than the what. More generally, insofar as attitudes are relevant to the explanation of behavior, the mediators of belief and desire are just as important as the propositions they determine.

It is thus natural on Russellian terms to expect that we would develop some mechanism for getting across information about the mediators of attitudes, as well as about their propositional objects. The Russellian grants that we have. We often use ascriptions like

(4) Odile believes that Twain is dead,
(5) Odile believes that Clemens is dead

to get across such information. For example, in the right sort of situation, perhaps one in which it's important how Odile would or would not express her belief, we might use (4) to convey that Odile believes the relevant proposition under 'Twain is dead'. Or we might take a use of 'Hammurabi believed that Hesperus was Phosphorus' to be communicating that Hammurabi believed the relevant proposition under the Babylonian sentence that is conventionally translated as 'Hesperus is Phosphorus'.

Taking the mediators of belief to be sentences, one might say that we often use an ascription

a believes that *S*

to get across that *a* believes the proposition determined by *S* under *S*, or under some sentence whose relation to *S* is, given the context of the conversation, clear enough.[8] But this, the Russellian insists, is a matter of pragmatic implication.

Why is it a *pragmatic* implication? Why isn't (4) *true* only if Odile believes the proposition expressed by 'Twain is dead' under that very sentence? The Russellian observes, for one thing, that (4) obviously can be true without this being the case, if, for example, she believes it under 'Twain est mort'. Furthermore, arguments like the context-hopping argument suggest that sentences such as

8 As I said, the text gives a sort of generic account of the pragmatic implication. Salmon (1986) suggests a number of pragmatic, non-truth-conditional implications that may be associated with an ascription of the form

a believes that S.

The most significant of these are two: (1) that *a* believes S (or "his sentence for" S) to be true and would assent to it. (2) Consider the function *f* that takes a person, time *t*, and the use of a sentence to the way the person would grasp the proposition expressed by the use, at *t*, were the proposition to be presented to him via the sentence. Given the existence of *f*, a use at *t* of

a believes that *S*

conveys, pragmatically, that *a* believes the proposition expressed by *S* under *f*(*a*, *t*, *S*).

Other Russellian suggestions on the nature of the pragmatic implications of attitude ascriptions are found in Richard (1983 and, esp. 1987a) and in Soames (1987b). (Of course, I no longer endorse the position in Richard 1983 and 1987a.)

(4) are true even when what they imply about the way in which a belief is held is false.

The Russellian's explanation of our anti-Russellian intuitions is that we mistake a common, important, pragmatic implication about the how of belief for truth-conditional content. Should someone suggest that Hammurabi believed that Hesperus was Phosphorus, we would (probably rightly) take him to be getting across that Hammurabi held the belief under a certain sentence, one we are certain he didn't believe it under. When we insist that his claim is strictly and literally false, we are (wrongly) confusing the implication with what was strictly and literally said.

This maneuver is perfectly cogent. Although it is a primitive fact about attitude ascriptions that they convey information about the way in which attitudes are held, it is arguably not a *primitive* fact that this information is relevant to the truth conditions of attitude ascriptions. We do not come equipped with a meter that reliably distinguishes between semantic and pragmatic implications. Examples like that concerning 'and' and temporal order help make the point that what seems for all the world like a truth-conditional implication may turn out not to be one.

The Russellian honors the intuitions about sentences like 'Hammurabi believes that Hesperus is Phosphorus' that seem to be so telling against his position. He points out, quite correctly, that many of our judgments of acceptability, even our refined ones, result from our reacting to what we infer from someone's use of a sentence, or what we infer from the use and our background knowledge and assumptions about why a rational person would make the utterance the person we are speaking with makes. The Russellian may agree with his critics as to what sort of evidence our judgments of acceptability are sensitive. They are sensitive, on his view, to evidence about the Russellian content of an attitude *and* to evidence about the way in which a belief is held – something very much like the sort of thing Fregeans have in mind when they speak of cognitive content. He simply disagrees as to how much of this evidence bears on the truth of the claim literally and strictly made by an attitude ascription.

It is worth observing on behalf of the Russellian that a semantic theory must be responsive to a number of things besides speakers' intuitions about whether a certain kind of use of a sentence is true.

Such theories must be responsive, for example, to intuitions about validity, to intuitions about the nature of the objects of attitudes (for example, that they are truth bearers as well as belief objects), and so on.

Such differing demands on a theory may well justify a theoretical decision that certain kinds of information, which at first seem central to the use of a sentence (and so ought to be taken to be truth conditional), are best taken to be non-truth-conditional. The Russellian, in pointing to the three considerations we reviewed earlier, is in effect using these sorts of considerations to justify moving implications about the how of belief into pragmatics. The fact that cognitive theories seem to do a rather bad job of accounting for the way in which we ascribe attitudes is particularly important in this regard.

Our sketch of Russellianism should make it clear that what really divides Russellians from non-Russellians – at least non-Russellians like the unregenerate Fregean – is not a dispute about the intelligibility of the notion of sense, or cognitive role, or some allied notion. There needn't even be much dispute between the Russellian and his opponents about what attitude ascriptions are used to say. What is under dispute is how much of what we say with a sentence like 'Odile believes that Twain is dead' is relevant to the sentence's truth conditions.

The Russellian prefers to speak about ways of apprehending a Russellian proposition or believing a proposition under a sentence (or a sentence's meaning, or under a particular representation). Modern Fregeans prefer to speak of ways of thinking about, or modes of presentation of, objects, properties, and states of affairs. Though there are undeniable differences in detail and emphasis, the overall picture of attitudes the two have is strikingly similar.[9] For

9 This is most obvious in the case of Fregeans like Forbes and McGinn, who are willing to look on the sense of a sentence as a way of thinking of a state of affairs, where states of affairs are congeries of individuals, attributes and relations, and logical operations – i.e., Russellian propositions. But a related point can be made, I think, about most contemporary Fregean theorists.

Of course, a Russellian will complain about the traditional Fregean's insistence that something like sense or cognitive value determines reference. And perhaps some Russellians do think that the notion of the cognitive value of a sentence, even stripped of its role as the determiner of reference, is somehow suspect. But Russellians, once they admit ways of grasping a proposition, or sentences as mediators of belief, allow the existence and importance of something like Fregean

each, belief and the other attitudes involve a sort of content individuated in broadly referential terms, as well as something broadly cognitive in nature, which in some sense relates the believer to the referential content of his attitude. As far as the semantics of natural language is concerned, the primary difference here seems to come in the answer to the question Does the information conveyed about ways of grasping a proposition, or ways of thinking of a reference, or whatever you want to call it, contribute to the truth conditions of an attitude ascription? Given the failures of Fregean accounts of attitude ascription, the Russellian may observe that it is time to consider seriously the idea that the answer to this question is simply no.

So runs the case for Russellianism. The natural, and I think correct, response to this case involves pointing to the strength of the evidence against the Russellian view. As I observed earlier, even though some of our intuitions favor the Russellian position, we have an enormous, stable body of contrary intuitions. These intuitions have a stability that intuitions like that about 'and' and temporal order apparently lack.

For example, other than using bribery, threats, hypnosis, or the like, there is simply nothing you can do to get most people to say that Jones believes that Tully was an orator, once they know that Jones sincerely denies 'Tully was an orator', understands it, and acts on his denial in ways appropriate thereto. In particular, pointing out that Jones can express something he believes with 'Cicero was an orator' seems simply irrelevant to most people. Even walking them through a version of the context-hopping argument produces at best befuddlement and not an admission that Jones, after all, believes that Tully orated. This is hardly an isolated case.

The situation thus seems somewhat different from the situation with 'and'. People in fact do tend to come around fairly quickly to the view that the connective expresses (only) the truth function that logic books are fond of saying it does.

The Russellian is correct when he says that our intuitions about truth conditions are not wholly reliable. But they are certainly not to be *ignored*. When sophisticated speakers have what amounts to an unshakable conviction about truth conditions – and our anti-

senses. The question is then whether this something has any interesting role in truth-conditional semantics.

Russellian convictions approach this – we have a compelling reason to look for a theory that honors those intuitions, even if there already exists a coherent theory that denies the intuitions. If such a theory is to be had, we should, all else being equal, embrace it.

Let me make a somewhat different point. There is an enormous, easily delineated body of attitude ascriptions that can reasonably be said to have as their *primary* purpose conveying information about the how of belief, not just information about the Russellian what. Among these are ascriptions used in the attempt to explain action, as in 'Randi waved because he wanted Hesperus to rise, and he thought that if there was waving, Hesperus would rise'. It is clear that, if these do explain behavior, they don't do so because of what they tell us about Russellian objects of belief. That Randi wants

⟨Rising, Venus⟩

and believes

⟨implication, ⟨the Russellian proposition that there is waving, ⟨Rising, Venus⟩⟩⟩

doesn't suggest in the least that Randi is disposed to wave. (Suppose he holds his wish under 'Hesperus rises' and his belief under 'If there is waving, then Phosphorus will rise' and is ignorant of the truth of 'Hesperus is Phosphorus'.)[10]

Of course, this isn't the only use of an attitude ascription whose primary point seems to be to convey information about the how, instead of just the what. Other examples are our claims about what the Babylonians did and didn't believe about Venus, about Jones – who thinks that Cicero orated, but not Tully – and so on. Such claims aren't really intended to explain behavior. They are meant to tell us what (in a nontechnical sense of 'what') the Babylonians and Jones do and don't believe.

By and large, the point of ascribing an attitude is to get across some information about the how of the attitude as well as its what, much as, by and large, the point of using 'or' is to express disjunction. I am aware that the path from use to truth is a slippery

10 Perhaps I should point out that the question Are folk-psychological attempts to explain behavior genuine explanations? is irrelevant to the argument. The point here is that we intend our uses of such ascriptions to be explanatory. Further, this intention is not obviously misguided, as it would be if we intended to explain behavior simply by appealing to the Russellian objects of attitudes. See the beginning of Section 4.

one. But surely the truth conditions of sentences are in great part a resultant of the way we use them, along with our intentions.

So suppose that a natural and otherwise satisfactory semantic theory made the relevant information a part of the semantic content of a sentence. Suppose that the theory did this without abandoning the insights of Kripke and Kaplan about reference and modality. And suppose that it accounted for quantification into attitude ascriptions, the context-hopping argument, and other evidence for Russellianism in a satisfactory way. Then surely it would be more reasonable to adopt the theory than to adopt Russellianism.

The second condition here – that the idea that the "information about the how" should fit into a coherent and theoretically satisfying semantic theory – is just as important as the first. If, for example, we could fit the idea into semantics only at the cost of making arguments like

a thinks that Twain is dead,
b thinks whatever *a* does,
Thus, *b* thinks that Twain is dead

invalid, then the cost of making the information semantic is arguably too high. After all, this *is* a valid argument. Relevant here are also considerations of elegance and naturalness of explanation. If, in making information about the how of belief semantic, a theory must make a large number of rather ad hoc maneuvers – such as the bifurcation between purely and partially Russellian propositions we considered earlier, as a response to the Russellian point about quantifying in – then we may finally agree that we would be better off, in doing truth-conditional semantics, if we embrace Russellianism.

Since information about the how seems central, in a vague but nonetheless important sense of central, to so many attitude ascriptions, whether Russellianism is tenable seems to depend on whether a semantic theory can make this sort of information semantic without running into the sort of problems we encountered in the preceding chapter, or into some different sort of muddle. The Russellian is correct in observing that there are no pretheoretic data that *demand* that the how be part of truth conditions. But there certainly is a great deal of evidence that *begs* us to put the how into truth-conditional content.

Perhaps this seems obvious enough. But critics of Russellianism sometimes don't appreciate that whether Russellianism is untenable depends mostly on how difficult it is to incorporate information about the how of belief into a semantic theory. As we have seen, it's possible to give a coherent, Russellian explanation of our anti-Russellian intuitions. And it is possible to tell a not unconvincing Russellian story in which, for example, the information relevant to the explanation of behavior by attitude ascription is a matter of pragmatics, not semantics.

To say this is to give the Russellian his due. If there really is no acceptable alternative to his view, we should swallow hard and accept it. But surely we should look a bit more before we swallow.

Appendix

I have heard it said that the context-hopping argument plays on something like a *de re/de dicto* ambiguity in sentences like (9). I myself now have reservations about the argument (see Section 4). But the *de dicto/de re* response, as I have heard it developed, seems to me implausible, in part because the distinction as it is usually drawn strikes me as implausible. More importantly, the reasons usually given for drawing it seem bad. I will begin by reminding the reader what the distinction is and why people have wanted to draw it. I will then outline two of the responses I have heard to the argument that involve the distinction and point out the costs they seem to incur.

The distinction I find implausible is one between readings or uses of attitude ascriptions like 'The man watching you thinks that you are in danger' or 'Odile thinks that Twain is fat'. Sometimes it turns out to be a semantic distinction, as in the case of Quine; sometimes it is a syntactic one, as it seems to be for many Fregeans. The rough idea behind the distinction is that in the *de dicto* reading, the t-clause is assigned something that captures the "true content" of a belief, as opposed to the *de re* reading, which only characterizes what the belief is about or only characterizes in part the true content of the belief. Often, the distinction is drawn with respect to occurrences of singular terms. In this case, it is often introduced by use of exportation: The *de re* reading of

Odile believes that Twain is fat

is suggested by

Twain is such that Odile thinks that he is fat,

while *de dicto* reading is supposed to be the one in which 'Twain' is not taken as exported, nor "as taking wide scope." It is generally agreed that the *de dicto* reading of an ascription is not implied by the *de re* reading. Authors differ about when, if at all, the converse implication holds.

Quine (1956) is in good part responsible for the current belief in the distinction. His own reasons for drawing the distinction are dubious. He observed that there is clearly a sense of

(1) Ralph thinks that someone is spying on us

that implies not merely that Ralph believes the proposition, that someone is spying on us, but that Ralph believes, with respect to some particular individual, that she spies on us. This sense is seemingly reached by giving the quantifier wide scope, yielding something like

(2) $\exists x$(Ralph believes that x is spying on us).

As is often observed, this alone gives us no reason to think that ascriptions like 'Odile believes that Twain is dead' or 'The man watching you thinks that you are in danger' are themselves ambiguous. What we have is a quantifier-scope ambiguity, such as we find in 'Someday, everybody in the room will be hungry'.

The position of the second 'x' in sentence (2) is an opaque one. That is, it is not open to substitutivity of identity, as is witnessed by the invalidity of one reading of

Ralph believes that the man in the corner is spying on us,
The man in the corner is the person in the corner who is not spying on us,
Thus, Ralph believes that the person in the corner who is not spying on us is spying on us.

So (2) involves quantification into an opaque position. Quine thought that such quantification in was impossible. So Quine proposed that 'believes' was itself ambiguous. Simplifying somewhat, the proposal was that 'believes' has a *de re* sense, on which term positions are open to substitutivity of identity and accept free variables bound by quantifiers outside the scope of the belief operator, and a *de dicto* sense, in which term positions are not open to outside quantification and for which substitutivity fails.

Why Quine thought that quantification into opaque position was impossible is obscure. Kaplan (1986) and Kazmi (1987) exhaustively survey various arguments Quine might have had in mind and find them, rightly, to be wanting. In any case, anyone who finds quantified modal logic – or, as Kazmi observes, quantification across temporal operators, as in '$(x)(x$ is a person in the room $\rightarrow$ someday $(x$ will be hungry))' – intelligible is prima facie committed to the intelligibility of such quantification.

The point is that Quine's motivation for drawing the *de re/de dicto* distinction was spurious. So unless someone can give us some other, better reason for postulating an ambiguity of Quine's sort, we have every right to resist arguments that begin by assuming that Quine stumbled on a genuine ambiguity.

Fregeans also sometimes draw something like a *de re/de dicto* distinction, although in a somewhat different way and for somewhat different reasons. Where Quine's distinction cashes out as a semantic ambiguity, the Fregean distinction cashes out as a syntactic one.

As noted in the text, a Fregean must tell an artful story about sentences like (2) in order to avoid saying that individuals are constituents of Fregean thoughts. Fregeans reinterpret single quantifiers like that in (2) as a pair of quantifiers, one being a standard objectual one, one ranging over senses. Thus, (2) becomes

(2') $\exists x \exists y (y$ is a sense that presents x and Ralph believes $^s y$ is spying on us$^s)$

So far, nothing has been said that would suggest that attitude ascriptions are intrinsically ambiguous; we simply have a somewhat idiosyncratic treatment of quantification in. But we are now on the way to dividing up attitude ascriptions according to the rough principle behind the *de re/de dicto* distinction. Sentence (2') doesn't specify "the total content" of Ralph's belief, according to a Fregean. It partially characterizes it and thus is seemingly different from a claim like 'Ralph believes that Susan spies', which does, on a naive Fregean account, give the total content of a belief.

But now think back on the conclusions of Chapter 2. There we saw that, in order to defend his view, the Fregean was reduced to a strategy in which much of the time, a sentence like 'Ralph believes that Susan spies' itself fails to characterize the total content of Ralph's belief. This is what we called the happy-face strategy, on which such ascriptions are syntactically *ambiguous* between a reading on which their names are exported and one on which names are left in the scope of the attitude verb. [Of course, the Fregean has to pursue such a strategy with regard to terms other than proper names. For example, it is obvious that he will have to treat demonstratives and indexicals in this way. Such a line is pursued, in various ways, in Peacocke (1981), Evans (1981), and Forbes (1987a).] Thus, the Fregean is led to posit a general syntactic ambiguity in attitude ascriptions, one that, according to him, reflects two different ways we ascribe attitudes: by specifying their "complete content" and by specifying their content "in part."

The nature of ambiguity, as well as the motivation for postulating it, are somewhat different in the case of the Fregean case than they are in the case of Quine. But I think we can say fairly at this point that the Fregean doesn't have a very good reason for thinking that attitude ascriptions are ambiguous either. It is not as if the distinction arises in a natural way within the context of a more or less satisfactory semantic theory. It has, rather, the air of a last-ditch attempt to defend a view of attitude ascriptions – the match of cognitive content view – that the facts show to be wrongheaded.

I don't think it is very plausible to think that there is a *de re/de dicto* ambiguity of any of the sorts usually postulated. To my knowledge, no one has ever given a very good reason for supposing that there is such an ambiguity. [Stich (1983) also argues against the existence of such an ambiguity, though he has somewhat different reasons than mine for rejecting the distinction.] Since it is implausible to think that the ambiguity exists, responses to the context-hopping argument that presuppose such an ambiguity are themselves also implausible.

I also find such responses to require us to say somewhat implausible things. Recall the sentences involved in the argument:

(6) I believe that she is in danger,
(7) I believe that you are in danger,
(8) The person watching me believes that I am in danger,
(9) The person watching you believes that you are in danger,
(10) I am the person watching you.

One objection I have heard based on the *de re/de dicto* distinction begins with the claim that an 'I' in the subject position forces a *de dicto* reading of an ascription. Given the privileged position of the first-person belief ascriber – who is better placed to know the content of the ascribee's beliefs? – perhaps this is not so unreasonable. If this is true, then a use of (7) by A would be a *de dicto* use.

If we accept this, we might reason as follows: What is controversial is that (7)'s *de dicto* reading is true in the case under consideration. It seems fair enough to say that B's use of (8) is true *de re*, but not *de dicto*; that were A to use (9), basing his use on B's use of (8), that would be true *de re*, but not *de dicto*. But we can't get from a true *de re* reading of (9) and the identity of (10) to the true *de dicto* reading of (7). At best, we can get from

(9) The person watching you believes you are in danger [true *de re*],
(10) I am the person watching you [true],

to

(7) I believe that you are in danger [true *de re*]

The response makes the *subject* position of a sentence like (9) opaque. On the view just adumbrated, (7) doesn't have a *de re* reading; the idea was that 'I' forced the *de dicto* reading. On this view, there exists no argument from (9) and (10) to (7) of the sort mentioned above, since there isn't a *de re* reading of (7)!

No matter how the details of this position are spelled out, I think, we lose the ability to substitute freely one term for another in the positions marked by the ellipsis in

. . . *believes that so and so.*

So the argument schema

(S) *a* believes that *S*,
    a = *b*,
    Thus, *b* believes that *S*

is not a valid one. This happens even if the *de re*/*de dicto* distinction gets reflected in whatever sort of form is appealed to in characterizing logical validity. For example, if we read the distinction onto forms by splitting the verb 'believes' into two verbs, 'B_r' and 'B_d' – for 'believes *de re*' and 'believes *de dicto*', respectively – then the schema

a B_r that *S*,
a = *b*,
Thus, *b* B_r that *S*

does not represent a valid pattern of inference, in that the truth of the premises does not ensure the truth of the conclusion.

Another version of this objection gives sentences (6) and (7) themselves both a *de re* and a *de dicto* reading. One can then preserve

132

the idea that schema (S), consistently interpreted, is a valid argument schema by saying that a sentence of the form of *a believes that S* has one form when read *de dicto*, another when read *de re*. One continues to say that it is only the *de re* reading of (8), as used by B, that is true and that only a *de re* reading of A's use of (7) follows from (8)'s *de re* use. One then continues the response to the context-hopping argument as above.

It is still true on this line that the surface form

a believes that *S*,
a = *b*,
Thus, *b* believes that *S*

is not valid, since the verbs may be interpreted differently. This strikes me as something of a drawback to this response, especially given the implausibility of the idea that *a believes that S* is ambiguous to begin with.

2. SAYING WHAT OTHERS THINK

In Section 1, I discussed a sort of generic Russellianism. It involved a picture of belief and the other attitudes as relations to Russellian propositions, relations themselves mediated by relations to natural language sentences. As should be clear from Chapter 1, I think the idea that the mediators of belief and other attitudes are *natural language* sentences is too simple-minded. Nonetheless, I think that generic Russellianism is a good first approximation to the truth.

For the purposes of this section and the next, I adopt the expository fiction that generic Russellianism really is the correct picture of the attitudes. Given that we are unsatisfied with the picture of attitude *ascription* that the Russellian offers us, what shall we offer in its place?

Consider the example of Hammurabi, who reputedly believed that Hesperus was Hesperus, but not that Hesperus was Phosphorus. If we allow ourselves to talk about belief blackboards and such, we can describe what the relevant facts are: There are two possible mediators of Hammurabi's belief. Pretend that they are

(1) $H = H$

and

(2) $H = P$.

Here 'H' is doing duty for the Babylonian word canonically translated 'Hesperus', 'P' for that canonically translated 'Phosphorus', and '$=$' for a Babylonian identity predicate. Hammurabi, presumably, had (1) written on his blackboard, but not (2). It is this fact, or one like it, that someone who utters

(3) Hammurabi believes that Hesperus is Hesperus; but
(4) Hammurabi doesn't believe that Hesperus is Phosphorus

is trying to get across. The question is, How do (3) and (4) get this across?

In some way or other, in uttering (3) and (4), the speaker uses 'Hesperus' to represent 'H', 'Phosphorus' to represent 'P', and 'is' to represent '$=$'. And thus, the 'that'-clause 'that Hesperus is Hesperus' represents (1), while the t-clause 'that Hesperus is Phosphorus' represents (2). (3) is true just in case what its t-clause represents is on Hammurabi's belief blackboard; likewise for (4). Since what (3)'s t-clause represents is on the board, while what (4)'s represents isn't, (3) is true while (4) is not.

It will be said, perhaps, that this is correct but that it leaves unanswered the most important question: How does 'Hesperus' come to represent 'H'? Given the argument of Chapter 2, we can agree that the right answer is *not* that 'Hesperus' has for us the same sense or cognitive role as did 'H' for Hammurabi. Is, perhaps, the fact that one of the expressions conventionally translates the other relevant here?

Well, of course it's relevant. But it is also an accidental feature of the example. Recall the case of Mutt, Jeff, and Odile from the beginning of the chapter. Mutt is asked if Odile believes that Twain is dead. The inquisitor wants to know how Odile will react to the question 'Is Twain dead?' Jeff is asked if Odile believes that Twain is dead. His inquisitor wonders whether Odile, pointing at Twain's picture, realizes that he's dead. Mutt knows she accepts 'Twain is dead'; Jeff knows that she does not accept 'that one is dead'. Mutt says she believes that Twain is dead, Jeff denies it.

Here Mutt's use of 'Twain' seems to represent Odile's uses of 'Twain'; Jeff's use of 'Twain' represents Odile's use of 'he' or 'that one'. The latter shows that t can represent t' without t being a conventional translation of t', or vice versa.

Beyond sameness of Russellian interpretation there is in an important sense *no* interesting connection between the expressions in

Jeff's t-clause and the expressions in Odile's belief mediator they represent. Beyond the identity of Russellian interpretation of 'Twain' and 'that one', there doesn't seem to be anything about the content of 'Twain' – in an intuitive sense of 'content' – that makes it an apt representative of Odile's use of 'that one'. The two needn't have the same cognitive content; neither need the one be a translation, in some meaty sense of 'translation', of the other, and so on.

The idea that there is something "intrinsic" to the content of Jeff's sentence that would make it represent one but not another of the mediators of Odile's belief is a mistake. 'Twain' can in principle represent any name, demonstrative, or indexical that Odile uses to refer to Twain. Of course, given contextual factors, there may be something that makes 'Twain' a more apt representative of 'that one' than other expressions the speaker might have used. Given the context of Jeff's remark, it is clear to all – that is, to Jeff and the inquisitor – that what is at issue is whether Odile accepts 'that one [Odile points at the picture] is dead'. Given the way the inquisitor asked his question – 'Doesn't she realize that Twain is dead?' – it is appropriate to use 'Twain' as a representative of 'that one'.

The right answer to the question – How does e in

Odile believes that . . . e . . . .

come to represent some expression (or class thereof) in Odile's belief mediators? – seems to go something like this: The interests and intentions of a speaker (and to some extent his audience) determine how expressions in a t-clause may be and are used to represent mediators of belief. Sometimes, for example, the speaker and audience are focusing on a specific name, term, or other way of representing something. This is what is going on in the case of Mutt and Jeff. This mutual focus produces a restriction on the use of 'Twain' to represent something about the how of Odile's belief. In Mutt's case, a restriction like – Use 'Twain' to represent 'Twain' – is operative. In Jeff's case, something like – 'Twain' is to represent only terms Odile associates with her current perceptual experience of Twain('s picture) – is operative.

The situation is a little like the situation with normal uses of a demonstrative like 'that' or an indexical like 'here' outside of attitude ascriptions. My cocking my finger, pointing, and saying, 'That is unusual' does not by itself determine a proposition, for the finger may be pointing at any number of things. It is only by reference to my intentions, which even I may have some trouble articulating, that one can tell what I said. The same point arises with sentences like 'It's dangerous here'. 'Here' might refer to the street, city, state, etc., as noted in Tatschek (1987).

In the case of 'that' and 'here', the intentions of the speaker help determine what uses of the terms refer to. In the case that interests us, the intentions of the speaker help determine what a use of 'Twain' in 'Odile believes that Twain is dead' can represent. (I say 'represent', *not* 'refer'. The view I am sketching is *not* one on which Mutt's use of 'Twain' refers to some token of 'Twain' that Odile uses.) The analogy with 'that' and 'here' is simply this: Which possible mediators of Odile's belief are relevant to the truth of a use of 'Odile thinks that Twain is dead' is in part a function of various contextually varying factors, including the intentions of the user, his interests, and his beliefs about his audience's interests. Likewise, which object is relevant to the truth of a use of 'that's unusual' in part depends on such intentions.

Of course, in some situations we are not focusing on how someone thinks about the objects and properties about which he has beliefs. In some contexts, as the Russellian is fond of pointing out, we just don't care about the how of Odile's belief, but only about the Russellian what. In these situations there is no restriction operative on what 'Twain' may represent, as long as it represents a name of Twain.

I will try in this and the next chapter to say a bit more about the relations between the intentions and beliefs of a speaker and the sort of restrictions ('Twain' is to represent 'Twain') of which I have spoken. But let's see if we can parley these remarks into an account of the overall semantics of belief ascriptions. (Other sorts of attitude ascriptions are to be treated, of course, in a similar fashion.)

Think of a t-clause as giving us two things. It gives us some Russellian referents − those of its constituents − and some expressions − those in the content sentence of the t-clause. 'That Twain is dead' gives us, for example,

(5) ⟨'is dead', 'Twain'⟩

and

(6) ⟨being dead, Twain⟩.

Things run most smoothly, I have found, if we fuse these into one item. Consider, then, what we get if we pair off the constituents of a sentence with their Russellian interpretations. If we do this with (5), for example, we get

(7) ⟨⟨'is dead', being dead⟩, ⟨'Twain', Twain⟩⟩.

Such hybrids are not Russellian propositions. They are not Fregean thoughts. They are fusions of things that represent – in this case, the expressions in a t-clause – with their Russellian interpretations. Perhaps we should give them a new name, since they are somewhat different from run-of-the-mill propositions. Since they are obtained by annotating the matrix provided by a sentence with the Russellian interpretations of its parts, we call them RAMs, for Russellian annotated matrixes.

Think of the believer. She accepts various sentences, each of which has a Russellian interpretation. Just as we can fuse the content sentence of a t-clause with its Russellian interpretation, mating (5) and (6) to get (7), so can we do this to each of the mediators of the believer's belief. If we do this for all of the mediators of her beliefs, we end up with a set of RAMs. This set encodes all of the facts about the believer that are relevant to the truth and falsity of belief ascriptions to her. Let's call this set the believer's representational system, or RS.[11]

When we ascribe an attitude using, say,

---

11 Some clarifications and caveats follow: In constructing RAMs for a token t-clauses to name, we pair off the types of expressions in the t-clauses with their Russellian interpretations. Thus, simultaneous uses of 'that Twain is dead' will (given identity of Russellian interpretations of their constituents) name the same thing.

In constructing RAMs from token accepted sentences to put into a believer's RS, we also pair off the types of expression tokens with their Russellian interpretations. For the purposes of this and the next section, I pretend that the notions of type in the two constructions are the same, and that in each case the type is public language word type.

In the case of the construction of RAMs for the RS, this is a (temporary) expository simplification. As I explain in Section 4 of this chapter and Section 2 of the next, a somewhat finer-grained notion of type is needed here. Since this notion of type is obtained in a relatively straightforward way from that of public language word type, I put off unveiling it until I have gone over the broad outlines of the view and met what seem the most likely objections to it.

The fact that this chapter ignores tense allows one other expository simpli-

(8) Odile believes that Twain is dead,

we seem to be saying something about the believer's RS, and not something simply about the collection of Russellian propositions believed. The remarks we made earlier suggest that what we are doing is saying (roughly) that the RAM our t-clause determines represents one of the believer's RAMs.

For our RAM to represent one of the believer's RAMs, it seems necessary (but not always sufficient) that our RAM be related to the believer's in a certain straightforward way. Putting the matter crudely, the necessary condition is that, stripped of their linguistic parts, the two RAMs amount to the same Russellian proposition.

Let's not rest with a crude statement of the condition. Call the pairs of things in RAMs, consisting of a vocabulary item and an interpretation, annotations. So $\langle$'Twain', Twain$\rangle$ is an annotation, $\langle$'he', Twain$\rangle$ is an annotation, $\langle$'is dead', being dead$\rangle$ is an annotation, and so on.

Say that a correlation is a rule (a function) that maps annotations to annotations and preserves reference. Suppose we have the annotations

$a:$ $\langle$'Twain', Twain$\rangle$,
$b:$ $\langle$'Clemens', Twain$\rangle$,
$c:$ $\langle$'Melville', Melville$\rangle$.

Then

$a \rightarrow a; b \rightarrow b,$
$a \rightarrow b; b \rightarrow b,$
$a \rightarrow a; b \rightarrow a;$
$a \rightarrow b; b \rightarrow a$

are all correlations. They are rules that take annotations to annotations and preserve reference. In contrast,

fication. In the text, I say such things as, if Odile accepts

(s) Twain is dead,

then a RAM of the form

(r) $\langle\langle$the type of 'is dead', being dead$\rangle$, $\langle$the type of 'Twain', Twain$\rangle\rangle$

gets added to Odile's RS. This is strictly speaking correct. But it is a little misleading, since the way I characterize types in this chapter is really a characterization of "momentary snapshots" or "temporal parts" of the full-blown types that I characterize in Section 3 of the next chapter.

My excuse for not introducing all of this material immediately is that it is easier to understand the view if I defer discussing niceties and complications until there is some call for them.

$$a \rightarrow b; \; b \rightarrow c,$$
$$a \rightarrow b; \; a \rightarrow a$$

aren't correlations: The first doesn't preserve reference; the second isn't a function. It is often convenient to speak as if correlations just mapped expressions to expressions, leaving the fact that annotations contain references as understood. For example, I will sometimes say things like such and such a correlation takes 'Twain' to 'Clemens' and 'Clemens' to 'Clemens'.

Take a RAM p and a correlation f (assume f is defined for all the annotations in p). Consider what we get if we systematically replace what is in p with its image under f. For example, if we begin with the RAM p determined by

Hesperus is Phosphorus

and use the correlation

f: 'Hesperus' $\rightarrow$ 'H'; 'Phosphorus' $\rightarrow$ 'P'; 'is' $\rightarrow$ '$=$',

we obtain the RAM – call it q – determined by

$H = P$.

When p, q, and f are related in this way – q comes from p via the correlation f – I say that p represents q under f.

The relation I mentioned earlier, that which is necessary for the truth of a belief ascription

Odile believes that S,

is that the RAM determined by the t-clause represents, under some correlation or another, a RAM in Odile's RS. So, for example, our old friend

(8) Odile believes that Twain is dead

is true only if the RAM determined by the t-clause

(7) $\langle\langle$'is dead', being dead$\rangle$, $\langle$'Twain', Twain$\rangle\rangle$

represents, under some correlation, a RAM in Odile's RS. As I remarked before, this is roughly equivalent to what the Russellian thinks to be necessary and sufficient for the truth of (7).[12]

12 Many Russellians grant its sufficiency but say that it is not quite a necessary condition. Note that the RAM that Hesperus rises after Hesperus does not represent the RAM that Hesperus rises after Phosphorus, since a correlation can't take 'Hesperus' to both 'Hesperus' and 'Phosphorus'. But many Russellians say that 'John believes that Hesperus rises after Hesperus' is true if John has a belief

But we don't think it to be *sufficient* for the truth of a use of (8). As mentioned earlier, sometimes we impose restrictions on the way an expression is to be used to represent parts of the mediators of someone's belief. Some contexts contain restrictions on the functions we may use to correlate our RAM (the one determined by the t-clause in an attitude ascription) and the RAMs in the subject's RS. When Mutt uttered (8), it was understood that 'Twain' was to represent 'Twain' and nothing else. So in evaluating Mutt's claim for truth, we are restricted in what correlations we can use. We can use only ones that map 'Twain' to 'Twain'. What Mutt said was true provided that his RAM, (7), represents one of Odile's RAMs under a 'Twain'-to-'Twain' correlation.

A context, then, provides a collection of restrictions on correlations. We can think of each restriction provided by a context as containing three things: a person u, an annotation a, and a collection of annotations S. For example, Mutt's context provides the restriction

Odile; ⟨'Twain', Twain⟩; {⟨'Twain', Twain⟩}.

A restriction involving u, a, and S tells us that, in evaluating an ascription of attitude to u, we are restricted to using correlations that map a to something in S. Mutt's restriction, for example, tells us that, in evaluating an ascription to Odile, we are restricted to using correlations that map 'Twain' to 'Twain'.

Our remarks can now be codified as follows: Taken in a context – call it c – an ascription of the form of

t believes that S

is true iff the RAM determined (in c) by *that S* represents a RAM in the representational system of what t names (in c), under a correlation that obeys all the restrictions operative in c. Or, a bit more loosely, the ascription is true iff the RAM *that S* represents one of t's RAMs, given the context's restrictions on correlations.

It should be tolerably clear how this proposal works in the case

he expresses with 'Hesperus rises after Phosphorus'.
    There are a number of interesting issues lurking here concerning the behavior of free variables and demonstratives within the scope of attitude verbs. I will discuss them at length in the first two sections of Chapter 4. I note in passing that correlations needn't be defined for every possible annotation. In general, they will not be. Correlations are in general (very) partial functions like the ones displayed in the text.

of Mutt, Jeff, and Odile. In the case of Hammurabi, too, matters seem relatively straightforward. Suppose we have heard the story of the ancient Babylonians, and say that Hammurabi believes that Hesperus is Hesperus, but not that Hesperus is Phosphorus. Given our focus on the way Hammurabi thought about the planets (note that the story is usually told thus – the ancients *called* Venus 'Hesperus' when they saw it in the evening), it is natural to suppose that we are operating under the restrictions

Ham: ⟨'Hesperus', Hesperus⟩; {⟨the Babylonian word that 'Hesperus' conventionally translates, Venus⟩},

Ham: ⟨'Phosphorus', Phosphorus⟩; {⟨the Babylonian word that 'Phosphorus' conventionally translates, Venus⟩}.

We can abbreviate here and represent the restrictions thus:

Ham: 'Hesperus' → the Babylonian it conventionally translates,
Ham: 'Phosphorus' → the Babylonian it conventionally translates.

Given these restrictions, as well as the noncontroversial assumptions – 'Hesperus' conventionally translates 'H', and not 'P'; 'Phosphorus' conventionally translates 'P', and not 'H'; the facts about what Ham accepted as given at the beginning of this chapter – it is clear that the RAM determined by 'Hesperus is Hesperus' represents one of Ham's RAMs relative to the context's restrictions, but that determined by 'Hesperus is Phosphorus' does not. The latter RAM,

⟨⟨'is', identity⟩, ⟨⟨'Hesperus', Venus⟩, ⟨'Phosphorus', Venus⟩⟩⟩,

can represent a RAM *only* of the form

⟨⟨e, identity⟩, ⟨⟨'H', Venus⟩, ⟨'P', Venus⟩⟩⟩

given the restrictions, where H and P are fixed as above. (Since there are no restrictions on 'is', e can be any piece of vocabulary.) Since this RAM is clearly not in Hammurabi's RS, the claim that he believes that Hesperus is Phosphorus is false.

A brief excursus

Before going further, I want to address a few technical niceties. The reader with little patience for such details might want to skim the next several pages and start again at the point in the text labeled 'End of excursus'.

141

What is said above doesn't quite determine the semantic value of 'believes' and other verbs of attitude. The verbs are to be treated as indexicals. So 'believes', for instance, has a single meaning (*character*, in David Kaplan's terminology); its interpretation (content) shifts across contexts. Following Kaplan, we can identify an expression's meaning with a rule that assigns to each context a suitable interpretation for the expression therein.

Let us suppose that in a context an n-place predicate's content is an intension, a function from n-tuples to sets of worlds. My gloss of the truth conditions of

(a) t believes that S

allows two sorts of answers to the question What's an appropriate intension for 'believes'? For the above is consistent with treating the verb as either a two-place or a three-place predicate. The first alternative is familiar enough and is, of course, what the surface syntax of (a) and related sentence forms naturally suggests. On the second alternative, (a) is treated at the level of logical syntax as an existential quantification:

(b) $\exists f B^3(t, \text{that } S, f)$.

More specifically, let $r(x)$ name the function that takes a context to the set of restrictions it provides. Use circumflexion to form function names, so that, for example, '$\hat{x}(\{w \mid x \text{ is bald at } w\})$' names the function taking x to the set of worlds at which it is bald. Let us write

$\text{Rep}(p, q, f)$

for 'p represents q under f'. Write

$\text{Obey}(s, f, u)$

for 'f obeys all the restrictions in s that are relevant to u'. [A restriction $\langle x, a, S \rangle$ is relevant to u iff $x = u$; f obeys the restriction if $f(a)$ is in S.] On the first alternative, the character of 'believes' is

$\hat{c}\hat{x}\hat{p}(\{w \mid \exists f \exists q (q \text{ is a RAM in } x\text{'s RS at } w \text{ and } \text{Rep}(p, q, f) \text{ and } \text{Obey}(r(c), f, x))\})$.

On the second alternative, the character is

$\hat{c}\hat{x}\hat{p}\hat{f}(\{w \mid \exists q (q \text{ is a RAM in } x\text{'s RS at } w \text{ and } \text{Rep}(p, q, f) \text{ and } \text{Obey}(r(c), f, x))\})$.

The two treatments assign the same truth conditions, in a fixed context, to simple ascriptions such as 'Odile believes that Twain is dead'.

An important difference between the two treatments arises with respect to how they are able to deal with uses of several attitude ascriptions within the context of a single discourse or conversation. Suppose I say something of the form

(c) Jones believes that S. He desires that T.

Or suppose that, in the course of a conversation, you and I each speak of various attitudes Jones has. A treatment of 'believes' and other verbs of attitude as three-place predicates makes it possible to assign (c) truth conditions suggested by

(c′) $\exists f(B^3(\text{Jones, that } S, f) \text{ and } D^3(\text{Jones, that } T, f))$,

as well as those suggested by

(c″) $\exists f B^3(\text{Jones, that } S, f) \text{ and } \exists f D^3(\text{Jones, that } T, f)$.

And something analogous is true for an assignment of truth conditions to the conversation you and I have about Jones. It does not seem that the first kind of assignment of truth conditions will be possible if we treat 'believes' and its friends as two-place predicates.

As I argue in discussing Kripke's puzzles about belief in Section 4, there are good reasons for thinking that discourses and conversations like (c) should often be assigned truth conditions along the lines suggested by (c′). So, I think, we should treat 'believes' and other propositional attitude predicates as three–place predicates.

This means that sentences of the form of (a) are existential quantifications "at the level of logical form." And so the propositions (i.e., RAMs) determined by uses of such sentences will contain components corresponding to existential quantifiers. In the informal exposition of RAMs I gave above, I said nothing about the structure or consituents of RAMs of this sort.

I ought to say something about them. Unfortunately, almost anything I say is bound to be controversial in somewhat irrelevant ways. The syntax of natural language quantifiers is a matter of contemporary dispute, and anything very specific I say about the RAM that something is tired is thus bound to offend one or another party to the dispute.

When in doubt, pretend that English is some familiar formal

language. I do assume that natural language quantification involves variables and variable binding, if not in surface syntax, then at a level of logical form. Thus, the RAM that something is tired will be something along the lines of

⟨⟨⟨'something', the semantic value of 'something'⟩, an annotation corresponding to a variable⟩, ⟨⟨'is tired', being tired⟩, an annotation corresponding to the variable⟩⟩.

In a model-theoretic account, we might deal with such RAMs as follows: First, we suppose that we have something, call it #, that is not among the possible interpretations of terms, predicates, quantifiers, or other expressions that appear in RAMs. The job of # is to indicate that what it is paired with in the construction of a RAM is a bound variable. Thus, the RAM for '∃x x is tired' will be

⟨⟨⟨'∃', the semantic value of '∃'⟩, ⟨'x',#⟩⟩, ⟨⟨'is tired', being tired⟩, ⟨x,#⟩⟩⟩.

Assume that the RAMs in an individual's RS that correspond to quantified sentences are so constructed that # marks (all and only) bound variables. We may then amend the definition of *p represents q under f* thus: p now represents q under f iff p represents r under f, in the former sense, where r is some "alphabetic variant" of q, and for any e and annotation $a = ⟨e,\#⟩$, there is an e' such that $f(a)$ is ⟨e',#⟩. The definition of alphabetic variant is straightforward, since # tells us exactly which annotations in a RAM behave as bound variables.

This leaves a number of issues open. I have not said anything that would fix the semantic values of the quantifiers; nor have I said anything that touches on issues concerning multiple quantification and compositionality. The latter issues are tangential to our main concerns, and I will therefore ignore them.[13] For our purposes, we may take the semantic values of the individual quantifiers to be functions that map the sort of condition associated with one-place predicates (i.e., functions from individuals to sets of worlds) to sets of worlds. For example, the semantic value of the existential quantifier takes a function f to the set of those worlds w such that, for some x, w is in $f(x)$.

Before returning to the main line of exposition, I want to mention a pair of somewhat technical complications. Although they are in

---

13 Most of what I have to say on this issue would be a recapitulation of Harold Levin's (1982) discussion of quantification in his Chapters 2 and 3.

a sense related problems, the first arises on either of the two treatments of the attitude verbs mentioned earlier; the second seems to arise only when we take 'believes' and its friends to be three-place predicates.

Here is the first problem. Consider an ascription such as

(J) John believes that Hammurabi believes that Hesperus is hot

in the context of a pure Russellian account of the sort discussed in Section 1. The Russellian assigns a relation to 'believes' and a structured entity to the t-clause. The assignment to the t-clause contains the semantic values of the expressions that occur in it. In the case of this sentence, the word 'believes' itself occurs in the t-clause; its semantic value thus goes into the proposition. So in this case we have a relation assigned to the main verb, the belief relation, trying to relate something that contains that very relation. This is more or less like a function taking itself for an argument – something that on the normal set-theoretic understanding of a function is impossible. Exactly the same sort of thing occurs in the account I have outlined.

Gupta and Savion (1987, p. 407) call this "a purely technical problem, one that deserves a purely technical solution"; they suggest adopting a set theory, like that developed by Peter Aczel, in which the axiom of foundation – which among other things prevents sets from being self-membered – is neither axiom nor theorem. In Aczel's set theory, functions can happily operate on themselves. (Aczel's theory is developed in Aczel 1988.)

I see no reason that we could not adopt such a solution, although I have not worked out its details. There are other technologies available here. What comes most naturally to (my) mind is a hierarchical treatment, one of the sort suggested either by the ramified theory of types or by some (propositional) version of a Tarskian hierarchy of languages. Such an approach declares verbs such as 'believes' to be systematically ambiguous. Although in

(J) John believes that Hammurabi believes that Hesperus is hot

it appears as if the same verb makes two appearances, this is not, on such an approach, really so. Rather, the initial verb is "of a higher level" than the embedded verb. The two verbs turn out to have different semantic values, and those of a higher level are functions that operate on (among other things) the semantic values of attitude verbs of a lower level. Once one invokes such a hierarchy, (J) no longer presents the problem just mentioned.

In such a treatment, not only does 'believes' come in levels, but propositions come in levels too: We cannot very well quantify over all propositions at once, since that would make the problem reappear with '(p) Odile believes that p'. Usually the treatment is accompanied by some sort of ambiguation of the quantifiers as well, since as one moves up the hierarchy, new entities become definable and are thus available to quantify over. In Section 4 of Chapter 4, when I discuss truth and truth predicates, I gesture at one way in which one might spell out the details of such a treatment.

Many find this sort of hierarchy objectionable. I invoke it not because I think it to be the best solution to the problem of a function seemingly operating on itself (or that of the liar paradox), but because it is a relatively familiar and straightforward approach to this (fairly ubiquitous) problem. I want to make it clear that the approach I am sketching does not force us to treat iterations of attitude verbs in natural language as unintelligible; I think the fact that they can be accommodated in a Russellian hierarchy suffices to show this. As I said, I have nothing against the sort of "technical fix" Gupta and Savion suggest.

The second problem I want to address is as follows: Consider again

(J) John believes that Hammurabi believes that Hesperus is hot.

Given our intention to treat 'believes' as a three-place predicate, we can quasi-regiment this as

$\exists f$(Believes (John, that $\exists gA, f$),

where '$\exists gA$' stands in for a regimentation of 'Hammurabi believes that Hesperus is hot'. Call the RAM named by '$\exists gA$' 'H'. As a whole, (J) is true only if H represents one of John's RAMs under some correlation. Now, H will contain an annotation in which the semantic value of the existential quantifier occurs. Supposing that this is the same quantifier as is prefixed to the sentence as a whole, a little reflection shows that, among the things in the range of this quantifier – and thus among the things contained in its semantic value on a normal set-theoretic treatment – will be various correlations. So the truth of (J) requires that some correlation operate on an annotation in which various correlations, including itself, occur. Once again, we have the specter of a function – this time a correlation, instead of the semantic value of 'believes' – operating on itself.

Though not the same complication as that involving 'believes', this does seem to be of the same ilk. The sort of technology that would solve the first problem would solve this one as well. In a hierarchical treatment, of course, what happens is that correlations themselves occur in levels, with correlations at higher levels operating on things that have lower-level correlations as parts. Given this, one can say the same thing about

$$\exists f(\text{Believes}(\text{John, that } \exists g A, f)$$

that we said about (J): Although it looks as though the same existential quantifier is appearing twice here, it is not, since the two quantifiers range over different domains. The range of the initial quantifier is (roughly) the range of the second plus certain correlations that operate on (things that include) the range of the first quantifier.

I return to a discussion of this in Section 4 of the next chapter.

End of excursus

Some comparison with Fregean theories is in order. You may be wondering how this account could succeed if Chapter 2's arguments were sound. After all, you may say, in the present account a t-clause acts more or less as a name of a Fregean thought or a conceptual role. When Mutt says, 'Odile thinks that Twain is dead', the t-clause is *really* naming Odile's sense or conceptual role for 'Twain is dead'; when Jeff uses the sentence, the t-clause is *really* naming her sense for, or the conceptual role of, 'that guy is dead'. This was exactly what Chapter 2 said a t-clause could not do.

This is exactly what a t-clause does *not* do on this account. We have made the content of a t-clause – what the t-clause, as a whole, names – a RAM, a fusion of some linguistic items found in a t-clause and some Russellian referents. Not only is this not a sense, on any standard view of sense, but what 'that Twain is dead' names does *not* change between Mutt and Jeff's contexts. In both cases, the t-clause names the RAM

(7) ⟨⟨'is dead', being dead⟩, ⟨'Twain', Twain⟩⟩.

147

What changes from context to context is not what the t-clause names, but what the t-clause can be used to represent. As the restrictions provided by the context change – as we go from

Odile: 'Twain'→'Twain'

to

Odile: 'Twain' → names of Twain Odile associates with her current perceptual experience of Twain,

what changes is which RAMs the RAM that Twain is dead is able to represent.

Recall that one Fregean theory we discussed (in Chapter 2, Section 2) was unacceptable because it made arguments like

Emily believes that Billy is riding a moped,
Rusty believes whatever Emily does,
Thus, Rusty believes that Billy is riding a moped

invalid. The Fregean view did this because it allowed the t-clause 'that Billy is riding a moped' to change its reference, as it migrated from premise to conclusion. Although the proposal I have made is a *little* like the proposal that a t-clause names its sense for the person under discussion, it doesn't have disastrous consequences like rendering the above argument invalid.

Let's see why this is. As explained in the excursus, our official policy is that 'believes' is a three-place predicate, with argument places that take names of a believer, a RAM, and a correlation. But let's first consider how the argument is analyzed if we treat 'believes' as a two-placed predicate, since it is marginally easier to see what is going on in this case. The argument will be ascribed the form

$B(e, \text{ that } B)$,
$(p)(B(e, p) \rightarrow B(r, p))$,
Thus, $B(r, \text{ that } B)$.

We will treat propositional quantification in the obvious way. The propositional quantifier ranges over arbitrary RAMs; $(p)A(p)$ is true just in case $A(p)$ is true for any assignment of a RAM to p. (So propositional quantification is objectual quantification. Exactly what RAMs there are for the quantifier to range over will become clearer in the next section.)

Naively speaking, an argument is valid just in case what its premises say jointly entail what its conclusion says. This naive definition ignores the fact that an argument's premises or conclusion might say different things in different contexts. We can't afford to ignore contextual variation in what sentences say. So we define validity by adapting the naive definition, requiring that premises and conclusion all be evaluated in the same context. That is, we say that an argument is valid provided that, no matter what context we may pick, what its premises say, when interpreted relative to the context, entail what its conclusion says, so interpreted.

It should be clear that this argument is valid. Think of a sentence *a believes that S* as saying the RAM *that S* represents one of *a*'s RAMs. Of course, the nature of the representation relation changes from context to context. But in asking whether the argument is valid, we can think of this relation as being fixed in one way or another by an arbitrary context. Then, the premises of the argument tell us that a particular RAM (say, that Rusty is riding a moped) represents one of Emily's RAMs and that, if a RAM represents one of Emily's RAMs, it represents one of Rusty's. Clearly, these claims guarantee the claim made by the conclusion, that the RAM that Billy is riding a moped represents one of Rusty's RAMs.

Now consider the argument when 'believes' is treated as a three-place predicate. In order to evaluate the argument for validity, we need to know how to represent its second premise. In Chapter 4, I will offer an algorithm that provides regimentations of arguments in which 'believes' occurs. The algorithm assigns the argument the form

$\exists f(\text{Believes}(e, \text{that } B, f))$,
$(p)(\exists f(\text{Believes}(e, p, f)) \rightarrow \exists f(\text{Believes}(r, p, f)))$,
Thus, $\exists f(\text{Believes}(r, \text{that } B, f))$.

(Observe that this awards uses of the second premise the same truth conditions as does the two-place predicate treatment.) The argument is clearly valid on this treatment, as long as the term *that B* doesn't switch its reference between premises and conclusion. And the 'that'-term *doesn't* do that. It does *not* refer to or name a sense or conceptual role or any other sort of cognitive critter. In this respect, the view outlined above is quite un-Fregean.

Be this as it may, someone may ask, 'Isn't all this a sort of closet Fregeanism, with expressions in t-clauses doing duty for the senses of expressions for those to whom we ascribe attitudes?'

I don't want to quibble about the epithet (or honorific, depending on your perspective) 'Fregean'. If you are willing to accept this account and it makes you feel better about things to call it Fregean, by all means do so. But we have wandered quite far from any *traditional* sort of Fregeanism. This view abandons the Fregean view that attitude ascription involves a match of nonreferential, cognitive content between a t-clause and some state of, or sentence accepted by, the subject of the ascription. Whether Mutt and Odile associate similar ways of thinking of Twain with their uses of 'Twain' is wholly irrelevant to the question Does, or could, Mutt use 'Twain' to represent Odile's uses of 'Twain'? In fact, one can comfortably hold the sort of view I am urging and insist that, in general, interpersonal comparisons of a sentence's cognitive role or sense can't be made. One could say, for instance, that such comparisons presuppose an isomorphism of the subjective probability functions that users associate with their sentences, a sort of isomorphism that, practically speaking, is never to be found.

Furthermore, nothing in the view even suggests that associated with a use of an expression, as a matter of the expression's meaning or otherwise, is some descriptive condition that determines the expression's reference. Here is no shade of the idea that sense determines reference.

It is also worth noting differences in the treatment of apparent quantification into attitude ascriptions. Frege thought it absurd that an individual should literally be part of what is named by a t-clause. So claims like

(9) There is a man such that Odile believes that he is dead

that seem to involve such "quantification in" must be treated gingerly by a traditional Fregean. The natural regimentation of (9) is suggested by

(10) $(\exists x)(x$ is a man & Odile believes that x is dead$)$.

If we treat the quantifier in the standard manner – and thus assign to the variable simply an individual, and not a sense, or an individual and a sense – (10) [and therefore (9)] presents a bit of a puzzle for Frege. We seem to have Odile believing something with an individual, instead of a sense, as a part – just what Frege said was impossible.

Of course, there are Fregean treatments of sentences like (9). We

150

looked at one such treatment in Chapter 2. The Fregean usually treats (9) somewhat as follows:

(10') $(\exists x)(\exists y)(y$ is a man & x is a sense that presents y & Odile believes 'x is dead').

He insists that (9) points to a complication in, not an objection to, his view.

For argument's sake, let us grant this: At the moment, we are interested only in differences between Fregean views and the present one. And sentences such as (9) certainly point to such a difference: We treat quantification in, in a straightforward Russellian way.

The Russellian says that, relative to an assignment to the variables, a sentence like 'x is dead' expresses the same sort of proposition as is expressed by a sentence like 'Twain is dead'. Indeed, if we assign Twain to 'x', 'x is dead' expresses the same Russellian proposition as does 'Twain is dead'. Therefore, (10) [and thus (9)] is just an existential generalization of

(8') Twain is a man and Odile believes that Twain is dead,

which, of course, is exactly what (10) *appears* to be.

Just as an open sentence determines a Russellian proposition relative to an assignment of individuals to its free variables, it determines a RAM relative thereto. For example, 'x is dead' determines

(11) $\langle\langle$'is dead', being dead$\rangle$, $\langle$'x', Twain$\rangle\rangle$

relative to an asignment of Twain to 'x'. Sentence (11) can represent a RAM in Odile's, or anyone else's, RS, just as well as the RAM

(7) $\langle\langle$'is dead', being dead$\rangle$, $\langle$'Twain', Twain$\rangle\rangle$

does. For example, suppose that we are in a context with no restrictions operative. Then a use of (9), which we suppose regimentable via (10), is true just in case there is a man X such that

(12) $\langle\langle$'is dead', being dead$\rangle$, $\langle$'x', $X\rangle\rangle$

represents one of Odile's RAMs. So it will be true if, for example, Odile has (7) in her RS. The view treats quantification into propositional position in a Russellian, and not a Fregean, manner.

Contexts often enough provide restrictions on the ways in which names – my generic term for ordinary proper names, demonstratives, and indexicals – that occur in a t-clause can be correlated with

151

the things that are parts of the mediators of a person's belief. For instance, Mutt's context provided the restriction

Odile: 'Twain' → 'Twain'.

Does something analogous happen with free variables? For instance, are there contexts that contain restrictions like

Odile: '*x*' → 'Twain'?

I believe – indeed, I insist – that the answer is no. There are patterns of inference which are undeniably valid and which require that correlations be unrestricted in the way in which they take an annotation like ⟨'*x*', Twain⟩ to an annotation. (Of course, a correlation is required to take ⟨'*x*', Twain⟩ to something whose second member is Twain, if it takes the annotation to anything at all.) Consider, for example, the argument

Odile believes that Twain is dead.
Thus, there is an *x* such that Odile believes that *x* is dead.

If, and only if, a correlation can map ⟨'*x*', Twain⟩ to anything it likes (so long as the mapee contains Twain), this is valid; for suppose that the premise is true. Then, relative to the restrictions in the context, the RAM (7) represents one of Odile's RAMs. Given that the restrictions in the context say nothing about what a correlation is supposed to do with ⟨'*x*', Twain⟩, it follows that there is a correlation that obeys the context's restrictions and that maps (8) to one of Odile's RAMs. So the argument is valid.

Another brief excursus

To find such a correlation, take one, call it *f*, that obeys the context's restrictions and maps (7) to one of Odile's RAMs. Now use the correlation just like *f*, save that it also maps ⟨'*x*', Twain⟩ to what *f* maps ⟨'Twain', Twain⟩ to. There must be such a correlation, since the context is silent on the treatment of variables.

The reader can validate that the proposed treatment of quantifying in also validates arguments from

b believes that *Faaa*,

where '*F*' is a three-place atomic predicate to any of the following:

$(\exists x)(b$ believes that *Faxa*); $(\exists x)(b$ believes that *Faxx*); $(\exists x)(b$ believes that *Fxax*); $(\exists x)(b$ believes that *Fxxx*); $(\exists x)(b$ believes that *Fxxa*).

There are certain somewhat controversial inferences, involving variables within the scope of 'believes' bound from without, that my account does not validate. For example, it will not validate the inference from

$(\exists x)(\exists y)(x = y$ and x is a planet and y is a planet and John said that he saw x rise, then y rise, then x set, then y set$)$

to

$(\exists x)(\exists y)(x = y$ and x is a planet and y is a planet and John said that he saw x rise, then y rise, then y set, then x set$)$.

This is far from transparently valid. Most people don't think the second claim follows from the first. So I don't think that failing to validate the inference is a defect. In fact, I think it's a virtue. Since a discussion of this matter is somewhat involved, I defer it to Chapter 4.

End of excursus

It would be misleading to say that the view of attitude ascriptions I am sketching has nothing in common with Fregean views. Like the Fregean, I see the truth of an attitude ascription as being sensitive to facts about the way an individual thinks about the objects and properties his belief is about. But I reject the mechanism the Fregean proposes to explain this sensitivity. I also want to be committed to as "thin" an account of ways of thinking as possible. I am somewhat dubious about the significance of comparisons of non-referential content across speakers and am trying to offer an account that avoids them. In fact, so far I have said nothing that commits us to a very interesting notion of *intra*personnal identity of non-referential content, among different expressions or "modes of thought."

I will address this subject later, when I discuss Kripke's Peter/Paderewski case and the retention of belief. What I will say won't come near to resurrecting anything like a traditional Fregean notion of sense. I will speak of different expressions realizing the same or different "ways of thinking" of an object x for a thinker y. But to say that two terms, t and t' represent the same way of thinking of x for y, it will turn out, is (roughly) to say that certain noncognitive conditions are fulfilled (e.g., both terms actually refer to x) and that y accepts the identity $t = t'$. Such senses even a Quinean could love.

3. WORRIES ABOUT WORDS

The traditional name for what a 'that'-clause names is *proposition*. Because RAMs are so different in makeup and function from most traditional candidates for propositions, I've made up a new moniker for them.

New terminology or no, it will be observed that I am individuating propositions extremely finely. If two sentences differ at all in what expressions occur in them, then they determine different RAMs; they express different propositions, to use the standard terminology. So different sentences of English – 'John is a doctor', 'John is a physician', to pick an example – invariably determine different propositions. Likewise for sentences of different languages – the proposition that snow is white is distinct from that determined by 'La neige est blanche'.

It's natural to worry that the presence of expressions in propositions, and the resulting fine distinctions among them, will lead to trouble. One worry is that my view is obviously incorrect, since it doesn't allow us to ascribe attitudes to speakers of foreign languages: If Odile doesn't speak English, then she won't have the RAM that Twain is dead – a RAM that contains the English 'is dead' – in her representational system, or RS. So 'Odile believes that Twain is dead' can't be true if Odile speaks no English – an unacceptable result.

This objection arises out of a confusion about the function of RAMs, and is thus not very serious. But there are more serious worries one might have about the words I have put in propositions – for example, that the view will succumb to the sort of objections that Church (1950) made to Carnap's and allied accounts of attitude ascription. Church believed he had discovered "an insuperable objection against . . . analyses that undertake to do away with [traditional] propositions in favor of such more concrete things as sentences." Church's objections, which are widely thought devastating, were to views according to which either t-clauses refer to linguistic items or the presence of a t-clause in a sentence makes it necessary to refer to linguistic items when giving truth conditions. Since I make t-clauses name entities that contain expressions, it might seem that Church's arguments could be turned against my proposal.

Another worry is that my view will bar us from identifying what sentences of different languages, or of the same language, say. Since the RAMs, that is, propositions, that John is a doctor and that John is a physician are different, isn't it false on this view that the sentences say the same thing? Isn't it likewise false that 'Snow is white' and 'La neige est blanche' say the same thing, given that propositions are RAMs? Isn't the view thus obviously false?

No. Neither Church-style objections nor those having to do with when sentences say the same thing pose any threat to the view sketched in the preceding section. So I will argue in this section, at any rate. Before considering these objections, however, it will be worth saying a little about the first objection I mentioned: that

(1) Odile believes that Twain is dead

would be false if all of Odile's RAMs were "made out of" foreign language sentences.

This betrays a confusion about the proposal of the preceding section. On that proposal, the point of (1) is not to say that Odile has the RAM that Twain is dead in her RS. Rather, in (1) this RAM is said to represent one of Odile's RAMs. There is no reason that the RAM that Twain is dead can't represent a "French RAM." Consider the correlation

'is dead' → 'est mort',
'Twain' → 'Twain'.

It should be clear that the RAM that Twain is dead represents the RAM determined by 'Twain est mort' under this correlation. If Odile has the latter RAM in her RS and (1) is used in a context without restrictions, then (1) is true. So much for that objection.

Although I didn't bother to point this out in the preceding section, the notion of a RAM is supposed to be a very general one. Obviously, I envision that there are RAMs that correspond to the sentences of all natural languages, ones that result from fusing the expressions of various natural languages with their Russellian referents. But there is no need to limit RAMs in this way. Take an arbitrary set of objects that could play the roles of parts of a language or system of representation – that is, take any set of things you like that could be "words." Now pair off these "vocabulary items"

155

with Russellian referents, as we do in forming RAMs for natural language sentences. The result is a RAM. One can think of such a RAM as representing, in a somewhat crude way, what it is for a certain sort of representation – one made out of the "vocabulary items" with which we started the construction – to have a certain sort of Russellian content. Such RAMs of possible, even if actually unspoken, languages are just as respectable as the RAMs yielded by the familiar natural languages we speak. So when occasions arise on which we want to speak of arbitrary RAMs – as, for example, when we want to treat propositional quantification – we shall suppose that among the RAMs are not only those that correspond to natural language sentences, but ones such as

⟨⟨Australia, being dead⟩, ⟨David Lewis, Mark Twain⟩⟩,

which corresponds to a sentence in a language in which David Lewis plays the role of the name 'Twain' and Australia plays the role of the predicate 'is dead'.

Let's turn to somewhat meatier objections to the view of the preceding section. For our purposes, we may take Church's major complaint against translational accounts of attitude ascriptions to be that they fail to get the truth conditions of attitude ascriptions right. For example, to the view that a sentence such as

(2) Seneca said that man is a rational animal

is to be analyzed as

(3) Seneca wrote (or uttered) a sentence S in some language L, and the translation of S from L into English is 'Man is a rational animal',

Church objected that (2) does not follow from (3), since the sentence 'Man is a rational animal' might have meant something different in English than what it in fact means. 'Man is a rational animal' might, for example, have meant that the lion is a rational animal if 'man' had meant what 'the lion' actually means. If this had been so and Seneca had written a Latin sentence saying that the lion was rational (but no sentence saying that man was rational), then (3) would be true without (2)'s being so. If we assign (2) the truth conditions of (3) – I take it that this is the most important part of the claim that (2) is to be analyzed as (3) – we would then be assigning (2) the wrong truth conditions.

One might argue that, in this instance, Church's argument was in one or another way misguided.[14] I won't pause to consider that question here, since the proposal I have made isn't at all like the proposal to assign uses of (2) the truth conditions of uses of (3). What I propose to focus on is whether introducing words into propositions *in the manner of the preceding section* results in an inappropriate assignment of truth conditions to sentences like (1) and (2).

14 The objection in the text can be evaded if one says that it is an essential property of English that 'Man is a rational animal' says therein that man is a rational animal. Church was aware of this. He gave an ingenious objection involving iterations of attitude verbs that shows that objections along the lines of that mentioned in the text can be made against Carnap's and allied views, even if it is assumed that an essential property of a language is that its expressions have the semantical properties they in fact have.

In the text, I don't spell out each of the objections made in Church (1950). I try to say enough so that anyone familiar with Church's piece will see that no objection that it suggests makes trouble for my view.

Church appeared to have a worry beyond the worry that Carnap's and allied accounts fail to give correct truth conditions. He apparently thought that Carnap was trying, or should have been trying, to give an *analysis*, in a Moorean sense, of attitude ascriptions.

Some of the arguments suggested in Church's article are of interest only if one assumes that Carnap was, or should have been, trying to give such an analysis of *Odile believes that Twain is dead*. Consider Church's (1950) observation: "Following a suggestion of Langford we may bring out more sharply the inadequacy of (3) as an analysis of (2) by translating into another language, say German, and observing that the two translated statements would obviously convey different meanings to a German (whom we may suppose to have no knowledge of English" (p. 98; numbering changed to conform with numbering in this text). This is quite correct: (2) and (3) translated into German clearly come to different things, since when we translate (2), what we get ('Seneca hat gesagt, dass der Mensch ein vernunftiges Tier sei') has no explict reference to linguistic items, whereas (3)'s translation will contain quotation names of English expressions. Church is presumably assuming that (a) one sentence provides an analysis of another only if the two sentences share a certain property – having the same meaning; (b) if two sentences have this property, then a speaker who understands them will know that they agree on this property; (c) the property in question is preserved by translation.

I myself doubt all three of these claims if 'analysis' is understood in such a way that 'knowledge is justified true belief' is taken to be (except for its falsity) a paradigm of the sort of thing we are after in philosophical analysis. But the important point here is that Church's observation is irrelevant, given that our project is simply to give a correct and illuminating account of the truth conditions of *Odile believes that Twain is dead*. To do that we do not need to give an analysis of the sentence in a Moorean sense. It suffices to explain, in a correct and illuminating way, exactly what situations – what worlds, if you like – are correctly characterized by various uses of the sentence. This doesn't require a meaning-preserving, Moorean analysis – something that is probably impossible anyway. Applications of the "Church–Langford translation test" to the proposal I am making I think to be simply irrelevant.

157

In objecting to Carnap's (1947) account of attitude ascription in *Meaning and Necessity*, Church considered the way in which Carnap would assign truth conditions to attitude ascriptions and their natural translations into foreign languages. He in effect argued that Carnap's account assigned different truth conditions to such pairs of sentences as

(1) Odile believes that Twain is dead

and its natural German translation,

(1') Odile glaubt, dass Twain tot ist.

The objection turned on the fact that, in giving the truth conditions for such sentences, Carnap made reference to certain linguistic entities. In the case of (1), reference was made to English and the sentence 'Twain is dead'; in the case of (1'), reference is made to German and 'Twain ist tot'.

On the present account, (1) has a part, 'that Twain is dead', which refers to something containing the parts of 'Twain is dead'; (1') has parts referring to German, and not English, expressions. So (1) and (1') on the present account, apparently make quite different claims: One says that Odile is related to an "English RAM"; the other says that she is related to a German one. One suspects that we, too, assign truth conditions to (1) and (1') in an objectionable way.

Let us then discuss pairs of sentences such as (1) and (1'). We begin with the treatment of the verb 'glaubt', the German equivalent of 'believes'. It is to be treated in just the way the English verb is. So 'glaubt', like 'believes', will be treated as an indexical. Its (constant) meaning will be something that, given a set of contextually supplied restrictions, pairs off believers and RAMs, relative to a correlation that obeys the context's restrictions: Given the restrictions operative in a context, 'glaubt' will pair off a person u and a RAM r just in case r represents one of u's RAMs under the correlation. So 'glaubt' behaves, in this respect, exactly as 'believes' does.

Although it is clear that 'glaubt' has the same kind of meaning as 'believes', it may not be clear whether it has exactly the same meaning as 'believes'. In fact, it may seem that it can't, since the German verb and the English verb "look at" different things. One

158

deals with RAMs manufactured from English sentences, the other with German RAMs.

However, there is no reason that the two verbs can't have exactly the same meaning. The meaning of 'believes' is a rule that takes us from a contextually supplied "translation manual" or "dictionary" (a set of restrictions) to the trios $\langle u, r, f \rangle$ such that r represents one of u's RAMs under f, and f "pays attention to the dictionary." All the language-specific information here is introduced by the dictionary, that is, by the contextually varying restrictions. The German verb realizes *exactly* the same function from translation manuals as the English does, and thus has exactly the same meaning as the English verb.

So we say of German sentences of the form of

a glaubt, dass *S*

just what we said of their English correspondents. The German is true, taken relative to a context, just in case the RAM determined by *S* represents, relative to the context's restrictions, a RAM in the RS of *a*. (I am ignoring the fact that German inverts the word order of the relative clause in a belief ascription. Nothing hangs on this.)

Now we are ready to discuss the sort of worry that Church raised about Carnap's account. I will discuss four worries you might have about the treatment of sentences such as (1) and (1').

(a) You might be worried that the account allows a use of

(1) Odile believes that Twain is dead

in one context to be true, while a use of

(1') Odile glaubt, dass Twain tot ist

in some other context is false. And this, it might be said, is quite unacceptable, since (1) and (1') are translations of one another.

Of course, I grant that (1) and (1') can be used in such a way that the uses have different truth conditions. But this is no objection. Remember that one of the motivations for this view is that (1) *itself* can be used in such a way that it says different things in different contexts. One reason for adopting the view is that a sentence like (1) seems to be used some, but not all, of the time to say something quite specific about the how of Odile's belief. The same is true of (1'). So the observation that the sentences might be used to say different things is hardly an objection to the theory.

159

(b) Someone might be tempted to object that, on the view I have sketched, *no* use of (1) can have precisely the same truth conditions as a use of (1'). If this were true, it would be a serious objection. But given what we said above, it should be clear that this is not true. Consider, for example, uses of (1) and (1') in contexts in which no restrictions are operative. As should be painfully familiar at this point, such a use of (1) is true iff the RAM that Twain is dead represents a RAM in Odile's RS. More generally, such a use determines the set of worlds in which Odile has in her RS a RAM that the RAM that Twain is dead represents. (I identify the truth conditions of a use of a sentence with the intension the use determines.)

But these are the truth conditions of a use of (1') in a context without restrictions. Such a use is true in case there is some way of correlating

⟨⟨'ist tot', being dead⟩, ⟨'Twain', Twain⟩⟩

with one of Odile's RAMs. Such a use of (1') picks out exactly the same set of worlds as does the use of (1) we considered. So (1) and (1') can be used in such a way as to have the same truth conditions.

Even when restrictions are operative, the two sentences can have the same truth conditions. For example, a use of (1) in a context with just the restriction

Odile: Map 'is dead' to 'is dead'

will have exactly the truth conditions of a use of (1') in a context with just the restriction

Odile: Map 'ist tot' to 'is dead'.

In general, any truth conditions that (1) can have (1') can have, and vice versa.

(c) Suppose that you and I are wondering whether Louis realizes that Hector is a Greek. We know that he realizes that Hector is a Hellene; we have just heard him say, 'Hector is a Hellene'. But this doesn't satisfy us. We want to know whether he realizes that Hector is a *Greek*. You say he does; I tend to doubt it.

In our context, the restriction

Hector: 'is a Greek' → 'is a Greek'

seems to be operative. Now, consider the natural German translation of

(4) Louis believes that Hector is a Greek,

namely,

(5) Louis glaubt, dass Hector ein Griechen ist.

We aren't thinking about this sentence; no one in our vicinity is using it. Let's pretend, in fact, that neither of us has so much as heard of the German phrase 'ist ein Griechen'. Restrictions being a function of our beliefs and intentions, it seems that there is no restriction in our context on 'ist ein Griechen'. The German predicate can be mapped to any expression that picks out the property of being a Greek.

Suppose that Louis holds a belief under 'Hector is a Hellene', but not under 'Hector is a Greek'. Given the restrictions operative in our context, your use of (4) will be false. But (5), its German translation, will be true, taken relative to our context, since the context's restrictions allow mapping 'ist ein Griechen' onto 'is a Greek'.

So we have a sentence and its natural translation into German; in our context one is true, the other false. This might seem objectionable: Taken relative to one and the same context, one might insist, a sentence and its natural translation into another language ought to say the same thing.[15]

I have a number of things to say about this objection. The idea that powers this objection is something like

(I) If a sentence type S of one language is naturally and correctly translated by a sentence type T of a second language, then there is no context relative to which S and T have different truth values.

There are cases that cast considerable doubt on (I). As I understand it, there is an animal, the woodchuck, for which English has two names, 'woodchuck' and 'groundhog', where French has but one, 'la marmotte'. So the French 'Louis croit que Chuck est une marmotte' can be translated as either 'Louis believes that Chuck is a woodchuck' or as 'Louis believes that Chuck is a groundhog'. Presumably, the two English sentences can diverge in truth value taken relative to a single context. We certainly might say, in the appropriate circumstances, that Louis believes that Chuck is a wood-

---

15 Ali Kazmi made this observation in commenting on a forerunner of this chapter at an APA symposium in Portland in March 1988. Kazmi is also responsible for the Church's theorem objection at the end of this section.

chuck but does not believe that he is a groundhog. But if this might be so, then, if we can assign any truth value at all to the French sentence relative to the context of the English, a French sentence and one of its natural English translations will diverge in truth value when taken relative to one and the same context. That is what principle (I) forbids.

So I am inclined to think that this objection is based on a false principle. I also think that the objection puts the cart before the horse. Whether (I) is true depends on what sorts of context sensitivity exist. We would expect (I) to break down completely if there were context-sensitive expressions whose interpretation depended on the intentions of users with respect to other expressions in the sentences in which they occur. This is exactly the way in which 'believes' and 'glaubt' behave on the view I'm sketching. When I use 'believes' in 'Odile believes that Twain is dead', I make a decision about what sort of thing 'is dead' is supposed to represent. Unacquainted as I am with Swahili, I make no decision at all about how I might use Swahili expressions to represent Odile's RAMs. So the Swahili translation of my utterance – taken, as it were, out of context and interpreted in an environment not designed for it – might well diverge in truth value from the English it translates.

The idea that there are expressions that behave in this way is perfectly coherent. If we can give an otherwise satisfactory explanation of how verbs of attitude behave that treats them as expressions of this sort, then the right thing to do is to modify principles like (I), not abandon the analysis. We thus have two reasons to reject the objection: It is based on a principle that seems to be false, and it begs the question about what sorts of context sensitivity there might be.

Digression

I will make a final observation about (I): Even ignoring attitude ascriptions, it is not transparently true. There are at least two ways to think of the notion of a context. We could think of a context as an actual, or counterfactual, historical situation in which a sentence is used, or could have been used, by someone. Or we could think of contexts as abstractions from such situations, as collections of items that are or might be provided by a context in the first sense. If we think of contexts in this way, we are free to idealize them –

for example, by building into the abstract representatives of a historical context things that intuitively are not present in what the abstractions represent.

Principle (I) is false if we think of contexts in the first way. Consider, for example, sentences containing so-called pure demonstratives like 'that' and 'this'. It is clear what the natural and correct translation of the sentence type

(6) That is a dog

into German is:

(7) Das ist ein Hund.

If we think of contexts as actual or possible contexts of utterance, and think of the reference of a demonstrative in a context as (partially) a function of the user's intentions with respect to a token of the demonstrative, it is clear that (6) and (7) can diverge in truth value with respect to the same context. Simply consider a context in which I utter (6) referring to some dog, but have no intentions whatsoever with respect to the German 'das'. Here (6) is true; (7) receives no truth value.

By idealizing the notion of context in the way mentioned above, we can try to rescue (I). We might think of contexts as sequences of items that are, or that fix, interpretations of context-sensitive elements. So a context might consist of an individual (who provides an interpretation for first-person pronouns); a time or an interval (which provides a value, or a range of values, for expressions like 'now'); perhaps a world (to deal with 'actually'); some standards of precision (to help with 'Italy is shaped like a nylon'); a sequence S of individuals (the first object demonstratively referred to, the second object demonstratively referred to, etc.); and so on.[16]

It is easy enough now to assign referents to the demonstratives in a sentence that isn't used in the context. For example, we might order the occurrences of demonstratives in a sentence in terms of left to right order, and assign the first demonstrative the first member of S, the second the second, and so on. This guarantees that (6), taken alone in a context, always agrees in truth value with (7), taken alone in the same context.

If we conjoin (7) with another sentence, we run into problems.

16 This is one of the accounts of contexts that can be extracted from Kaplan (1977). The two accounts of demonstratives mentioned in the text are also, in essence, Kaplan's.

If the first member of S in a particular context is Rex the dog, whereas the second is Kitty the cat, then (6) will be true, relative to the context. But (7), as it occurs in

(8) Das lauft, und das is ein Hund,

will not be true, since the second 'das' now refers to Kitty the cat, not to a dog.

There are other ways to try to force (I) to be true. For instance, we could deny that (6) is translated by (7). We could say that (6) is not strictly speaking a sentence type, and so we can't really talk about what does and does not translate (6). Perhaps we could say that only when supplemented by a demonstration is (6) a sentence type; a translation of (6), thus supplemented, is (7), supplemented with the same (type of) demonstration.

There are problems with this. For example, it is not clear that, in order for a demonstrative to refer, it must be accompanied by a demonstration. I might utter (6) when a certain beast is salient and thereby refer to the beast without pointing or otherwise demonstrating it in any straightforward sense of 'demonstrating'. (I need not even see it, so long as I know that there is but one beast salient.) More importantly, if this *is* true of sentences like (6) and (7), why shouldn't the same sort of thing be true of sentences like (1) and (1′)? That is, why shouldn't it also be true that whether 'Odile glaubt, dass Twain tot ist' translates 'Odile believes that Twain is dead' depends on what restrictions are associated with each?

I hope the reader will agree that principles like (I) are problematic when applied to sentences containing expressions like 'that', whose interpretation depends partially on the user's intentions. For such sentences, I think, we ought simply abandon (I) altogether. We may continue to talk of one sentence type translating another but admit that a type and its translation needn't agree in truth value at the same context. Or we can instead talk of a sentence, taken relative to a particular context, as being (or failing to be) a translation of some other sentence, taken relative to the same or different context; we can salvage the truth behind (I) by remarking that S in c translates S^* in c^* only if S in c has the same truth conditions as S^* in c^*. But this principle is much weaker than (I) and isn't sufficient to generate the original objection.

End of digression

164

(d) Church's objections to Carnap raise one more issue. Church himself noted that his objection to Carnap was really forceful only in the case of iterated attitude ascriptions like

(9) John believes that Hammurabi believes that Hesperus is hot

and their translations into foreign languages.

What will we assign to a t-clause in which 'believes' occurs, like 'that Hammurabi believes that Hesperus is hot'? What we need to know is whether, in constructing a RAM for this, we pair off 'believes' with its meaning (the rule for getting from context to interpretation) or with its interpretation in a particular context. It is clear that most indexicals and demonstratives should be paired off with their interpretations. For example, in a context in which I am speaking, the t-clause in

(10) John believes that I am fat

should name the RAM

(11) ⟨⟨'is fat', being fat⟩, ⟨'I', me⟩⟩.

The exception to this rule are the verbs of attitude. In constructing the RAM 'that Hammurabi believes that Hesperus is hot', 'believes' is paired off with its context-independent meaning. We also think of those RAMs in the believer's representational system that correspond to sentences in which 'believes' or another verb of attitude occurs as being constructed out of the verb's meaning, not out of the verb's interpretation in the believer's context.

If we proceed in this way, there is nothing particularly puzzling about iterations of 'believes'. Consider, for example, (9) and its natural German translation

(9') John glaubt, dass Hammurabi dass Hesperus heiss ist glaubt.

The t-clause of the English names a RAM whose constituents and structure can be read off the quasi-regimentation

$\exists f$ Believes (Hammurabi, that Hesperus is hot, f).

This RAM looks something like this:

(E) {[⟨the English existential quantifier, its semantic value⟩, ⟨'f', #⟩], [⟨'believes', its meaning⟩, [⟨'Hammurabi', Ham⟩, the RAM that Hesperus is hot, ⟨'f', #⟩]]}.

(See the first excursus of Section 2 for an explanation of the function of #.) The German 'dass-'clause names something whose constituents and structure can be read off

$\exists g$ Glaubt(Hammurabi, dass Hesperus heiss ist, g).

This RAM looks something like this:

(G) {[⟨the German existential quantifier, its semantic value⟩, ⟨'g', #⟩],
   [⟨'glaubt', its meaning⟩, [⟨'Hammurabi', Ham⟩, the RAM determined
   by 'Hesperus ist heiss', ⟨'g',#⟩]]}.

If you examine the two RAMs, you will see that there is no difference between them in terms of the semantic values with which expressions are paired off. For example, since 'believes' and 'glaubt' have the same meaning, the only difference between the annotations

⟨'believes', its meaning⟩,
⟨'glaubt', its meaning⟩

lies in their first elements.[17] Indeed, the only difference between the RAMs (E) and (G) is in the vocabulary items they contain. If we translate the English expressions in (E) into German and reletter bound variables, replacing 'f' with 'g' what we obtain is (G).

This is just the sort of relation that the RAMs named by the complements of

(1) Odile believes that Twain is dead,
(1') Odile glaubt, dass Twain tot is

bore to one another. So what we will say here is exactly parallel with what we said about (1) and (1'). When restrictions are absent, whatever (E) can represent (G) can, and vice versa. If (9) is taken in a context with no restrictions and John accepts 'Hammurabi believes that Hesperus is hot', then (9) relative to the context is true: We can correlate the RAM named by (9)'s t-clause with John's RAM, since 'believes' in our RAM is paired off with its meaning, which is exactly what it is paired off with in John's RAM. (Note that it doesn't matter whether there are restrictions at work in John's context that are not at work in ours.) It's easy enough to work out

17 Of course, I am supposing that the semantic values of the existential quantifiers in English and German are the same. This assumption might be challenged. There is a simple argument in its favor. Existential quantifiers ought to be assigned the same semantic values if they range over the same things. But surely our quantifiers and those of our Bundesrepublik brethren do range over the same things.

that the natural German translation of (9) will be true, too, if used in a context without restrictions. In fact, the translation will have, taken in its context, the same truth conditions. And even when restrictions are operative, (9) and its translation can determine the same set of truth conditions.[18]

Let's turn to another sort of worry mentioned at the beginning of this section, that since 'Snow is white' and 'La neige est blanche' determine different propositions, the sentences can't say the same thing. Whether this is so depends on the semantics of 'says' as it is used in sentences like " 'La neige est blanche' says that snow is white." A first approximation to the semantics of 'says' as it is used here is this: Call the RAM determined by the French sentence p, that determined by 'Snow is white' q. Ignore for the moment the fact that in different contexts the RAMs can represent different things because of variations in restrictions. Then we may speak without qualification about what RAMs the RAMs p and q might represent.

Given that 'la neige' is to be treated syntactically as a unit, it seems clear that the RAMs p and q have the same "representational potential": If p represents a RAM r, so does q, and vice versa. To say that 'Snow is white' and 'La neige est blanche' say the same thing is to say that they have the same representational potential. To say that 'La neige est blanche' says that snow is white is to say that the RAM that the French determines has exactly the representational potential that the RAM that snow is white does. Since the two RAMs do have the same representational potential, the French sentence indeed says that snow is white.

This is only an approximation, since we ignored the fact that we can talk about a sentence determining a RAM, or about a RAM representing other RAMs, only when things are relativized to a

18 Someone might pose the following objection: Why should (8) be true just because John accepts 'Hammurabi believes that Hesperus is hot'? The truth of (8) requires that the RAM (E) represent one of John's RAMs. Since (E) contains a quantifier, it can represent only RAMs that contain such. But there is no existential quantifier in 'Hammurabi believes that Hesperus is hot'.

In one sense it is probably true that 'Hammurabi believes . . .' doesn't contain an existential quantifier: The surface structure of the sentence probably doesn't contain one. It doesn't follow that there isn't an existential quantifier in some other structure the sentence has. In particular, it doesn't follow that there is no quantifier in what is generally referred to as the sentence's logical form. As I observed in Chapter 1, it is the logical form of a sentence that is relevant to what proposition is expressed by it.

context. The idea that, strictly speaking, we can evaluate what a sentence says only when it is taken relative to a context is quite standard. Everyone agrees that it makes no sense to ask what 'I am fat' says if a context of interpretation isn't specified; it surely makes no sense to ask if it's true. 'Boston is ugly' seems to say different things in different contexts: Today, it expresses the proposition that Boston is ugly today; yesterday, it expressed the proposition that Boston was ugly yesterday.

So we should treat sentences like

(12) 'La neige est blanche' says that snow is white

and

(13) 'La neige est blanche' and 'Snow is white' say the same thing

as ellipses for things of the form of

(12') 'La neige est blanche' taken relative to context c says that snow is white

and

(13') 'La neige est blanche' in context c and 'Snow is white' in context c' say the same thing.

'The same thing' is to be cashed out as a propositional quantifier: 'There is a p such that each sentence says p'. We can incorporate the context relativity of what RAM a sentence determines and of what a RAM can represent as follows: Let's say that a RAM p's profile in a context c is the rule that assigns, to each world, the class of pairs $\langle u, q \rangle$ such that p represents (under some correlation or other obeying c's restrictions) q, and q is in u's representational system at u. The idea of a RAM's profile is just a generalization of the notion of a RAM's representational potential discussed earlier. We can also speak of the profile of a sentence (of a particular language) relative to a context: This is just the profile, in the context, of the RAM the sentence determines in that context.

Now we can say that *"S" in context c says that T*, taken in a context c' is true iff the profile of S in c is the same as the profile of T in c'. *"S" in c and "T" in c' says the same thing*, taken in a context c'', will be true just in case there's a RAM p such that the profile of S in c and the profile of T in c' are identical with the profile of p in c''.

Let's look at an example or two. We may suppose that claims of the form of

"*S*" says that *S*

with *S* an English indicative sentence, are generally elliptical for ones of the form of

"*S*" in this context says that *S*,

where 'this context' refers to the context of utterance. Barring a failure of reference in *S* (given which, intuitively, the sentence expresses no proposition at all), it should be clear that such claims are always true: Sufficient for their truth is that the profile of *S* in the context is identical to itself.

Suppose that we imagine 'Snow is white' taken relative to a context c with no restrictions operative; suppose 'La neige est blanche' taken relative to c', which has no restrictions. Then (ignoring subtleties concerning tense), it is clear that (13) will be true.

Of course, there will be cases in which a claim like

(14) the English sentence 'Snow is white' in c does not say that snow is white

come out true. For example, if the context relative to which (14) is taken contains no restrictions, but c contains a restriction like

Odile: 'is white' → 'est blanche',

then (14) comes out false. For the profile of 'Snow is white' in c is different from what it is in the context of utterance: There will be some worlds in which Odile has a RAM, call it r, "made out of" 'Snow is white' in her RS. So the profile of the English sentence in the context of utterance will map these worlds to ⟨Odile, r⟩, whereas its profile in c will not so map these worlds.

Something like this is true on most views of propositions. [Admittedly, there are "more opportunities" for (14) to be true on my view than there are on other views of propositions.] Almost everyone agrees that a sentence like 'Reagan is thinking' says different things at different times. So if c is a context earlier than the present, then ' "Reagan is thinking" in c doesn't say that Reagan is thinking' is, on almost everyone's view, true.

Are the "extra opportunities" I give a sentence like

'Reagan is thinking' in c says that Reagan is thinking

to be false a problem? I don't think so. Suppose we take seriously the claim that 'Odile believes that Reagan is thinking' can vary in truth value from context to context. Then it is surely true that, while in some contexts it is true that Odile believes what is said by the sentence 'Reagan is thinking', in other contexts it is *not* true that Odile believes what is said by the sentence 'Reagan is thinking'. So the sentence must be said, in some sense, to say different things in different contexts

On the view I am defending, the idea that there is some one thing that is the proposition that Reagan is thinking is literally correct but quite misleading. It is literally correct because there is one thing that 'that Reagan is thinking' names – the RAM that Reagan is thinking. It is perniciously misleading because it suggests that an attitude ascription like 'Nancy thinks that Reagan is thinking' simply says that Nancy has this very object "in her psychological ken."

In a certain loose sense, there are *many* propositions that Reagan is thinking: Besides that picked out by 'Reagan is thinking', there is the one picked out by the German 'Reagan denkt', that picked out by 'Reagan penst', and so on. These are all propositions that Reagan thinks, insofar as the sentences that express them all say the same thing – that Reagan thinks – and insofar as having any of them in one's representational system can count, in some contexts, as believing that Reagan is thinking. But, as I have cut up the pie, all these propositions are literally distinct.

This goes against conventional philosophical wisdom. Most people think that the proposition that snow is white simply *is* the proposition expressed by 'La neige est blanche'. I don't have a snappy argument to show that this is a confusion. But I do think the theory I'm sketching explains a good deal about the way in which we ascribe attitudes and talk about what sentences say. The theory demands that we give up this belief about propositional identity. Giving up the belief seems a relatively small price to pay. After all, we can still truly say that 'Snow is white' and 'La neige est blanche' say the same thing. And this seems to be what lies at the root of the intuition about propositional identity.

As before, the price is a somewhat more extreme version of the price that other theories have to pay. As we saw in Chapter 1, there are good reasons to build into propositions the structure of the sentences that express them. Once we do this, we have to deny certain intuitions about propositional identity – for example, the intuition that the proposition that A and B is the proposition that B and A. As we saw there, it wasn't clear that we were *required* to hold onto this intuition in order to explain other, seemingly more fundamental intuitions. For example, we could deny the identity and still say that, necessarily, whoever believes that A and B, believes that B and A. Likewise, one can say that 'A and B' and 'B and A' say the same thing without insisting that the sentences determine the same proposition, by deploying a version of the strategy I am outlining here. The point is that the difference between the sacrifice the theory I am presenting makes, with respect to our beliefs about propositional identity, and that made by many other theories is one of degree, not of kind.

Let me mention a last worry about propositional identity. We sometimes name propositions. We call the proposition that first-order logic is undecidable 'Church's theorem'; that all and only the Turing computable functions are effectively computable, 'Church's thesis'; and that for any integer n greater than 2, there are no x, y, and z such that $x^n + y^n = z^n$, 'Fermat's last theorem'. Having named them, we go on to use the names in attitude ascriptions. We say that Marie Bernard doubts Church's thesis, that Ralph can prove Church's theorem, or that Francis believes Fermat's theorem.

Now, there are a number of ways of expressing Church's theorem and thesis, as well as Fermat's theorem. For example, Church's theorem can be expressed with 'First-order logic is undecidable' or as 'First-order logic is not decidable'. Church's thesis, as well as being expressible as above, can be expressed by saying that all and only the effectively computable functions are general recursive. Fermat's theorem is surely the claim that for n greater than 2, and x, y, and z, $x^n + y^n \neq z^n$. In general, I assign different RAMs to the different sentences that all count as Fermat's theorem; likewise for Church's thesis. It would even seem that the syntax of the two formulations of Church's theorem I have given, which differ between 'is not decidable' and 'is undecidable', are sufficiently different so that the RAMs I would assign to them will be distinct.

So what do expressions like 'Church's thesis' name on my account? One worries that there is no nonarbitrary way to single out a proposition for it to name. The two propositions mentioned above are equally good candidates for the thesis, and neither of them happens to be the thesis that Church actually expressed: Church gave another gloss of computability, which, as it turns out, is provably equivalent to the two I have mentioned. So now we have three candidates for the nominatum of 'Church's thesis'. Logicians will point out that there are many more. Surely I have to say that 'Church's thesis' doesn't name anything, a disastrous result. Likewise for 'Church's theorem' and 'Fermat's theorem'.

This is a problem that *every* theory about propositions seems to face. Most Russellians, for example, distinguish between the proposition that there is no $n > 2$ such that for any x, y, and z ..., and the proposition that for any $n > 2$, there is no x, y, and z. ... The very fact that one might be surprised to learn that, if there is no ..., then for any ... is, in any case, a reason for the Russellian to make such a distinction.

Presumably the Russellian will say that there is a *range* (perhaps somewhat vague) of propositions that "count" as Fermat's theorem. In some contexts, it is clear which of the members of the range 'Fermat's last theorem' is supposed to name. If, for example, Francis says, 'I can prove Fermat's last theorem' and he has some one favored way of expressing the theorem, then we can take him to have said (probably falsely) that he is related to the proposition determined by this way of expressing the theorem by the relation of being able to prove. In other contexts, there may be no non-arbitrary candidate for the role of the theorem. Perhaps we know that Ralph believes Fermat's theorem but have no idea what versions of it he would recognize. In this case, the Russellian could quite aptly suggest that we treat 'Fermat's theorem' somewhat like a free variable with a restricted range (the set of things that count as Fermat theorems); 'Ralph believes Fermat's theorem' is true, provided that some assignment to "the variable" from its range makes the sentence true. I would say the same thing.

It is not as if those who favor structureless propositions are really much better off in this regard. Consider, for example, someone like Stalnaker who takes propositions to be sets of worlds. As we saw in Chapter 1, in order to avoid making the claim

Mary believes that $2 + 2 = 4$

entail the claim

Mary believes that for any $n > 2$, there are no x, y, and z such that $x^n + y^n = z^n$,

172

Stalnaker took such claims to be, typically, metalinguistic. When we say that Mary believes that, for $n > 2$, there are no x, y, and z such that $x^n + y^n = z^n$, Stalnaker told us, what we are typically saying is something like this: Mary believes that 'for $n > 2$, there are no x, y, and z such that $x^n + y^n = z^n$' says for $n > 2$ that there are no x, y, and z such that $x^n + y^n = z^n$.

How will Stalnaker treat a claim like 'Ralph believes Fermat's theorem'? Surely we don't want this to follow from 'Ralph believes that $2 + 2 = 4$', given that we don't want 'Ralph believes that, for any $n > 2$, there are no x, y, and z such that $x^n + y^n = z^n$' to follow from it. So Stalnaker must also assign a metalinguistic proposition to 'Fermat's theorem'. But just as the Russellian and I have ever so many structured propositions to choose from, as possible nominata for the term, so Stalnaker has ever so many metalinguistic claims that are equally apt candidates for Fermat's theorem. The choice for Stalnaker is no less and no more arbitrary than it is for the Russellian or for me.

I am not saying that this poses a particular problem for Stalnaker's view. Stalnaker can solve this problem with an analogue of the way I suggested the Russellian and I might solve it. Rather, I am pointing out that the above problem is a problem for everyone. Although there are good reasons for being dissatisfied with Stalnaker's view – as we saw in Chapter 1 – this is not one of them. Nor is it a reason for being worried about the present account of propositions.

4. APPLICATIONS AND AMPLIFICATIONS

In this section, I first say a little about the explanation of behavior by attitude ascription. Then I discuss some puzzle cases: Kripke's puzzles about Pierre, Peter, London, and Paderewski, and the context-hopping argument of Section 1 of this chapter.

In discussing explanations of behavior by ascription of attitude, I presuppose the truth of psychological sententialism, discussed and defended in Chapter 1. I also assume that folk-psychological explanations – by which I mean garden-variety attempts to explain behavior by ascribing beliefs, desires, and other attitudes – typically are explanations. So, for example, I assume that the sorts of cases in which we would be inclined to offer

(1) Randi wanted Hesperus to rise; and he thought that, if there was waving, then Hesperus would rise

as an explanation of

(2) Randi waved

and, by and large, cases in which (1) gives the crux of a genuine explanation of (2).

This may make it seem that I am begging the most important question about belief–desire explanations: Are they *really* explanations? But my interest here is not in whether folk psychology is idle folklore, but in whether the common idea – that what a sentence like (1) says can explain Randi's waving – can be accommodated by the sort of account I'm sketching.

As I pointed out at the beginning of this chapter, on a Russellian view, this idea is somewhat puzzling. On Russellian terms the idea that what makes a claim like (1) true tends also to make (2) true is a mistake. What makes (1) true for a Russellian is just that Randi had some way of desiring-true the proposition that Hesperus rises and some way of believing-true the proposition that, if there is waving, then Hesperus rises. Since there needn't be much of a relation between these ways of getting to the propositions, what makes (1) true isn't something that makes, or tends to make, it true that Randi waves.

I suggested that this was an unhappy state of affairs. So it had better be the case that, on my view, what makes uses of (1) true – at least the uses of (1) that would be made by behavior explainers – is a state that is at least a plausible candidate for one that makes, or tends to make, Randi wave.

It is plausible to think that, if Randi accepts a sentence of the form

$$W \to Rh,$$

where W is a sentence with the truth conditions of 'there is waving', Rh is a sentence in which 'h' names Hesperus, 'R' picks out the property of rising, and he "desires-true" a token of Rh, this will make, or tend to make, him wave.[19] So if there is the right sort of relation between Randi's being in this sort of state (or having a

---

19 I remind the reader that 'acceptance' is used in a quasi-technical sense in this book, as explained in Chapter 1, Section 5.

representational system that corresponds to it)[20] and the truth conditions our account assigns to (1) – say, the truth of (1) guarantees that Randi is in this sort of state – then the account I am sketching will make the idea that (1) explains (2) a reasonable one.

(1) involves more than one ascription of attitude. It therefore could be evaluated in a number of ways. Suppose we are evaluating (1) in a context without restrictions. It seems natural to evaluate it serially: First we evaluate the first conjunct, then the second. Suppose we find that there is a correlation under which the RAM that Hesperus rises represents a RAM in the appropriate part of Randi's RS. Perhaps the correlation

(r) *Randi*: 'Hesperus' → 'Hesperus'; 'rises' → 'rises'

will make the RAM that Hesperus rises represent a RAM in Randi's system of desires.

Now we turn to the second conjunct. There seem to be several ways we can proceed. On the one hand, we might decide to use only correlations that extend, in the straightforward sense, correlation (r). Or we can simply ignore what we did in evaluating the first conjunct of (1), and ask if there is some correlation or other that will make the sentence we are now looking at true. Or we might just start all over again and ask, Is there some correlation that makes both conjuncts true?

If Randi's RS is arranged in certain ways, which procedure we pick will make a difference to our evaluation of (1) as a whole. For example, suppose that Randi had a belief that he would express with

(3) If there is waving, then Phosphorus rises

and a desire that he would have expressed

(4) Hesperus rises.

And suppose he was innocent of the fact that Hesperus is Phosphorus. Then (on a natural elaboration of what Randi's overall RS

---

20 As defined in Section 2, a representational system consists only of RAMs that correspond to sentences "believed-true." Obviously, we can expand the notion of an RS so that an individual's RS is a family of sets of RAMs, with each set corresponding to one of the individual's attitudes. So the expanded RS will contain the set of "desire RAMs," "doubt RAMs," etc., as well as a set of "belief RAMs." In the text I have quietly shifted to this way of thinking of an RS.

is like) the first and third strategies will make the first conjunct of (1) true, the second false; the middle strategy makes the conjunction as a whole true.

I think it is a mistake to look for some one strategy that we invariably apply in cases like this. There is, rather, a most natural strategy, which is roughly the third: When we have multiple ascriptions of attitude to someone, we try to evaluate them using one correlation, one that obeys whatever restrictions the context may provide. This strategy has the effect of coordinating the information that attitude ascriptions individually provide; it also makes such ascriptions relevant to the explanation of behavior. This last claim should be clear enough. Suppose we resolve to evaluate (1) using a single correlation: We treat it as the claim that, for some f obeying the context's restrictions, the RAM that Hesperus rises represents one of Randi's desires under f, and the RAM that, if there is waving, then Hesperus rises represents, under f, one of his beliefs. Then (1) won't evaluate as true unless Randi holds beliefs and desires under sentences of the forms of $W \rightarrow Rh$ and Rh. This makes the idea that (1) gives us a reason for thinking that Randi waved a coherent one. In general, if the premises of a belief–desire explanation of action are evaluated using a single correlation, they will not be jointly true unless the agent whose action we are trying to explain is in a state that it is reasonable to think would tend to make him act in the appropriate way. So given that we are supposed to evaluate the premises of belief–desire explanations in this way, the belief that such explanations are genuine is reasonable enough – which is just what we wanted to show.

That we typically use a single correlation for evaluating multiple ascriptions to an individual seems reasonable enough. I am suggesting that we should think of this strategy as being built into the semantics of sentences like (1). That is, in the appropriate circumstances – and circumstances in which (1) is used in the attempt to explain behavior are invariably such – (1) is true only if a single correlation makes each conjunct true. Such uses of (1) are to be assigned truth conditions reflecting this: (1) so used says something true only at worlds in which Randi's beliefs and desires have the sort of structural relation that (1)'s content sentences have to one another.

If this is so, then it is sometimes inappropriate to assign truth conditions to a use of an attitude ascription in isolation from the

176

conversation or discourse in which it occurs. In the relevant cases (1) is an existentially generalized conjunction prefixed with a quantifier binding (implicit) variables in each of (1)'s conjuncts. (There is obviously a rather strong analogy here to the Fregean happy-face strategy discussed at the end of Chapter 2.) Asking what each conjunct of (1) says, in isolation from the discourse as a whole, is a bit like asking what 'x is a cookie' says taken in isolation from '$\exists x(x$ is a cookie and x crumbles)'.

More generally, a sentence like 'Randi believes that Hesperus is rising' is best thought of as an *open* sentence. In a conversation in which a number of attitude ascriptions occur, the free variables of the ascriptions may be jointly bound by a single quantifier ("implicit to the conversation"). They need not be: Each might be bound by its own quantifier. Or, putting the same idea slightly differently, when a conversation contains multiple ascriptions of attitude, the ascriptions are sometimes to be interpreted jointly – and thus true only if an assignment of the same correlation to the free variables makes all true – and sometimes interpreted singly.

What is needed here is some general notion like *Conversation C taken as a whole is true* or *Conversation C as a whole has truth conditions such and such*, of which the usual notions of the truth of a single sentence, or of its truth conditions, are a special case. It is not as if such a notion is needed to explain only the semantic properties of attitude ascriptions.[21] Narratives and tensed discourse also provide examples of sets of sentences whose truth conditions seem most sensibly assigned as a whole, and not individually.

Explanatory digression

Let us consider a simple example. Suppose that yesterday John took an antacid and then got indigestion. Suppose that I say, thinking myself to be making a literally correct narrative report of what happened yesterday,

21 Hans Kamp and Irene Heim have argued that such notions are necessary to explain anaphoric pronouns. Kamp and Hinrichs have argued that such notions are necessary to explain the semantic properties of tensed discourse. Kamp and Nick Asher have applied Kamp's general framework to the treatment of attitude ascriptions. See Kamp (1981, 1985), Hinrichs (1986), Heim (1982), and Asher (1986). A good introduction to the ideas behind Kamp's approach is given in Partee (1984).

(5) John got indigestion. He took an antacid.

In this case, I have gotten things wrong. It seems clear that (5) is false; it's not clear that there is much point in assigning truth values to the constituents of (5). (5) as a whole makes the claim that, at some time yesterday, John got indigestion and, a decent interval thereafter, took an antacid. This claim is wrong. But there is not much point in deciding whether 'John got indigestion', *as I used it*, is true or false. After all, I had no opinion on the time yesterday he got indigestion, save that it occurred before his antacid taking.

One might observe that we *can* assign truth values to the constituent sentences of (5). We can decide, for instance, to make 'John got indigestion' true provided that at some time yesterday he got it, and the second sentence true provided that, after the relevant time, he took an antacid. This would make the first sentence true, the second false.

There is no doubt that we could make such assignments. But it is not clear why we should prefer an approach that makes (5) false by making such assignments to one that resolutely treats (5) in a holistic fashion. For one thing, there are other ways to make such assignments to the individual sentences. It would be no more arbitrary in the case above to make the second sentence true, the first false. Furthermore, it is not altogether clear whether a strategy that treats each sentence of (5) individually really assigns independent truth conditions to each sentence. Exactly what truth conditions does my use of (5)'s first sentence get? Perhaps the same truth conditions as 'at some time yesterday, John got indigestion'. But then, if we can assign truth conditions to the second sentence of (5) at all, it would seem that it would be taken as saying the same as something like 'Yesterday, John took an antacid sometime after he got indigestion'. If we apply this strategy to longer narratives, it would seem to make each successive sentence in a narrative encode all of the information assigned to earlier sentences of the narrative. This is surely somewhat bizarre.

End of digression

I return to this topic in Chapter 4. There, I will suggest the bare bones of a procedure for assigning truth conditions to dialogues with multiple occurrences of attitude ascriptions. For now, all we need agree on is that a sentence of the form

x believes that S. x believes that T

can be read or evaluated in two ways: Jointly, so that it is properly regimented as

$$\exists f(\text{Believes}(x, \text{ that } S, f) \ \& \ \text{Believes}(x, \text{ that } T, f)),$$

and individually, so that it is regimented as

$$\exists f\,\text{Believes}(x, \text{ that } S, f) \ \& \ \exists f\,\text{Believes}(x, \text{ that } T, f).$$

Let us turn to a discussion of some puzzle cases, beginning with Kripke's case of Pierre. We reviewed the case of Pierre in Chapter 2. Of it, Kripke writes, "This is the puzzle: Does Pierre, or does he not, believe that London is pretty?" Kripke argues successively that

(6) Pierre believes that London is pretty

is (or at least seems) true (focusing, of course, on Pierre's "French" beliefs); that

(7) Pierre believes that London is not pretty

is (or at least seems) true (focusing now on Pierre's "English" beliefs); but that they can't both be true, because Pierre, a leading logician "would *never* let contradictory beliefs pass. And surely anyone, leading logician or no, is in principle in a position to notice and correct contradictory beliefs if he has them" (Kripke 1979, p. 257).

What would count as a solution to this sort of puzzle? I suppose that, all else being equal, we want to preserve as much of our pretheoretic intuitions about sentences (6) and (7) as possible. So ideally, a solution to the puzzle will provide a way of saying that both (6) and (7) are true – that is, the uses Kripke makes of them, when he ascribes truth to them, are true uses – and yet (6) and (7), taken together, can't be true, for more or less the very reason Kripke gives.

One nice thing about the view I've been sketching is that it does allow us to say something like this: It seems plausible to say that one way in which what I have been calling restrictions on correlations come to be operative is that, if the speaker is focusing on how someone expresses his beliefs, thinks that his audience is so focusing (and thinks his audience thinks he knows that they are so focusing), then the appropriate restrictions tend to come into play.

So when Kripke begins walking us through the puzzle, focusing on Pierre's "French" beliefs, we might expect the restriction

Pierre: 'London' → 'Londres'

to be operative. This will make (6) true. Then Kripke asks us to focus on a completely different aspect of Pierre's cognitive structure, his English-language beliefs. The old restriction is no longer operative, and a new one,

Pierre: 'London' → 'London',

comes into play. So (7) is true. Then Kripke asks us, in effect, to answer the question Can both of these be true together? And he observes that they seem to imply that Pierre is in some sense irrational.

And this is quite correct. The most natural way of evaluating (6) and (7) when used together is jointly, using a single correlation function. So any natural way of evaluating the conjunction of (6) and (7) makes it false. And it is false for just the reason Kripke gives: It suggests that Pierre is irrational, accepting some sentence and its negation. It is (roughly) in this sense that anyone with contradictory beliefs is in a position to recognize such and correct it. (I will make this claim more precise below.)

I do have to say that there is a way of interpreting the conjunction of (6) and (7) so that it is true. If we are in a context in which no restrictions are operative and we interpret the ascriptions singly, and not jointly, then both (6) and (7) will be true. I don't think that this is a disaster. First of all, as I argued above, this is a very unnatural way to evaluate multiple ascriptions. So I think I may fairly say that the account I have been presenting leads us to expect that there will be at best a weak inclination among speakers to say that both (6) and (7) are true, if they are presented together. And this is what we do seem to find.

And we do have *some* inclination to say that in the case of Pierre both are true. Most of us are inclined to reason as follows: well, (6) *is* true. And, gosh, (7) *is* true. So I guess (gulp) their conjunction is true.

Let's turn to the case of Peter and 'Paderewski'. It might appear that this case presents a problem for my view. The case is like that of Pierre and 'London'/'Londres'. Peter hears one day of a famous musician, Paderewski, and thinks to himself 'Paderewski had musical talent'. He hears on some other day of a Polish statesman, Paderewski. Thinking that politicians are poor musicians, he thinks to himself, 'Paderewski did not have musical talent'. We have, Kripke urges, exactly the same sort of puzzle about

(8) Peter believes that Paderewski had musical talent,
(9) Peter believes that Paderewski did not have musical talent

as we did concerning (6) and (7).

In the case of Pierre, it was clear that I could say, for example, that in certain contexts (6) is true and (7) is false. We needed only to consider a context in which the restriction 'London' → 'Londres' was operative. It would seem that I can't say this sort of thing about this case, for here there seems to be but one sentence type, that of

Paderewski had musical talent,

which is such that Peter accepts tokens of both it and its negation. So it seems that, no matter what restrictions are operative, if (8) is true, so is (9). So, it appears, I have to treat like cases (Pierre and Peter) in unlike ways.

Some might say that the expression 'Paderewski' in Peter's spoken dialect is ambiguous: Appearances to the contrary, Peter does not accept some natural language sentence and its negation. I would prefer not to say this. 'Paderewski' is presumably not ambiguous in *our* spoken dialect; arguably, Peter's spoken dialect is ours. In any case, I think there are better things to say about the case of Peter.

Let's go back to the picture of belief that we are working with. The states that underlie true attitude ascriptions on this picture are what we called in Chapter 1 states of acceptance. As long as we don't forget the warnings of Chapter 1 about acceptance and to-kening, it will do no harm to think of acceptance as a matter of having sentence tokens written inside of the head, maybe on a blackboard next to the pineal gland. We should think of a believer's representational system, the set of RAMs we quantify over in giving truth conditions for attitude ascriptions, as being determined some-how by what is written on the blackboard.

Up to now, I have been pretending that the way the blackboard determines the RAMs is the way suggested by the following example: If a public language sentence token of the form Fa is on the blackboard, then a RAM of the form $\langle\langle d, e\rangle, \langle b, c\rangle\rangle$ is in the representational system, where b is the type of a, c is the referent of the relevant token, d is the type of F, and e is the Russellian referent of the relevent token. On this picture Peter would have a RAM and its negation in his representational system. (I haven't defined a negation of operation for RAMs, but it's obvious, I think, how to go about it.)

The tale of Peter shows that the relation between the blackboard and the RS is not *quite* this straightforward. Peter treats different tokens of 'Paderewski' as representations of different things. This should require that such tokens make different contributions to his RS.

The obvious way to effect this is by distinguishing between the public language word type of a mental term token and what we might call the token's representational type for the tokener.[22] Although all of Peter's 'Paderewski' tokens are of the same public language word type, all these tokens aren't of the same representational type for him. Rather, these tokens divide up into two classes for Peter, one of which (speaking crudely) contains the musical 'Padereweski' tokens, the other the political ones.

Allow for the moment that the distinction between public language type and representational type is perfectly transparent and that we can define, for each tokener x, an equivalence relation *t and t' are of the same representational type for x* on mental term tokens. Then we can speak simply of *the* representation a mental term token t determines. We identify it with the set of tokens t' of the same representational type for the tokener as t. We can now use representations, instead of public language word types, to construct RAMs for the RS. To return to the example above: Suppose a token of the form Fa is on the blackboard. Then there is a RAM of the form $\langle\langle d, e\rangle, \langle b, c\rangle\rangle$ in the representational system, where b and d are the *representations* determined by a and F, and c and e are as before.

If we can do this, then the cases of Pierre and Peter really are parallel. Peter has two representations of Paderewski; Pierre has two representations of London. Peter uses one representation to think Paderewski thus and so, and another to think him not thus and so. Pierre, likewise, uses one representation to think London

---

22 The notion of a representation should, of course, be extended to predicates and other sorts of expression. I will discuss only how terms – and then only certain sorts of terms – determine representations.

so and thus, another to think it not so and thus. And in talking and thinking about Peter and Pierre, we sometimes use 'Paderewski' and 'London' to represent one of their representations, and sometimes we use the terms to represent the other.

At this point I will spell out enough of the details of the notion of a representation so that it's clear that the cases of Pierre and Peter really are parallel on my view. What is needed is an answer to the question: Under what conditions are two mental term tokens t and t' part of the same representation? For the moment, let us simplify matters by limiting attention to the case in which both t and t' are tokens of public language names.

As I see it, there will be two sorts of conditions that, together, will be necessary and sufficient for two tokens to determine the same representation. The two sorts of conditions are what we might call "outside" and "inside" conditions. For tokens of proper names of a natural language, the outside condition is that they be of the same public language name type.

Of course, there are a number of ways of characterizing the notion of 'same name'. There is a sense in which Aristotle the philosopher and Aristotle the husband of Jackie had the same name: Their names are, in modern English, orthographically and phonologically the same. When I speak of two tokens being tokens of the same name, I certainly do *not* mean that they are *simply spelled or pronounced the same*.

Part of what makes for sameness of name in the requisite sense is being part of the same "causal chain" of transmission.[23] So the

23 The idea of a causal chain of transmission is due to Kripke (1980), who suggests the following picture of how a name token refers: There is an initial event – perhaps an ostensive baptism, perhaps a use of a description to fix a reference, perhaps something else – that associates a token with an individual in such a way that the token refers to the individual. Further, there are certain relations that preserve reference and that constitute a chain of transmission of a name. Kripke observes that "when the name is 'passed from link to link', the receiver of the name must, I think, intend when he learns it to use it with the same reference as the man from whom he heard it" (p. 96).

This gives a picture of name tokens forming a sort of tree of transmission, with a single token (or some relatively small set of tokens) forming a base node and later tokens being connected with the base via the sort of links Kripke emphasizes. (I do not suppose that very much more than what I have just mentioned is involved.) In suggesting that this condition is not sufficient for name identity, no criticism of Kripke is intended; Kripke (1980) is not concerned with questions of word identity.

The idea that membership in the same tree of transmission is important for outside condition is one that is in part broadly causal in nature. To be parts of the same representation, proper name tokens have to be residues of the same causal or historical chain, in the sense in which this notion is used in the causal theory of names.

Given that two tokens are tokens of the same name only if they satisfy such a condition, they determine the same representation only if they are names of the same thing. So 'Aristotle', when it names the philosopher, will not determine the same representation as it does when it names the shipping magnate. And 'Hesperus' and 'Phosphorus' do not determine the same representation, being parts of different "chains of transmission".

I think of membership in the same chain of transmission as being necessary but not sufficient for two tokens to be of the same name. Thus, being in the same chain is not a sufficient condition for satisfying the outside condition for determining the same representation. Since the other conditions for sameness of name are irrelevant to Peter and Paderewski, I defer discussing them.

The interior condition, for when two tokens determine the same representation, is a "recognition condition." I will speak somewhat intuitively about this. Usually when we hear someone talking about someone, we know (or think we know) who is being talked about. We hear someone say, 'Reagan was going to bomb Nicaragua', and we simply assume that it is the former president who is being discussed, not his wife, son, or daughter, much less an animal-rights philosopher or erstwhile White House chief of staff.

When this is true – when, intuitively speaking, we recognize the subject of discussion – it seems appropriate to think that we are in some sense "filing" or "grouping" the token of 'Reagan' we are "processing" along with certain other tokens on our blackboard ("presidential tokens") and segregating it from certain others. In such a case, the new token of 'Reagan' bears the interior relation for sameness of representational type to the presidential tokens. Suppose that in this case it was the president that was being discussed. Then, since both outside and inside conditions are satisfied,

word identity is due to Kaplan, who introduced the idea in the unpublished lecture mentioned in the text. What I say about name identity owes a good deal to this lecture and discussions with Kaplan. I don't know whether he would endorse what I say in the text. After this book was sent to press, I read Devitt (1981), who anticipates the idea that word identity is a function of causal chains. This book contains a valuable discussion of the notion of a causal chain.

the new token of 'Reagan' and the older presidential tokens will all determine the same representation.

The interior condition just sketched is to be understood in such a way that tokens that have different referential values can satisfy it – such tokens can be "recognized as naming the same thing." In variants of the case above, for example, you might have been wrong: Regan the animal–rights philosopher, outraged at the plight of ferrets in Managua, was the subject of the conversation. In this case, the outside condition on sameness of representation would not be fulfilled, although the interior condition would be.

In summary, two proper name tokens are part of the same representation for a person provided (a) they are of the same word type, and (b) that person groups them together, that is, he manipulates them as if they named the same thing.

Return now to the case of Peter. Peter has a token of 'Paderewski has talent' on one place on the blackboard, a token 'Paderewski has no talent' somewhere else. It is quite clear, I hope, that on any way of spelling out the inside conditions I have been talking about, the "talented" tokens of Paderewski will not determine the same representation as do the "untalented" ones. Let's call the representation the talented tokens determine 'P_t', the representation the untalented ones determine 'P_u'. Peter's RS will contain the RAMs

$\langle\langle$'not', negation$\rangle,\langle\langle$'is talented', being talented$\rangle, \langle P_u,$ Paderewski$\rangle\rangle\rangle$,
$\langle\langle$'is talented', being talented$\rangle, \langle P_t,$ Paderewski$\rangle\rangle$.

Since P_t and P_u are distinct, this is much like having an RS that contains the RAMs determined by 'Hesperus is hot' and 'Phosphorus is not hot', or those determined by 'London is not pretty' and 'Londres est jolie'.

Given this refinement of our characterization of a representational system, we can treat the case of Peter in just the way we treated the case of Pierre. When we think or talk about this case, we do, after all, tend to focus on the different ways in which Peter represents Paderewski to himself. This, in turn, brings into play restrictions that make our use of 'Paderewski' in sentences like

(8) Peter believes that Paderewski has musical talent,
(9) Peter believes that Paderewski did not have musical talent

represent one or another of Peter's representations, in the sense of representation adumbrated above. That is, we tend to switch back and forth between using

Peter: 'Paderewski' → P_t

and

Peter: 'Paderewski' → P_u.

As in the case of Pierre, there are contexts in which (8) is true and (9) is not and ones in which (9) is true and (8) is not. And we feel uncomfortable with the idea that there is some way to make both (8) and (9) true, as well we should; for on the natural way of making both of these true – by using one correlation to interpret both – their joint truth implies that Peter accepts a sentence of the form

(10) Tp,

and a sentence of the form

(11) not: Tp'

and that he has "filed" the relevant tokens of p and p' together, as tokens that pick out the same thing. For if (8) and (9) are made true under a single correlation, then the subject terms of the tokens of (10) and (11) Peter accepts determine the same representation. This requires that Peter take them to represent the same thing. Sentences (8) and (9), taken in this way, portray Peter as irrational: They have him saying that so and so is talented and *the very same so and so* is not talented. It is in this sense that anyone with contradictory beliefs is, in principle, in a position to recognize such and correct it.

I will say a little more about the notion of representation just introduced. The notion raises a number of issues. One has to do with "name tokens" in beliefs we have on the basis of our perceptual experience. If I see someone enter the room, I will typically come to have a belief about that person, that she is entering the room, even without having a natural language proper name for her. On the picture I am working with, this implies that I am in a sentential state with a constituent that represents the individual in question. We can stretch the word 'term' in such a way that these constituents, as well as natural language proper names, count as terms.

One wants to know a number of things about such terms. For one thing, one wants to know what they *are*. Are they images, something that can be defined in terms of images, or something else? One wants to know, when two of them determine the same representation, what the outside condition the terms satisfy will be. And one wants to know whether a natural language proper name and such a term can determine the same representation. An allied set of questions arises with respect to the use of natural language demonstratives, like 'this' and 'that', in thought. The use of these is typically connected with perceptual experience of one kind or another. One wants to know when two demonstratives determine the same representation and whether a use of 'that' ever determines the same representation as a natural language proper name.

I raise these questions at the moment so that the reader, to whom they perhaps occurred long ago, will know that I am aware of them. I will address some of them – in particular, questions about demonstratives and representation – in the next chapter.

I return to issues connected with representations and names of public languages. I said that membership in the same causal chain of transmission is necessary, but not sufficient, for sameness of name type. What else, then, is necessary?

One might be tempted to say that two tokens must be spelled or pronounced the same, in order to count as the same word. But as Kaplan observes (in an unpublished lecture), this is quite contrary to intuition: Orthographic or phonological distortions don't destroy identity of word type, at least up to a point. The man from Nebraska who says 'KAR-ter' presumably uses the same word as the Bostonian who says 'KAHRT-ta'. The fact that the British spell it 'colour' doesn't make it a different word from our 'color'.

Though these observations are correct, I think there is nonetheless something to the idea that orthography and pronunciation are relevant to the identity of a name or word. I propose (though I don't think it's a very original thought) that we think of a name type as something along the lines of a practice or ritual of referring to an individual.[24] Now let us ask, In general, what determines whether two acts are performances of the same practice or ritual?

Part of what makes up a ritual (type) is a standard or canonical format for it. For example, there is a canonical format for celebrating mass. In general, a token can deviate to some extent from a ritual's standard and still count as a token of the ritual, though of course there are limits. You can (probably) celebrate mass without saying all the prayers at the foot of the altar; if, however, you

---

24 What about empty names? Well, there are empty practices, aren't there? Consider what an atheist might say about a practice like the mass, the point of which is (partially) to worship God.

neglect to consecrate the host, what you do doesn't count as celebrating mass.

Part of what goes to make up a name, qua ritual of referring, is a certain canonical orthography and pronunciation.[25] When we acquire the ability to refer to someone using a name, picking up the name from others, we typically intend to conform to the prevailing standards for spelling or uttering the name, just as we intend to refer to whomever our teachers refer to using the name. Subsequent productions of the name thus have a canonical orthography and pronunciation, one that the tokens themselves may or may not realize. Thus, given a token of a name, we can ask what its canonical spelling and phonetics are. We can't, however, be assured that this can be read off the token itself.

It is plausible to think that such factors are relevant to word identity. Roughly, two simultaneously produced tokens are tokens of the same name only if their canonical morphophonetics are identical. (This, by the way, justifies what I glibly assumed in discussing Pierre, that 'London' and 'Londres' are different words.)

When we think about nonsimultaneously produced tokens, we can see that matters are a bit more complicated than this suggests. Note that the canonical form for a ritual can evolve over time. What counts as a mass today (probably) wouldn't have counted as such in 325; arguably, token masses of 325 and token masses of today are nonetheless tokens of the same ritual in some fairly important sense. The mass, that is, the type of ritual that Catholics perform on Sundays, has evolved without turning into a new ritual.

The same is true for words. Their pronunciations or spellings may evolve without a destruction of word identity. For example, it is apparent, from looking at the poetry of the time, that in the 1600s 'love' and 'move' had canonical pronunciations that made them rhyme; not today, however.

I am trying here only to give the reader some idea of what I have in mind for the outside conditions on sameness of representation; I am not trying to spell out a theory of word identity. So I won't try to spell out the conditions under which nonsimultaneously produced tokens are tokens of the same word. I do, however, want to mention one further complication: Just as practices can evolve,

25 This is oversimplified: Many words have a number of acceptable spellings or pronunciations.

so one practice can split into two, as the mass fragmented, with schism and Reformation, into a variety of Sunday practices. Something analogous can happen in the case of names.

Suppose that someone receives tokens of 'Donnellan' at different times and doesn't recognize them as being the same, even though they are parts of the same tree of transmission. This might easily happen if, for example, the tokens are transmitted orally and are pronounced differently: DON-al-n and don-NELL-n. That the recipient of the two tokens of 'Donnellan' doesn't recognize the same word twice over is not, in itself, distressing. But suppose that our friend is not the only person who receives the two phonetically distinct tokens. Suppose that everyone who has any name of Donnellan is familiar with the alternative pronunciations. Many realize that these give two ways of referring to the same person, but a fair number do not. After a time, perhaps half of the community treats the phonetic difference as marking a difference in person named.

Once this happens, we in the know will find ourselves pointing out to people that DON-al-n is don-NELL-n, reporting that poor Smith doesn't realize that DON-al-n is don-NELL-n, and so forth. Intuition strongly suggests that we now have two different words.[26]

---

26 One might suppose that, in order to honor certain intuitions, we *have* to say that at the end of the story the public language DON-ell-n and Don-NELL-an are distinct words. (Let's abbreviate the phoneticisms with D and D'.) After all, it seems quite obvious that one might say that poor Smith does not know that D is D', although of course he knows that D is D. So, it seems, it should be possible to make both ascriptions true using a single correlation. But if D and D' determine the same word in our spoken language, then a correlation has to treat them in the same way.

Suppose we *did* say this for the case in question. It is clear that we can and often do introduce new words into our idiolect when the situation calls for it. For example, we temporarily or permanently christen an individual previously unknown when we need a way to refer to him. We can do this even if the individual already has a name.

If we can do this in ignorance, we ought to be able to do it even when we know what the individual is called. For the purposes of explaining what someone thinks, we can temporarily resolve to use the two different phoneticisms as different names. We seem to do this sort of thing in the Paderewski case. If pressed to explain exactly what Peter does and does not believe, we employ the neologisms 'Paderewski the musician' and 'Paderewski the politician' to ascribe beliefs to Peter: Peter, we say, believes that Paderewski the musician was talented musically; he does not believe that Paderewski the politician was. If we suppose that these are introduced as new, albeit temporary, vocabulary items, then we can take such ascriptions as literally correct characterizations of what Peter does and does not think, assuming that the obvious restrictions are being employed by the speaker. Surely we can say the same sort of thing about the ascriptions

If we think of words in the way I have been suggesting – as being analogous to rituals like the mass – this intuition isn't all that puzzling. Certain changes in the mass, if they are set in the right sort of social situation (e.g., schism), can make a change in the ritual performed. In the case of certain sorts of schisms – those in which the split revolves around how one is to perform a certain part of a ritual, say – it seems quite natural to say one ritual may split into two.

This is the case with certain changes in orthography or phonetics. If an allowable variation in pronunciation or vocabulary becomes rigidified into two different practices, that may mark the transformation of one word into two. Or if a word is taken over from one language to another, it may come to count as another word, either because it has acquired a new canonical orthography and pronunciation, or because of other differences between its use in the parent language and its use in the other language.

At the beginning of the Donnellan case, 'Donnellan' is a word that may be pronounced indifferently in two different ways. It is like the plural of 'matrix', which may be spelled 'matrices' or 'matrixes'. Over time, a number of users have acquired the belief, and passed it on, that there are two words here with different canonical pronunciations. The bare fact that enough speakers come to think that the differences in pronunciation mark a difference in what the word picks out seems sufficient to make for different words, just as the beliefs of the schismatics, the accompanying differences in their Sunday practices, and the ensuing split in the society seem to make one ritual into two. Since my topic is attitude ascription and not word identity, perhaps I have said enough on the latter subject.

I close the chapter with a discussion of the context-hopping argument – CHA, for short – of Section 1. The setup for the argument has A watching B and speaking to her on the phone, innocent of

to Smith. (Graeme Forbes, in defending a Fregean account, has made observations along these lines.)

Thus, I don't think that we are *forced* in the D/D' case to say that, after a time, we have two different names of Donnellan in order to explain how we can say that Smith believes that D is D, but not that D is D'. Nonetheless, I find myself somewhat sympathetic to the claim that we have two different names of Donnellan in the case in question. (Some people think that the fact that the names would still be spelled the same means that we would not have different names. But the case can be altered so that this would not be so: Imagine the story told of a preliterate society.)

the fact that the woman spoken to is the woman being watched. A thinks the observed to be endangered, but not the one spoken to. The argument revolves around the sentences

(a) I believe that she is in danger,
(b) The man watching me believes that I am in danger,
(c) The man watching you believes that you are in danger,
(d) I am the man watching you,
(e) I believe that you are in danger,

and goes as follows:

1. Suppose (a) is true in A's context [or that A could use (a) truly]. Suppose further that A alone watches B, and so (d) is true in A's context (and so a use thereof by A would be a true one).
2. Given 1, (b) is true in B's context [a use of (b) by B in her context would be true].
3. If the last is true, then (c), taken relative to A's context, is true (a use of it by him would be a true use).
4. But given the truth of (c) and (d) in A's context (that uses thereof by A would be true uses), it follows that (e) is true in A's context (its use would be a true one).

The argument was offered in support of the thesis that if

x believes that ... t' ... ,
$t' = t''$

are true relative to a context (would be true if a speaker were to use them), then so is (so would be)

x believes that ... t'' ... ,

where t' and t'' are proper names, demonstratives, or indexicals. Since each step of the argument seems quite reasonable, it presents something of a puzzle: If the argument doesn't establish what it is supposed to, what is wrong with it?

Let's begin by distinguishing between two versions of the argument. Think of contexts as representatives of facts, about (potential) speakers and their environments, which are relevant to the interpretation of context-sensitive items. So contexts are something like tuples consisting of an agent (for 'I', 'me', etc.), a time (for 'now'), a world (for 'actually'), something that establishes interpretations for pure demonstratives, standards of precision ('France is square'), a set of restrictions, and so on. Let us also assume that, if we stick to one world, there corresponds to each person p and time t at most one context. Then we can let '$C(x, y)$' name the partial function that assigns to a person x and time y the context, if any, he then determines.

Given this, we can talk naturally enough about the truth of a sentence that contains context-sensitive elements, even relative to a context in which the sentence is not used. 'I am happy' is, for example, true relative to C(me, yesterday at two o'clock), provided I was happy yesterday at two. Whether I said 'I was happy' yesterday at two o'clock is irrelevant to the truth of the sentence in the context.

One way to understand the argument from 1 to 4 is this: Let t be some time after A has noticed B to be in danger. We assume that (a) and (d) are true in $C(A, t)$; we make no assumption that A uses them in the context. Then we reason simply that if (a) is true in $C(A, t)$ [abbreviate: $C(A, t) \vdash$ (a)], then $C(B, t) \vdash$ (b); if $C(B, t) \vdash$ (b), then $C(A, t) \vdash$ (c); and if $C(A, t) \vdash$ (c), (d), then $C(A, t) \vdash$ (e). In all of this, we ignore what A and B might or might not actually be saying. Perhaps, to simplify matters, we assume that, at t, each of them is thinking and talking about some wholly irrelevant matter.

One might also take the argument dynamically. Suppose we think of A and B as using (a), (b), (c), and (e) sequentially in a conversation that begins at t. Then the argument would be something like this: Given that $C(A, t)$, $C(B, t + 1)$, $C(A, t + 2)$, and $C(A, t + 3)$ are the contexts of use of (a), (b), (c), and (e), we have

$C(A, t) \vdash$ (a)   (by assumption),
If $C(A, t) \vdash$ (a), then $C(B, t + 1) \vdash$ (b),
If $C(B, t + 1) \vdash$ (b), then $C(A, t + 2) \vdash$ (c),
So, since $C(A, t + 3) \vdash$ (d), $C(A, t + 3) \vdash$ (e).

If you don't think that 'believes' is context sensitive, the two ways of thinking of the argument come to much the same thing: In particular, embedding (a) through (e) in a conversation doesn't have any relevant effect on their interpretation. But once we take 'believes' to be context sensitive, it is clear that the two ways of understanding the argument might well make a difference to what we say about it.

What other conversants say and do is often relevant to the interpretation of certain expressions. As Lewis (1979a) observes, one can change the standards of precision, and thus the interpretation of 'is square', simply by saying 'France is square'. Under the old standards, the sentence might not have counted as true; Lewis claims that since we generally try to adjust such standards to make conversational contributions true, simply saying that France is square may, for the purposes of the conversation, make it so.

Likewise, when a conversant ascribes an attitude to someone, we may try to accommodate her by adopting whatever restrictions we take her to be using. So embedding a use of, say, (c) in a conversation may make it subject to restrictions that it wouldn't otherwise have been subject to.

Let's evaluate each version of CHA.[27] As I have sketched the first version, we ignore whatever A and B might actually say, pretending they are talking of matters irrelevant to the argument. In this version of the argument, whether (b) is true or false in B's context is really completely irrelevant. What is relevant is what restrictions are operative in A's context, $C(A, t)$. In particular, we need to know whether

(R1) A: 'you' $\rightarrow$ 'you'

or some other restriction on 'you' is operative.

As I have said, I think of what restrictions are operative as being in large part a function of the communicative intentions of a speaker. Given that A and his conversant aren't thinking about what A believes, I am inclined to say that $C(A, t)$ contains no restrictions that concern A. (Of course, if A *were* to turn his attention to what he believes, restrictions would arise.) So on this version of the argument, we may agree, both (c) and (e) are true in A's context. This version of the argument is perfectly sound.

But it certainly does *not* follow that, if A were to use (e), his use would be true. More generally, the argument lends no support to the idea that, for *any* context c, if $c \vdash x$ believes that $\dots t \dots$, and $c \vdash t = t'$, then $c \vdash x$ believes that $\dots t' \dots$. That is, the argument, as presently construed, does not show that we may freely substitute one name of something for another in a belief ascription. As remarked, if A *were* to turn his attention to what he believed, this would tend to bring new restrictions into play, and this would affect the truth of (c) or (e) or both. For example, if at t, A were, out of the blue, to utter (e), this would tend to bring (R1) into

27 In what follows, I ignore complications that arise when we allow that truth conditions should be assigned in the first instance to whole conversations or discourses.

play: It seems correct to say that, in a first-person ascription, expressions are generally governed by "homophonic restrictions." Thus, (e) would be false. More generally, the above argument notwithstanding, there are contexts in which coreferential names have differing restrictions attached to them and thus are not freely intersubstitutable after 'believes'.

Someone might object that, however we think of contexts, a context that represents my situation at a time t should assign to a sentence S whatever truth value it would have had if I had used S at t. Thus, since (e) would have been false, if A had used it at t, it should come out false relative to $C(A, t)$.

But counterexamples to the principle on which this objection is based abound. Kaplan (1977), for example, observes that we would assign truth to 'I am not talking', taken relative to a context with me as silent agent. But if I had uttered it, it wouldn't have been true. Or suppose I do say, 'France is square', and thereby speak truly. It still might be true that, *had* I instead said 'France is not square; it's hexagonal', I *would* have spoken truly, since my counterfactual utterance and its accompanying counterfactual intentions would have fixed the standards of precision so that it was true.

The first version of CHA does nothing to establish the validity of a general principle of substitutivity. When interpreted so that (a), (b), (c), and (d) are taken as part of an ongoing conversation, CHA is somewhat more interesting. Let's pick up the argument at the point at which B utters

(b) The man watching me believes that I am in danger

in $C(B, t + 1)$. Suppose we flesh things out so that B is inspired to do this by seeing A frantically waving at her. We may suppose that the operative restriction in $C(B, t + 1)$ is

(R2) A: 'I' → terms that A associates with his current visual experience of B.

Now A uses

(c) The man watching you believes that you are in danger

in $C(A, t + 2)$. What restrictions does this context contain? As observed earlier, in normal conversation, we will try to accommodate our partners, adopting whatever restrictions they adopt. Of course, when a restriction involves a context-sensitive expression in the way (R2) does, we don't adopt the very restriction our partner uses, but a corresponding one. In the case of A and B, we may expect A to adopt

(R3) The man watching you [that is unbeknownst to A, A himself]: 'you' → terms that the watcher associates with his current visual experience of B.

I don't say that A consciously resolves to adopt (R3), or even that he could articulate a version of (R3). Rather, I say that we generally intend that we should not speak at cross-purposes with others. This intention makes it generally appropriate to say that, when one speaker is using a restriction, other speakers in the same conversation should be said, given that they don't disagree with the first speaker, to have that restriction, or a corresponding one [in the way that (R3) corresponds to (R2)], operative in their context. This idea is just an extension of the idea that the most natural way to interpret a number of ascriptions of attitude to a single individual is via a single correlation function.

Thus, since $C(A, t + 2)$ is a context following B's use of (b), and since B's utterance involved (R2), $C(A, t + 2)$ involves (R3). It seems fair enough to suppose that $C(A, t + 2)$ won't contain other restrictions having to do with A, save those that might be present as a result of A's earlier use of 'I believe that she is in danger':

A: 'she' → 'she'
A: 'is in danger' → 'is in danger'.

So (c) is true in $C(A, t + 2)$, since its RAM represents one of A's RAMs under the context's restrictions.

A now utters (e). As I have suggested, first-person ascriptions of belief are generally accompanied by homophonic restrictions, ones that require an expression to represent itself. One reason for thinking that there are such restrictions is that they are needed to ensure that, by and large, when we say, 'I *don't* believe that S' what we say is correct. It would seem that the restriction

(R1) A: 'you' → 'you'

is thus operative in $C(A, t + 3)$. But there is no reason to think that (R3) has ceased to be operative. The context thus contains restrictions that, as a matter of fact, can't be satisfied. A does not associate 'you' with his current perceptual experience of B. So (R3) rules out correlations that map 'you' to 'you'; but (R1) requires such.

In this case, A's use of (e) is "twice over false." Since the context contains restrictions that can't be jointly satisfied, it turns out to be false. But even if some of these were removed – if we removed (R3) from the context – it would still be false, for the RAM determined by A's use of 'You are in danger' doesn't represent one of A's RAMs under a correlation obeying (R1).

The most likely objection to this account of the argument is that it threatens the validity of the inference pattern

(S) *a* believes that *S*,
    a = *b*,
    Thus, *b* believes that *S*.

After all, pretending that A utters (d) at *t* + 3, we have

C(A, t + 2): The man watching you believes that you are in danger [true],
C(A, t + 3): I am the man watching you [true],
C(A, t + 3): I believe that you are in danger [false].

Note that in making this objection we are forced to skip from one context to another in evaluating premises and conclusion. If we restrict attention to a *single* context in evaluating premises and conclusion, the objection doesn't go through. In fact, (S) is perfectly valid, provided that validity is a matter of the truth of the premises, taken in a context, guaranteeing the truth of the conclusion *taken in the very same context.*

And surely we should want to define validity in this way anyway. The argument

It is now 3:00,
3:00 is the time when Harold stands on his head,
Thus, it is now the time when Harold stands on his head

is surely valid. But if we evaluate the first premise at 3:00 and evaluate the second premise and conclusion at 4:00, the premises of the argument come out true, and the conclusion false.

4

Some issues in logic and semantics

> I... beg the reader not to make up his mind against the view –
> as he might be tempted to do, on account of its apparently
> excessive complication – until he has attempted to construct a
> theory of his own on the subject.... This attempt, I believe,
> will convince him that, whatever the true theory may be, it
> cannot have such a simplicity as one might have expected be-
> forehand.
>
> Bertrand Russell, "On Denoting"

Chapter 3 set out the rudiments of a view of the semantics of attitude
ascriptions. It suppressed discussion of complications and subsidiary
issues. In this chapter, I address a few of the issues ignored in
Chapter 3.

I begin by discussing quantification. The account of quantification into attitude ascriptions I have given violates Leibniz's law,
the principle that universal closures of

If $x = y$, then if $\ldots x \ldots$, then $\ldots y \ldots$

are invariably true. This principle has been said to be fundamental
to objectual quantification; thus, the fact that my account violates
it might be thought to be a defect. I argue that violating the principle
is no defect, since Leibniz's law is no law of quantification theory:
A language's quantifiers may one and all be objectual without the
law being true of it. In fact, I will argue, there is good reason to
think that English is such a language.

In Section 2, I make good on the promise of the last section of
Chapter 3 to provide an account of demonstratives and representations. Section 3 takes up some issues having to do with tense and
the retention of belief. I offer an account of what it is to retain a

belief, as well as an account of the semantics of ascriptions that imply that belief has been retained, ascriptions such as

Throughout the game, she believed that Jabbar was on the court at the game's beginning.

This section also addresses the assignment of truth conditions to dialogues containing multiple ascriptions of attitude and to truth functionally complex sentences involving attitude ascriptions, such as

If Mary doesn't believe that Dan is tired, she wishes that he come.

I have observed that the truth conditions of a consecutive use of

(1) Peter believes that S

and then

(2) Peter believes that T

or of a use of their conjunction need not be the intersection of the truth conditions of individual uses of (1) and (2). The conjunction of (1) and (2) has, on my view, two readings; likewise for the dialogue of (1) and (2), and for various other ways of compounding the sentences. This means we need a general account of how many readings a sentence or dialogue has. In Section 3, I try to provide the beginnings of such an account.

Section 4 says a little about RAMs as truth bearers. Finally, Section 5 discusses something thus far assumed without comment: If an attitude ascription

(3) Rex believes that S

is true, then there is agreement in reference, between constituents of the sentence S and the constituents of some state of Rex's. Many find this implausible. They point to ascriptions of attitude to animals, children, and aborigines. They claim that such ascriptions are by and large true – many dogs do believe, for example, that their masters feed them. But, they say, it is implausible that such creatures share our concepts, and so it is implausible that the sort of referential agreement I say is necessary for the truth of (1) exists in these cases. I take up a version of this objection involving higher nonhuman animals like dogs and defend the requirement of referential agreement against it.

198

1. QUANTIFICATION AND LEIBNIZ'S LAW

Leibniz's law is first and foremost a principle about first-order languages with identity. Taken as such, it can be formulated as follows:

(L) Any universal closure of a sentence of the form of

$$x = y \rightarrow (S \rightarrow S')$$

[where S' differs from S at most in having some free occurrences of x (or y), where S has free occurrences of y (or x)] is true.

Examples of sentences that (L) tells us are true are

$(x)(y)(x = y \rightarrow (Fx \rightarrow Fy))$,
$(x)(y)(x = y \rightarrow (Rxa \rightarrow Rya))$,
$(x)(y)(x = y \rightarrow (Lxyx \rightarrow Lyxy))$.

Since we aren't free to stipulate the syntax of natural languages as we stipulate those of formal languages, formulating versions of (L) for English and such will be a bit tricky. For example, we will have to explain what we might mean by saying that a sentence of English is a universal closure of a sentence of the form of *if $x = y$, then, if S, then S'*. And we might have to replace or supplement talk of variables with talk about pronominal reference. But there seems to be no reason that we couldn't formulate a version of (L) for English, or French, or German.

Many, probably most, logicians and philosophers have held that (L) is central to objectual, Tarski-style quantification: If the quantifiers of a language are objectual, these philosophers say, then (L) *must* be true of the language. For example, Richard Cartwright writes that the truth of instances of (L) is "a fundamental constraint, consequent upon the intended interpretation of '=' and of devices of quantification." Quine and Kaplan have made similar claims.[1] Given the widely held belief that 'all', 'every', and other English devices of quantification are objectual, it would follow that a version of (L) is true of English.[2]

---

1 Cartwright (1979, p. 304); Quine (1960b, pp. 167–8); Kaplan (1986, p. 235).
2 (L) is to be distinguished from the principle of substitutivity as well as the indiscernibility of identicals. The former is the principle

(S) If a and b are any terms, then if $a = b$ is true (possibly relative to an assignment), then, if $S(a)$ is true, so is $S(b)$.

The latter is the principle

(I) For any x and y, if x is y, then any property of x is a property of y.

(S) is much broader than (L) and is apparently falsified by the truth of sentences

I believe that the idea that (L) is fundamental to objectual quantification is a mistake: All of a language's quantifiers may be objectual, and yet sentences of the language that are instances of (L) may be false. I think I can prove that this is so, and presently I will give the proof.

I also doubt that (L) is true of English. Before getting immersed in the details of quantification theory, let's look at a case that suggests that (L) fails for English. Suppose that John says to you,

Last night, I observed the planet Hesperus and then the planet Phosphorus. I was disappointed; I wanted to observe Phosphorus and then Hesperus.

The next day, you want to tell me what John told you about his astronomical exploits and desires, but you have forgotten the names of the two planets. Certainly, you would speak truly if you reported,

(1) There are planets x and y: John said that he observed x and then y, and he wanted to observe y and then x.

But it seems that you would not speak truly, if you were to say,

(2) There are planets x and y: John said that he observed x and then y, and he wanted to observe x and then y.

Suppose that John has never spoken about planets save during your conversation. Given that the quantifier 'There are planets' is objectual, it seems to follow, since (1) is true, that the assignment of Hesperus to 'x' and to 'y' makes the sentence

John said that he observed x and then y, and he wanted to observe y and then x

true. Given the objectuality of the quantifer and the falsity of (2), it seems that no assignment to the variables of

John said that he observed x and then y, and he wanted to observe x and then y

makes it true. But this means that

(3) If $x = y$, then: if (John said that he observed x and then y, and he wanted to observe y and then x), then (John said that he observed x and then y and he wanted to observe x and then y)

like 'Twain is Clemens, and Odile thinks that Twain is dead, and Odile doesn't believe that Clemens is dead'. Principle (I) is, of course, true. In arguing against (L), I am not arguing against the trivial truth that things that are one share their properties.

200

is false, if we assign Hesperus to 'x' and Phosphorus to 'y'. So the universal closure of (3) is false. This certainly seems to be a counterexample to (L).

The account of attitude ascriptions that I gave in Chapter 3 does not make (1) and (2) agree in truth value. It does not make universal closures of (3) logical truths. Consider, for example, the way it treats (1) and (2). It will simplify exposition here if we treat the content sentences in (1) and (2) as if they were atomic sentences. So let's assimilate them to '$Oxyyx$' and '$Oxyxy$', respectively. We may then think of the 'that'-clauses (t-clauses) of (1) and (2) as naming, relative to an assignment of some object V to the variables 'x' and 'y', the RAMs

(4) $\langle\langle\text{'}O\text{'}, O\rangle, \langle\langle\text{'}x\text{'}, V\rangle,\langle\text{'}y\text{'}, V\rangle, \langle\text{'}y\text{'}, V\rangle,\langle\text{'}x\text{'}, V\rangle\rangle\rangle$
(5) $\langle\langle\text{'}O\text{'}, O\rangle, \langle\langle\text{'}x\text{'}, V\rangle,\langle\text{'}y\text{'}, V\rangle, \langle\text{'}x\text{'}, V\rangle,\langle\text{'}y\text{'} V\rangle\rangle\rangle$

respectively, where O is the interpretation of 'O'. The inference from (1) to (2) fails because the fact that (4) represents one of John's RAMs doesn't guarantee that (5) does.

Suppose, for example, that the only RAM in the "assertion section" of John's RS is that determined by '$Ohpph$', where 'h' and 'p' name V. This RAM – call it R – is just like (4), except it contains 'h' and 'p', respectively, where (4) contains 'x' and 'y'. Suppose there are no restrictions operative. Clearly, (4) represents R, since R comes from (4) under the correlation

'O' → 'O'; 'x' → 'h'; 'y' → 'p'.

Speaking intuitively, (4) represents R because of this correlation, which translates the sentence from which (4) is made, '$Oxyyx$', into the sentence from which R is made, '$Ohpph$'.

For (5) to represent R, we must be able to translate '$Oxyxy$' as '$Ohpph$' using some correlation. But this can't be done. For example, the correlation

'O' → 'O'; 'x' → 'p'; 'y' → 'h'

translates '$Oxyxy$' as '$Ophph$'. The correlation

'O' → 'O'; 'x' → 'h'; 'y' → 'p'

gets us '$Ohphp$', which isn't what we want either. Mapping both 'x' and 'y' to 'h' yields '$Ohhhh$'.

Intuitively, what is happening is this: Note that there is a sort of *structural* difference between the sentence John used in his assertion and the content sentence of the intuitively false (2). The sentence John used is of the form *Aabba*. The content sentence of (2) is of the form *Aabab*. It is just this sort of difference in structure that is responsible for the fact that (5) can't represent *R*. Likewise, I would say, it is the difference in structure between the content sentences of (2) and what John said that makes (2) false. And it is the difference in structure between (1)'s and (2)'s content sentences that explains the difference in their truth values in John's case and the consequent failure of (L).

I motivated the account of Chapter 3 by suggesting that an attitude ascription conveys information about the "how" of belief, as well as information about the Russellian what. Although I didn't point it out at the time, it should now be clear that some of the information thus conveyed is a sort of structural information. Cases like the above, I think, give support to the claim that attitude ascriptions convey this sort of information and, consequently, that (L) fails for English.

People find the claim that (L) fails in English distressing because they think (a) that English quantifiers are objectual, Tarski-style quantifers, but (b) that (L), as Cartwright suggests, is a consequence of the quantifier's objectuality. As I intimated, I think that (b) is mistaken. Let me see if I can convince you of this.

What determines whether a quantifer is objectual? The obvious answer is this: An objectual quantifier is one whose semantics is properly given in terms of a Tarski-style definition of satisfaction. For example, what makes Q an objectual universal quantifier is that an analogue of the following principle gives satisfaction conditions for sentences of which Q is the main operator:

(S) A sequence s satisfies QvS iff every sequence s' that differs from s at most in what it assigns to v satisfies S.

Here is another way of expressing this criterion of objectuality: Associated with each open sentence of a(n interpreted) language is what we may call a *condition*. The notion of a condition can be cashed out in a number of ways. Often, conditions are identified with extensions, or with constructions from extensions and entities such as times and/or possible worlds. Sometimes they are taken to be creatures of darkness such as properties. No matter how we understand the notion, a condition will be something that determines, or is even identical with, an extension (which we may take, for present purposes, to be a set of sequences). To say that a sequence s satisfies a sentence is to say that it is in the extension of the condition determined by the sentence.

Our first criterion of objectuality may thus be rephrased in terms of the contribution that the quantifier makes to determining a condition. We could, for example, say that for Q to be an existential objectual quantifier is for it to determine a condition in accord with this rule: The condition determined by QvS has a sequence s in its extension just in case some sequence like s (except perhaps in what it does to the variable v) is in the extension of the condition determined by S.

This way of characterizing objectuality is in keeping with the intuitive underpinning of the notion. For Q to be objectual is for it to be the case that the only thing relevant to whether s satisfies QvS (or to whether QvS is true) is what sequences satisfy S. Each of our characterizations of objectuality makes it a necessary and sufficient condition for the objectuality of Q that the satisfaction conditions of QvS depend only on the satisfaction conditions of S itself.[3]

Let us turn to variables. What is the role of the variables in languages with objectual quantifiers? Clearly, one is to supply an object, relative to an assignment. It is in terms of the objects assigned to the variables by a sequence that we characterize the notion of the extension of the condition determined by a sentence. For example, in a standard Tarskian account of satisfaction conditions for a language with an atomic predicate 'is prime', we begin with a clause to the effect that, for any variable v and sequence s, s satisfies (and thus is in the extension of) v *is prime* just in case what s assigns

---

3 Some languages whose quantifiers are substitutional will accommodate a sort of Tarskian definition of satisfaction. Take, for example, a language whose syntax is that of first-order logic, with constants and identity. Suppose that we defined an interpretation I for the language as something that assigns truth values to atomic sentences, subject to the restriction that, if $I(t = t')$ is true, and $B = A(t/t')$, then I treats A and B in the same way. Go on to define truth for the language in a standard substitutional way.

If we suppose that all of the constants of the language name things, then we may say that, relative to the domain of things named by the language's constants, the quantifiers of the language can be treated as Tarskian. I will ignore this fact in the text. The counterexamples to (L) that I discuss, both that involving 'Fx_1' and 'Fx_2' and that involving attitude ascriptions, involve languages for which truth is definable in a natural, Tarskian way by direct assignment of satisfaction conditions to sentences, and not in the accidental manner of the above example.

to v is prime. That this is a task of the variables is, I take it, familiar enough.

It is not always noticed that the variables have another task, at least in familiar first-order languages. One who has noticed this is Quine (1966), who writes:

> Basically, the variable is best seen as an abstractive pronoun: a device for marking positions in a sentence, with a view to abstracting the rest of the sentence as predicate. Thus consider... 'Some number x is such that $x^3 = 3x$'. ... The variable can be eliminated ... : we could say 'Some number gives the same result when cubed as when trebled', thus torturing the desired complex predicate out of '$x^3 = 3x$' with a modicum of verbal ingenuity. In more complex examples ... use of 'x' is the only easy way of abstracting the jagged sort of predicate which we are [interested in]. Where the variable pays off is as a device for segregating or abstracting a desired predicate by exhibiting the predicate sentencewise with the variable for blanks. (p. 228)

According to Quine, one syntactic role for variables (along with connectives and quantifiers, and even closed terms) is to expand the stock of predicates of a language, beyond the primitive or 'simple' predicates. Put another way, variables encode operations that map predicates to predicates. Semantically speaking, a role of the variables (along with the quantifiers and connectives) is to encode a set of operations on the conditions that are associated with primitive predicates or sentences of the language in which they occur.

This idea shouldn't be terribly foreign. What, after all, makes 'x loves y' and 'x loves x' different semantically? Put somewhat simply, Quine's answer is that the sentences determine different conditions (roughly, those of loving and self-loving, respectively); it is one of the roles of the variables to get us from simple predicates, such as 'loves' and 'kisses', and the conditions they determine to complex predicates and the conditions that they determine.

It is not implausible to think that a complete explanation of the role of the variables, in familiar first-order languages anyway, is given thus: Variables are used both to help determine what condition is associated with a sentence and to supply individuals relative to an assignment. On this view of the variables, a sentence of ordinary first-order logic such as

(6) $Ayxy$

might be more explicitly written as

(7) $\text{Ident}(A)[x, y]$.

Here, Ident is an operation that maps a three-place condition (viz., a condition whose extension can be represented as a set of triples) to a two-place condition. In (7) we have one syntactic device, the operator 'Ident', playing the role of predicate abstractor; other syntactic devices, the variables and brackets, supply objects. In (6), economy triumphs, with one device, the variables, doing both jobs.

We have an account of what makes the quantifiers and variables of a language objectual. As we will now see, it does not follow from the fact that a language's quantifiers and variables behave as just characterized that (L) is true of the language. This, I think, makes it dubious that (L) is fundamental to objectual quantification. In fact, not only does consideration of our description of the role of the variables make it obvious that (L) is not a tenet of objectual quantification theory; it suggests a number of ways in which a language with objectual quantifiers and variables might come to violate (L).

Whether (L) is true of a language depends upon how conditions are associated with the sentences of the language. For example, (L) strongly suggests, although it doesn't require, that open sentences that are alphabetic variants determine the same condition; (L) requires that sentences that are alphabetic variants apply to all the same things. Of course, we are used to thinking of open sentences and conditions in this way: How, it might be asked, could '$A(x)$' be true of things of which '$A(y)$' wasn't true? Mere relettering of an open sentence couldn't change what it is true of!

I disagree. Why is it a fact about objectual quantification, as opposed to a fact about the first-order languages with which we are familiar, that 'Fx_1' and 'Fx_2' determine the same condition? One can give a Tarski-style definition of truth for a language in which '$(\exists x_1)(Fx_1)$' and '$(\exists x_2)(Fx_2)$' may differ in truth value, but the quantifiers and the connectives receive their usual Tarskian treatment.

To give such a definition, one first needs to explain, for each simple predicate, the conditions under which a sequence satisfies atomic sentences in which the predicate occurs. Suppose we think of 'F' as, by itself, having the same meaning as the English predicate 'prime'. Then the *usual* way to begin a definition of truth for a language with the predicate 'F' will be to suppose some enumeration of the variables and to lay down a clause to the effect that

A sequence s satisfies 'F' followed by the ith variable iff what s assigns to the ith variable is prime.

The truth definition goes on to treat truth-functional and quantified sentences in the familiar Tarskian way.

But there are *many* other ways to assign conditions to the atomic sentences of a language that allow a Tarskian treatment of connectives and quantifiers. Here's one: Let G be a set of some (not all) of the integers; suppose in particular that it contains one but not two. Then, instead of the above clause, use

A sequence s satisfies 'F' followed by the ith variable iff [what s assigns to the ith variable is prime and i is in G].

This assigns a determinate condition (taken as a set of sequences) to each atomic sentence involving 'F'. One can now go on, without incoherence, paradox, or any particular problem, to define truth for the language as a whole *exactly* as one would in the usual case. In particular, the quantifiers may be treated in the Tarskian way described above. Of course, many of the usual quantificational metatheorems cannot be proven for such a language. But this, it can be said, shows that these metatheorems are not true of every language containing objectual quantifiers.

Many will claim to find the closed sentences of the resulting language incomprehensible. It is clear why, in such a language, '$(\exists x_1)(Fx_1)$' and '$(\exists x_2)(Fx_2)$' can diverge in truth value: The formulas cash out, respectively, to something like '$(\exists x_1)([C(`Fx_1\text{'}](x_1))$' and '$(\exists x_2)([C(`Fx_2\text{'})](x_2))$', where the bracketed predicates are stipulated to express the conditions determined by the object language sentences. This, some might argue, militates against understanding the object language '$\exists$' as an existential quantifier: '$(\exists x_1)(Fx_1)$' doesn't seem to say something is an F.

But this is because '$(\exists x_1)(Fx_1)$' *doesn't* say something is an F in this language; rather, it says something more complex, depending on the nature of G, the set involved in the clause assigning conditions to sentences in which 'F' occurs. In the language under consideration, the 'x_1' in 'Fx_1' helps to determine what condition is determined by the open sentence in a way that differs from the way it does in first-order logic. It does not follow that the quantifiers (or the variables) are nonobjectual. In a sense, the variables here behave just as they do in familiar first-order languages: They provide objects, relative to an assignment, and they help to determine conditions. It is just that their contribution to determining a condition is somewhat different from the contribution they make in the familiar first-order case.

This, it seems to me, settles the matter of whether (L) is fundamental to objectual quantification. Admittedly, languages that violate (L) in *this* way are of little, if any, interest as vehicles for representing natural language, since it seems obvious that natural languages do not violate (L) in just this way. Nonetheless, the example serves to make the theoretical point.

Let us return to the subject of attitude ascriptions. In a language that realizes the proposal of Chapter 3, a perfectly determinate condition is associated with open sentences like

John said that he observed x and then y, and he wanted to observe y and then x

and

John said that he observed x and then y, and he wanted to observe x and then y.

If we think of conditions as sets of sequences, we may say that the condition associated with the first sentence is the set of sequences s such that, where $s('x')$ is X and $s('y')$ is Y, the RAM

$$\langle\langle 'O', O\rangle, \langle\langle 'x', X\rangle, \langle 'y', Y\rangle \langle 'y', Y\rangle, \langle 'x', X\rangle\rangle\rangle$$

represents one of John's "assertion RAMs." (Remember that we are assimilating the content sentences here to atomic sentences.) To the second sentence is assigned the condition that is the set of those sequences such that, where X and Y are as above, the RAM

$$\langle\langle 'O', O\rangle, \langle\langle 'x', X\rangle, \langle 'y', Y\rangle, \langle 'x', X\rangle, \langle 'y', Y\rangle\rangle\rangle$$

represents one of John's assertion RAMs. Given this, an existential closure of one of the sentences is true just in case some sequence is in the condition determined by the sentence stripped of its quantifiers. This is a perfectly objectual treatment of the quantifier. I conclude that Leibniz's law is not essential to an objectual treatment of the quantifiers. So to adopt the proposal of Chapter 3 does not require us to abandon the idea that quantification in English is objectual. It seems to me quite certain that English quantification is usually objectual. (*Maybe* it is not in some locutions such as 'There are numbers . . . '.) And it is very plausible to think that the inference from (1) to (2) discussed at the beginning of this section is not truth preserving. And so I also conclude that English, and presumably other natural languages, are languages whose quantifiers are objectual, but for which (L) fails.

2. DEMONSTRATIVES AND REFLEXIVITY

There is a sense of 'beliefs' in which a person's beliefs can be identified with the RAMs in (the belief sector of) his RS. Some of these beliefs contain more than one occurrence of an annotation $\langle r, u \rangle$, where r is one or another representation. I will call such beliefs reflexive. For example, the belief that I express with 'If I shake hands with Dukakis, then Dukakis's wife will smile' is thus reflexive: It contains two occurrences of the annotation $\langle r, \text{Dukakis} \rangle$, r being the representation determined by occurrences of 'Dukakis' in my thought.

We often ascribe reflexive beliefs to one another. If you try to explain why I thrust out my hand by saying, 'He thought that if he shook hands with Dukakis, Dukakis's wife would smile; he wanted her to smile', then you would ascribe a reflexive belief to me. The belief ascription's 'that'-clause names a RAM containing two occurrences of $\langle$'Dukakis', Dukakis$\rangle$, and thus will be true only if I have a reflexive belief, since the RAM the t-clause names can represent only a reflexive RAM.

The example is one of a belief expressed and ascribed with sentences involving proper names. But the same sort of thing can occur with beliefs expressed and ascribed by sentences involving demonstratives. I may think, 'If I shake his hand, then his wife will smile'; you may say, 'He thinks that if he shakes his hand, then his wife will smile'. Often, though not invariably, the belief I have and the belief you ascribe will be reflexive. We need some account of when beliefs realized by sentences containing demonstratives are reflexive and when ascriptions involving demonstratives ascribe reflexive beliefs. In Chapter 3 I ignored issues having to do with demonstratives and indexicals. It is time to fill in some of the gaps.

The first question to address is, How do demonstratives in the sentences we accept determine representations? I will concentrate here on uses of "true demonstratives," that is, deictic uses of expressions like 'this,' 'that', 'he', 'she', and 'it'.[4] If we extend the account

4 What we say about the explicit use of demonstratives in thought should carry

of Chapter 3 to the case of demonstratives, we will say that two term tokens, be they proper names or demonstratives, determine the same representation just in case they are tokens of the same representational type for the tokener. What shall we say about the representational types of demonstratives?

In Chapter 3 I suggested we think of proper name types of public languages as something along the lines of practices or rituals of referring to individuals. Token uses of a particular name are then token performances of a particular ritual. Now, paradigm deictic uses of 'this', 'that', 'him', and so on are, in important ways, unlike such uses of proper names. When I use 'him' on an occasion to refer to Miles Davis, I am not participating in a conventional practice of using 'him' to refer to Miles Davis. In a sense, 'him' is here being used as a temporary, "one-time name" of the trumpeter. This suggests that we might treat each thought token of a demonstrative as determining its own representation: Each such use is the exercise of a "one-time ritual" of referring to an individual. In the terminology of Chapter 3, we award each use of a demonstrative token its own representational type.[5]

This strategy perhaps sounds as if it couldn't possibly succeed. At least sometimes when I think, 'He's tall, but the man to whom he's talking is taller', I have a reflexive belief in virtue of so thinking. But here we have a sentence with different tokens of demonstratives in it. Since the above proposal would make each token determine a different representation, the RAM the sentence determines won't

over to beliefs that are acquired in the course of everyday perceptual experience, e.g., the belief you had (even before reading this sentence) that you are holding this book. It is plausible to say that this belief involves a constituent that represents the book, one connected with your current perceptual experience of it. Stretching the term 'term', we can call such constituents terms. They are like natural language expressions, insofar as they represent individuals. Perhaps they can even be assimilated to some demonstratives, on some of their uses, insofar as sentences containing deictically used demonstratives are often ones expressing such beliefs.

As will become apparent, I try to treat demonstratives in thought in a way that more or less ignores the fact that they are terms of a public language to begin with. If we can thus deal with them satisfactorily, we can reasonably hope that what we say will carry over in a relatively straightforward fashion to perceptually acquired beliefs.

5 I don't think that this is true of every demonstrative and indexical. In particular, it's not true of typical uses of first-person pronouns such as 'I': I do have a ritual, in the appropriate sense of 'ritual', of referring to myself in the first person. In this book I do not address the issue of belief *de se*. I have discussed the semantics of *de se* ascriptions of attitude elsewhere (Richard 1983, Sec. 2); what I have said there, I think, can be adapted to the current treatment of attitude ascription.

be reflexive. So much for the above proposal. Call this, for future reference, the reflexivity objection.

Actually, I don't think that this is a particularly damaging objection. But before we discuss it, let's look at alternative proposals. So far as I can see, there are two sorts of alternatives. One characterizes a nontrivial relation of being of the same word type for demonstratives and identifies sameness of representational type with something along the lines of being of the same word type (for some suitable notion of word), having the same referent, and being grouped together. The other alternative makes sameness of representational type for demonstratives a matter of sameness of referent and being grouped together.

Here is what is wrong with the second alternative. Suppose I am looking at a ship. I think (correctly), 'This [bow] is this [stern]', and 'This [bow] is a ship and this [stern] is about to leave the harbor'. (An analogous example appears in Perry 1977.) I group the four demonstrative tokens together. That is, the four tokens satisfy the interior condition on sameness of representation from Chapter 3. Because of this, I should have a reflexive belief about the ship – that it is a ship and it is about to leave the harbor. So it would seem that a RAM of the form

(r) $\langle \ldots \langle R, \text{the ship}\rangle \ldots \langle R, \text{the ship}\rangle \ldots \rangle$

ought to go into my RS, in virtue of my tokening the sentence 'This is a ship and this is about to leave the harbor'. And on the present proposal, one does, since all four tokens determine the same representation.

But now suppose you are standing next to me and think, 'This [the bow] is this [the bow], but this [the bow] is not this [the stern]'. I then think to myself, 'He thinks that this [bow] is not this [stern], but of course he thinks this [bow] is this [bow]'. All else being equal, my thought is true. However, although you don't group all of your demonstrative tokens together, I group all of mine together. If the latter fact implies that all the demonstrative tokens in my thought determine the same representation, then my thought about your thought won't, on the present proposal, be true; for then I would be thinking that a certain RAM does and does not represent one of your RAMs.

This sort of objection seems to apply to many versions of the first alternative mentioned earlier, on which demonstrative tokens

d and d' determine the same representation if they are coreferential, grouped together, and are of the same (relevant) word type. Obviously this happens if we group all tokens or all coreferential tokens of 'this' together as tokens of the same word. One might appeal to (some of) the perceptual experiences that accompany a thinker's use of demonstratives in order to forge an appropriate notion of word type. For example, one might say that some aspect of the thinker's experience in using a demonstrative serves to fix its referent and then say that sameness of type is a matter of sameness or similarity of relevant accompanying experiences.

If identity is required, versions of the reflexivity objection will reappear. If I think,

This is that, but he doesn't think this is that,

with all four demonstratives accompanied by somewhat different experiences (and coreferring), I may nonetheless have a reflexive belief in virtue of my thought. If it is only similarity that is required, we will almost certainly still be saddled with versions of the ship objection: Suppose I think the above-displayed sentence with the same demonstration accompanying the this's and another demonstration accompanying the that's, but ones similar enough to make all the demonstratives determine the same representation.

I think we should return to the original proposal and say that different tokens of demonstratives in thought always determine different representations. Thus, when I think to myself, 'This [bow] is a ship and this [stern] is about to leave the harbor', the two occurrences of demonstratives, given that they are occurrences of different tokens, determine different representations. The RAM in my RS that corresponds to this sentence, then, will be one of the form

$$\langle \ldots \langle\{d\}, \text{ the ship}\rangle \ldots \langle\{d'\}, \text{ the ship}\rangle \ldots \rangle.$$

(Remember that we identify representations with sets of tokens.) Even in thinking 'This [bow] is a ship and this [bow] is grey', the two occurrences of 'this', if occurrences of different tokens, determine different representations.

Why isn't the reflexivity objection fatal to this proposal? Basically because a person may accept sentences without explicitly tokening them. Distinguishing between tokening a sentence and accepting it, as we did in Chapter 1, we may say that, in general, when someone accepts a sentence token $S(t_1)$, accepts a token $S'(t_2)$, and groups the tokens t_1 and t_2 together, she also accepts the sentence tokens $S(t_2)$ and $S'((t_1)$. For example, if I accept a sentence of the form 'This is a ship and that is about to leave', where the two occurrences of demonstratives are occurrences of distinct tokens, and I group the tokens together, I also accept a sentence of the form 'This is a ship and this is about to leave the harbor', where the two occurrences of demonstratives are occurrences of the very same token. It is in virtue of accepting such a sentence that I have a reflexive RAM, one of the form of (r), in my RS.

This is a rough rule of thumb, not an inviolable truth. It is probably possible that someone believe that A and believe that B without believing that A and B. So it is probably also possible that someone believe that this is that and this is a ship without believing that that is a ship. There are, after all, some pretty dim bulbs out there. So it seems possible that someone group two demonstrative tokens t and t' together – which is tantamount to accepting $t = t'$ – and accept t *is* F, but still not accept t' *is* F.

This account requires us to say that a single term *token* can make a number of appearances in a sentence and can appear in a number of sentences. I don't see why this shouldn't be so. After all, one term token can appear in a number of 'places' in one set. Consider, for example, the set consisting of {the first token of 'a' in this book} and {the first token of 'a' in this book, the first token of 'b' in this book}. And it is easy enough to imagine (nonlinear) inscriptions of sentences in which one word token makes a number of appearances. Consider the following:

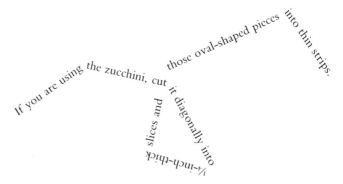

Somewhat more to point is the discussion of Chapter 1, Section 5, which gave examples of cases in which a number of sentences were accepted as a result of the tokening of one sentence or the "storage" of a "table of relations" among concepts. Given that these are examples of accepting sentence tokens, they are plausibly cases in which one token simultaneously appears in a number of sentences.

As I said earlier, it is not *invariably* the case that, when I group together tokens t and t' and accept $A(t)$, I also accept $A(t')$. Sometimes this is a matter of my failing to see the consequences of what I think; sometimes not. When I group together t and t', I may accept *John believes that t is F* but not accept *John believes that t' is F*. But this is not because I have failed to draw a consequence of my beliefs.

On this account there is a difference between the way demonstratives function inside and outside of attitude verbs: there is a loose closure of the set of sentences one accepts under "demonstrative identity elimination," but only for occurrences of demonstratives outside the scope of attitude verbs. I think this is acceptable. After all, the inference from $t = t'$ and *John believes that t is F* to *John believes that t' is F* isn't valid to begin with.[6]

Let us now consider the use of demonstratives in public language ascriptions of attitude. Suppose that someone says, 'He believes that this is a ship and this is about to leave the harbor', with both demonstratives naming the same thing. Such ascriptions sometimes are, and sometimes are not, ascriptions of a reflexive belief. If the sentence is spoken by someone who unwaiveringly points at one ship, it is probably intended as, and probably is, the ascription of a reflexive belief. If it is spoken by someone who points at different parts of a ship, ignorant of the fact that he is pointing to the same thing both times, it is probably intended as, and is, an ascription of a nonreflexive belief.

This means that it is not a perfectly mechanical matter to go from

---

6 There are probably alternative ways of characterizing the relations between the sentences one accepts and the contents of the RS. For example, one might say that, typically, if I accept tokens $S(t_1)$ and $S'(t_2)$ and group the tokens t_1 and t_2 together, then, provided the tokens are coreferential, two RAMs appear in my RS in virtue of my accepting $S(t_1)$, one with the representation determined by t_1 and one with that determined by t_2; and the analogous thing is true about my acceptance of the other sentence. As observed in the text, there will be certain exceptions to this rule.

We could say this, denying that I accepted the corresponding sentences. My preference is for the treatment in the text, since it keeps the relations between accepted sentences and RAMs in the RS somewhat tidier. But I would not argue with someone who insisted on proceeding in this way.

the surface form of an ascription in which demonstratives occur to its logical form. A t-clause whose surface form is suggested by

(s) that A(this, this)

will sometimes name a RAM of the form suggested by

(a) $\langle \ldots \langle \text{'this}_1\text{'}, u \rangle \ldots \langle \text{'this}_1\text{'}, u \rangle \ldots \rangle$,

sometimes one of the form

(b) $\langle \ldots \langle \text{'this}_1\text{'}, u \rangle \ldots \langle \text{'this}_2\text{'}, u \rangle \ldots \rangle$,

and sometimes one of the form

(c) $\langle \ldots \langle \text{'this}_1\text{'}, u \rangle \ldots \langle \text{'this}_2\text{'}, v \rangle \ldots \rangle$,

where u is not v.

Which of (a) through (c) will a particular use of (s) determine? Well, we often enough have the intention to ascribe a reflexive belief. If, when we say, 'He thinks that A(this, this)', we would say yes in response to a question like 'Did you mean that he thinks that A(this, the very same thing)?', there is reason to think that such an intention was present. If such an intention was present and the two demonstratives in the t-clause of 'He believes that A(this, this)' refer to the same thing, then the t-clause names a RAM of the form of (a). If this is not the case, then the t-clause names a RAM of the form of (b) or (c), depending on whether or not the demonstratives name the same thing.[7]

Multiple occurrences of demonstratives and other terms in public language sentences raise some other issues about the relation between public language sentences and the RAMs they determine. Consider anaphoric reference within a t-clause. Suppose that someone says, 'He believes that this is a ship and it is about to leave the harbor'. Intuitively, we have the ascription of a reflexive belief. It may not be clear how I can say that this is so. After all, won't the RAM named by the t-clause look like this:

(d) $\langle \ldots \langle \text{'this'}, \text{the ship} \rangle \ldots \langle \text{'it'}, \text{the ship} \rangle \ldots \rangle$

---

7 I assume that we have an infinite series of distinct demonstratives, 'that$_1$' 'that$_2$', etc., for constructing RAMs for English sentences. We can make the rough rule more mechanical by giving a recipe for picking which of these demonstratives to use in constructing a RAM for a given sentence.

The rule in the text is only a rough one because it doesn't tell us what to do for cases such as that of a t-clause 'that A(this, this, this, this)', where some terms name one thing, some another.

instead of like this:

(e) ⟨ . . . ⟨'this', the ship⟩ . . . ⟨'this', the ship⟩ . . . ⟩?

This depends on how we treat anaphoric pronouns within t-clauses. We don't have to transcribe mechanically an anaphoric 'it' in a t-clause as 'it' in passing from the anaphor to the annotation it determines. We should transcribe anaphoric 'it' as the expression on which it depends for its reference in passing from anaphor to annotation. This would give us a reflexive RAM as nominata of the t-clause in the above case.[8]

Consider ascriptions of the form *a believes that A(d, d')*, where *d* and *d'* are distinct demonstratives that are intuitively reflexive ascriptions. Suppose, for example, that Phil Donahue is talking to me. He says, 'Mary says that you wrote a book in philosophy, and [at this point Phil turns to address the audience] he is proud of it'. The use of 'he' is accompanied by a demonstration of me, and everything after 'say' is supposed to be within the verb's scope. (To flesh out the case, imagine the audience applauding madly.) Phil uses 'he is proud of it' to capture part of Mary's assertion (and not as an editorial comment). It is plausible to say that Phil's statement is the ascription of a "reflexive assertion," in a sense like that in which other sentences are ascriptions of reflexive beliefs. Again, it may be difficult to see how I can say this, since the RAM the t-clause determines is apparently one that looks thus:

⟨ . . . ⟨'you', me⟩ . . . ⟨'he', me⟩ . . . ⟩

instead of one that looks thus:

⟨ . . . ⟨e, me⟩ . . . ⟨e, me⟩ . . . ⟩.

Suppose we agree that what Donahue said was true only if someone made a reflexive assertion about me. It is not altogether clear that this requires that Donahue's t-clause name a reflexive RAM. Suppose that we allow that a context may supply restrictions that simply say that certain expressions must be mapped to the same thing, for example:

8 Again, this is too simple-minded a rule to work for all cases. For one thing, we may have an anaphoric chain of the form

Chastin . . . he . . . he . . .

or even, perhaps,

Chastin . . . the philosopher . . . he . . . .

Mary: Map 'you' and 'he' to the same thing.

If there can be such restrictions (and why shouldn't there be?), then Donahue's utterance may have the required truth conditions even if the RAM he uses is not reflexive.[9]

There are other ways of dealing with this sort of case, of course. Donahue intends to say that Mary has said something reflexive about me. Surely his intentions can, to a certain extent, affect what RAM his t-clause names. Suppose that someone shifts terms in ascribing attitude, for rhetorical effect or because of a shift in his perspective on the object under discussion, but still means to be ascribing a reflexive attitude. In such a case, the uttered sentence will be of the surface form

a V's that $A(d, d')$,

where d is the first demonstrative occurring after the attitude verb. Given the intention of the speaker, we may take his t-clause to name a RAM of the form

$\langle \ldots \langle d, d$'s referent$\rangle \ldots \langle d, d$'s referent$\rangle \ldots \rangle.$

This case raises the following issue. Suppose that Phil says, 'So you wrote a book in philosophy, and – ladies and gentlemen, can you believe it – he [I am demonstrated] is proud of it'. A third party can presumably say with truth,

(1) Phil says that Richard wrote a book in philosophy, and he [or Richard] is proud of it.

I think it is a fact about the way we talk that, when someone assertively utters a sentence of the form $A(d, d')$, where d and d' are (possibly distinct) demonstratives, neither of which occurs within the scope of an attitude verb and which are such that the speaker correctly takes the two tokens to refer to the same thing, we are willing to report him as having made a reflexive assertion. That is, such a use of a sentence suffices for the addition of a reflexive RAM to the assertion sector of the RS.

To accommodate this, I suggest that we allow a one–many cor-

9 Even given only the sort of restrictions discussed in Chapter 3, one can make Donahue's utterance reflexive simply by picking one representation for both demonstratives to be mapped to. But this will not handle the most interesting version of the case, in which Donahue has no current opinion on how these people said what they did.

respondence between assertively uttered sentences and RAMs in the assertion sector of the RS. The relevant rule is suggested as follows: For an utterance of $A(d, d')$ satisfying the above conditions, we add to the assertion sector of the RS RAMs of the following forms:

$\langle \ldots \langle\{d\}, \text{ the referent of } d\rangle \ldots \langle\{d'\}, \text{ the referent of } d\rangle \ldots \rangle$,
$\langle \ldots \langle\{d'\}, \text{ the referent of } d\rangle \ldots \langle\{d'\}, \text{ the referent of } d\rangle \ldots \rangle$,
$\langle \ldots \langle\{d\}, \text{ the referent of } d\rangle \ldots \langle\{d\}, \text{ the referent of } d\rangle \ldots \rangle$.

We saw in Chapter 1 that something like this was going to be true of assertion anyway. Someone who assertively utters, 'Phil is a man and Oprah is a woman', has certainly said that Oprah is a woman and Phil is a man. So if propositions are as structured as the sentences that express them, we will have to put two propositions into the set of propositions asserted for each assertively uttered conjunction. This is so not just on the account of attitude ascriptions I am giving, but on any account that takes propositions to be sententially structured. For example, it is true on Russellian accounts.

Suppose that someone utters a sentence of the form $A(d, d')$, where d and d' are ordinary proper names of the same object, and the speaker groups them together. Should we add multiple RAMs to the RS according to the above recipe? I am inclined to think not. It seems to me that Merv's saying, 'If Twain wrote *Huck Finn*, then Clemens wrote *Tom Sawyer*', and knowing that Twain is Clemens does not make it the case that Merv said that, if Clemens wrote *Huck Finn*, then he (or Twain) wrote *Tom Sawyer*.

Scott Soames would disagree. In fact, Soames (1987b) suggests that the following is true: If someone assertively utters a sentence of the form $A(d, d')$, where d and d' are demonstratives or proper names naming a thing u, then we can truly say *He said that $A(t, t)$*, where t is any proper name or demonstrative naming u. Likewise, whoever has a belief expressible by such a sentence $A(d, d')$ has an attitude ascribable with $A(t, t)$. Here is a case he thinks helps make his point:

Professor McX, looking through the open back door of the faculty lounge, sees Y walking down the hall. . . . A few seconds later Y passes by the front door. . . . [McX remarks during this]

(2) Who is in the department? Let me see. He (pointing to Y as he passes the back door) is a professor in the department and (turning) he (point-

ing to *Y* as he passes the front door) is a graduate student in the department.

On the basis of this, the following . . . seem[s] clearly true. . . .

(3) McX says that I am a professor in the department and I am a graduate student in the department. (Spoken by *Y*.) (Soames 1987b, 116–17; numbering altered)

It seems to me not at all clear that (3) is true. Consider first a slightly simpler example: As McX makes his two demonstrations, he says, 'He [back door] is chasing him [front door]'. It is perfectly natural in such a case for us to say to *Y*, 'McX said that you are chasing yourself', or for *Y* to say, when he hears the details of the story, 'Ha! McX said that I was chasing myself'.

It seems clearly true that ascriptions involving explicit reflexives are ascriptions of reflexive attitudes.[10] But such an attitude is not present in this modification of Soames's case. McX, after all, did not say and did not think that anyone was chasing himself. So it is clear that in this case what we are naturally inclined to say is something that we know, with a little reflection, to be false.

The simplified case seems pretty much parallel with the original one. If *Y* is going to attempt to say what McX said without circumlocution or adopting a rather odd way of expressing himself, he has no choice but to use a sentence like (3). This is because it is very odd, and potentially confusing, to refer knowingly to oneself in normal conversation with something other than a first-person pronominal construction. So it would be very odd, and potentially confusing, for *Y* – given that he is going to make any attempt at all to report McX's confused dictum – to use a sentence interestingly different from (3). Something analogous would be true of a second-person version of (3) spoken to *Y*. So we have the basis for an explanation of why it seems so natural for *Y* to utter (3).

In the simplified case, though a sentence ascribing a reflexive attitude was a natural one to use, such a sentence was false. I would say that much the same thing was true of Soames's original case. Observe that the intuition that *Y* can truly utter (3) seems as strong as the intuition that, if *Y* can truly say (3), then *Y* can also truly say,

10 Soames (1987b, Sec. 8) appears to agree that this sort of account of reflexives in attitude ascriptions is correct.

(4) McX says that I am a graduate student in the department who is a professor.

Or, to make a related point, the intuition that (3) is true seems about as strong as the intuition that, if (3) is true [i.e., if McX said (and thought) that Y was a graduate student in the department and Y was a professor therein] and McX is a fellow with normal logical prowess, then McX, if he reflects on what he thinks, will come to believe that there is a graduate student in the department who is a professor.

Now it is clear that (4) is not true in this sort of case, and it is clear that McX, no matter how great his logical prowess, will not have the belief in question. So we have *at best* two intuitions here, one that pulls one way, another that pulls in another. In fact, given the parallel between the simplified Soames case and the original, it seems that our considered intuitions pull only one way, against Soames's conclusion.

Soames's example doesn't really make the point he wants it to make. In any case, there is a good reason for thinking that an ascription of the form *He thinks that A(t, t)*, for any name or demonstrative *t*, is an ascription of a reflexive belief. We would like the truth of the premises of a belief/desire explanation of action to make it reasonable to think that its conclusion is true as well. This will generally be so, however, only if *He thinks that A(t, t)* ascribes a reflexive belief. That is, the reflexivity of *He believes that A(t, t)* is a prerequisite for its being generally reasonable to think that folk-psychological explanations are explanations. This should be obvious. Consider

Randi kissed Ann and Marsha because Randi thought that, if he kissed Ann and Marsha, then Ann, but not Marsha, would stay, and Randi wanted Ann, but not Marsha, to stay.

Only if the multiple occurrences of 'Ann' and 'Marsha' induce the sort of reflexivity we have been discussing would the truth of the belief and desire ascriptions give one a reason to think that Randi might have tried to kiss the two. Otherwise, the above explanation is no better than one like

Randi kissed Ann and Marsha because Randi thought that, if he kissed Ann and Marsha, then Ann, but not Marsha, would stay, and Randi wanted Ann, but not Marsha, to stay.

where, it so happens, Ann is Peggy and Natasha is Marsha.

3. BELIEF RETENTION

This section is about retaining beliefs and other attitudes through time. Its focus is on the truth conditions of ascriptions such as

(1) Throughout the game, John believed that Jabbar was on the court at the game's beginning

and

(2) Throughout the game, John thought that Jabbar was guarding Byrd,

which say that an individual has held an attitude throughout a period.[11]

Up to now I have ignored the fact that the objects of the attitudes contain times and expressions that determine them. For example, the proposition that Nixon is now (viz., 12:22 PM, Eastern standard daylight savings time, June 14, 1988 A.D.) rich contains the time 12:22 and so on as a constituent:

$$\langle\langle\text{'now'}, 12{:}22\rangle, \langle\langle\text{'is rich'}, \text{being rich}\rangle, \langle\text{'Nixon'}, \text{Nixon}\rangle\rangle\rangle.$$

Such a proposition is "eternally" true or false. That is, given a world w, the proposition is either true at w *simpliciter* – true at every time in w – or false *simpliciter* at w, depending on Nixon's financial status at 12:22. I take such eternalism to be a feature of all propositions expressed by natural language sentences, even those like 'Nixon is rich' in the simple present. I have argued for this elsewhere (Richard 1981, 1982; see also Salmon 1986) and won't repeat the details here.

One might say that a sentence like 'Nixon is rich' contains a "tacit occurrence" of 'now', and explain the eternalism of the propositions it expresses in that way. I prefer to say that it contains a tacit occurrence of a present-tense operator – call it "pres' – that when unembedded behaves semantically like 'now'. Thus, at 12:22, 'Nixon is rich' determines the proposition

$$\langle\langle\text{'pres'}, 12{:}22\rangle, \langle\langle\text{'is rich'}, \text{being rich}\rangle, \langle\text{'Nixon'}, \text{Nixon}\rangle\rangle\rangle.$$

The difference between 'now' and 'pres' comes out in certain embeddings, such as

(3) Mary believed that Nixon was rich,
(4) Mary believed that Nixon would be rich now.

11 I tend to focus on belief retention, to the exclusion of the other attitudes.

We might regiment these respectively as

(3') P(Believes(Mary, that pres (Nixon is rich))),
(4') P(Believes(Mary, that now (Nixon is rich))),

where 'P' is the past-tense operator. When embedded as in (4'), 'pres' behaves somewhat like a bound variable whose possible values are determined by the embedding tense operator. 'Now', however, takes the time of the context of use as semantic value no matter how it is embedded. Thus, (3') is true in a context c iff at some time t earlier than the time of c, Mary believed something represented by

$\langle\langle$'pres', $t\rangle$, $\langle\langle$'is rich', being rich$\rangle$, $\langle$'Nixon', Nixon$\rangle\rangle\rangle$.

Sentence (4') is true, taken in c, iff Mary believed at some such t something represented by

$\langle\langle$'now', the time of $c\rangle$, $\langle\langle$'is rich', being rich$\rangle$, $\langle$'Nixon', Nixon$\rangle\rangle\rangle$.[12]

Let us turn to belief retention. There are two phenomena that might be labeled persistence or retention of belief. First of all, there is the sort of persistence typified by someone like myself, who believed in 1972 that Nixon was president and has continued to believe that: in 1972 I had a belief I would have expressed with 'Nixon is now president', and now I have a belief I would express with 'Nixon was president in 1972'. In this case, there is no change through time in the truth conditions of what I believe: I preserve a certain (Russellian) content through time. I will call this A-type persistence.

Contrast this with the sort of persistence involved when someone thinks something to be true of every time in an interval. For example, since 1972, I have thought that Nixon is a crook: At each time t since 1972 I have had a belief I could express at t with 'Nixon is now a crook'. Here the truth-conditional content of my beliefs changes with time. Nixon could have reformed in the 1980s; if he had, what I used to believe would have been and would still be true – he *was* a crook – but my current belief would be false. Call this B-type persistence.

---

12 The structure of the RAM is supposed to reflect the view that 'now' is a sentence operator. Some details of an analogous treatment of tense are given in Richard (1982). Salmon (1986) contains an interesting discussion of the semantics of tense and attitude ascription.

It is natural to identify A-type persistence with a continued relation to a single object of belief. The persistence of my belief that Nixon was president in 1972 is naturally thought to consist in my continued relation to the proposition that Nixon is president in 1972. Analogously, B-type persistence is naturally identified with continued relation to a part of a proposition, a proposition minus a time.[13] Can the account I have been developing concur with these identifications?

There are two senses in which a proposition, that is, a RAM, can be an object of someone's belief. First of all, it can be a member of his RS. Let's say that in this case the RAM is a direct object of belief. A RAM p might also be said to be an object of u's belief because the sentence

u believes that S

is true, and *that* S names p. Let's say in this case that p is an indirect object of u's belief. u's indirect objects of belief are those RAMs that represent his direct objects of belief.[14]

It's plausible to think that A-type persistence requires that a RAM continue to be an indirect object of belief during the period in which belief is retained. In fact, we might as well take this to be definitive of A-type persistence: To say of x and p that x's belief p persisted throughout a period I is to say that, for each t in I, at t, x believed p. In this sense, belief retention clearly involves a continued relation to a single proposition.

Does A-type persistence require that some RAM continue to be a direct object of belief? Do sentences such as

(5) Since yesterday, John thought that yesterday was hot,
(6) All during the game, John thought that Mariam was married in 1972

imply that there is RAM p that is a direct object of John's belief throughout the relevant interval? It certainly seems wrong to say that the truth of (5) or (6) requires that the sort of RAM characterized in Chapter 3 and the preceding section continue to be in

---

13 If I were wrong about all of the objects of the attitudes being eternal, B-type persistence would probably reduce to A-type persistence. If, for example, 'Jabbar is guarding Byrd' were temporally neuter, in the sense of determining the same RAM at different times, then 'All during the game, John thought that Jabbar was guarding Byrd' could be seen as saying that, throughout the game, John had a belief whose truth-conditional content was that of the relevant RAM.

14 Of course, what counts as one's indirect belief objects shifts across contexts.

John's RS. As we have set things up, the contents of the RS are a function of sentences accepted: The general rule is that, if I accept S at t, and, at t, S determines the RAM p, then p goes into my RS at t. Now it is often the case that to retain a belief I accept different sentences as time goes by. To retain the belief that I had yesterday because I accepted 'Today is hot', today I accept 'Yesterday was hot'. These sentences determine different RAMs, containing as they do different demonstratives. So here is a simple case in which persistence of belief is not a matter of maintaining a relation to a single RAM.

Even when I retain belief by continuing to accept a single demonstrative-free sentence, the sentence will typically determine different RAMs at different times. In forming a RAM for the RS from an accepted sentence, we pass from the word tokens in the sentence to the representations they determine. For tokens of public language proper names, such representations were identified in Chapter 3 with certain sets of like-typed tokens. For a fixed thinker, the representation token t of public language name type T determines, at a given time, is the set of those mental tokens of type T that the thinker groups with t.

A person might group name tokens differently at different times. For example, Peter might finally learn that there is only one Paderewski. If we pretend that Peter is always related to the same total set of mental 'Paderewski' tokens, this means that his 'Paderewski' tokens determine different representations at different times. A "talented" token of the term determines one representation before his discovery (what we called P_t in Chapter 3, Section 4); it determines another, the union of P_t and P_u, after the discovery. So some of Peter's demonstrative-free sentence tokens – 'In 1887, Paderewski played the piano', for example – determine different RAMs at different times, since the term 'Paderewski' determines different representations at different times.

We wouldn't want to say that this keeps Peter from retaining the belief that in 1887 Paderewski played the piano, from the time he first hears of Paderewski the musician. Apparently, belief retention is not a matter of retaining a direct relation to the sorts of things we put in the RS in Chapter 3.

So what is it to retain a belief? Kaplan (1977) makes some useful observations about this in *Demonstratives*. Recall that Kaplan speaks there of believing a Russellian proposition under a sentence's character. The rough idea is that, when a person accepts a sentence S, he believes its Russellian content under the meaning of S. Kaplan asks:

Suppose that yesterday you said to me, and believed it, 'It is a nice day today'. What does it mean to say, today, that you have retained *that* belief? It seems unsatisfactory to just believe the same content under any old character – where is the *retention*? You *can't* believe the content under the same character. [Because today 'It is a nice day today' determines a different content.] (pp. 537–8)

Kaplan expands on this in a famous footnote:

[Suppose] I first think, 'His pants are on fire'. I later realize 'I am he' and thus come to think 'My pants are on fire'. Still later, I decide I was wrong in thinking 'I am he' and conclude 'His pants were on fire'. If, in fact, I *am* he, have I retained my belief that my pants are on fire simply because I believe the same content, though under a different character?... This does not capture my sense of *retaining a belief*. (p. 538)

I think Kaplan's idea can be vaguely glossed as follows: Belief retention requires some sort of *internal* continuity. Though he doesn't suggest what sort of continuity is needed, what naturally occurs to one is this: At a minimum, for me to retain a belief throughout a period, it has to seem to me throughout the period that I am believing the same thing. To retain a belief, not only must I believe the same Russellian content, I must (in principle) be in a position to recognize at later times that I believe the same content.

Whether Kaplan intended this, and whether he intended it as a commentary on the truth conditions of claims of the form

Since such and such a time, he has believed that S,

I think there is a use of such sentences on which their truth requires belief retention in (what I take to be) Kaplan's sense. Normal uses of such sentences, I think, say that belief retention in this sense has taken place. And this isn't true simply of beliefs held or reported with sentences involving explicit demonstratives. Suppose at game's beginning John accepts 'Jabbar is now on the court'; at game's end, he accepts 'Alcindor was at game's beginning on the court'. He accepts 'Jabbar is not Alcindor' throughout the game. I am inclined to say that it is then false that, throughout the game, John believed that Jabbar was on the court at game's beginning.

If we accept this much, we need to give a clearer account of the

224

sort of internal continuity needed for belief retention. Here is a very simple account, prompted by a simple example. Suppose I think, 'That's a planet' at t_1. Later, I am told, 'That was Venus', and I accept it. Later still, I forget having seen Venus (I remember *that* I saw it), but still I accept 'Venus is a planet'. Concentrate upon my representations of Venus. At a time t_1, I use 'that' to represent the planet. At a later time t_2, I have (a) a "trace" of the former 'that' (I remember, 'That was a planet') and (b) a name 'Venus' of the planet; I group these together. At a still later time t_3, I have only 'Venus'. There is a fairly simple sort of continuity between the names of Venus here: At sucessive times, we find either "memory traces" of earlier terms or terms grouped with such traces. A simple view would be that it is this sort of continuity that is the essence of attitude retention. For future reference, let us call this a name-perpetuation view of belief retention.

I think such a view is correct. Many people don't; presently, I discuss some of their objections. First, let's see in outline how such a view fits into the account of attitudes and their ascription given in Chapter 3.

Think of the representations and RAMs discussed up to now as momentary snapshots or temporal parts of temporally extended representations and RAMs. Given the believer's blackboard at a time t, we have thus far formed representations by selecting certain sets of tokens on the blackboard *at t* that the believer grouped together *at t*. We formed the RAMs that were to occupy the believer's RS *at t* from these representations. Such representations are synchronous; we now call them synchronous representations, or s-reps, for short. Diachronic representations, d-reps, for short, are certain temporally indexed sequences of s-reps, ones that display the sort of interior continuity present in the Venus example just given. (Equivalently, d-reps are functions from times to s-reps whose ranges are related in the appropriate way. Below, I treat d-reps as functions when convenient.)

Once we have the notion of a d-rep in hand, the modifications of the account of Chapter 3 are pretty obvious. Until now, we have said that, when *Fa* appears on the believer's blackboard, the RAM

$$\langle\langle sr(F), rr(F)\rangle, \langle sr(a), rr(a)\rangle\rangle$$

goes into the believer's RS, where *sr(e) is the s-rep e determines*, *rr(e)* its Russellian referent. Now that we are taking time and tense into account, we say this: If e is an expression on the blackboard at t and e determines the s-rep s at t, then, for any d-rep d of the believer, if $d(t)$ is s, then e determines d at t. If Fa appears on u's belief blackboard at t, F determines the d-rep d_F at t, and a determines the d-rep d_a at t, then the RAM

$$\langle\langle d_F,\ rr(F)\rangle,\ \langle d_a,\ rr(a)\rangle\rangle$$

goes into u's RS at t.

We now take the correlations involved in the truth conditions of attitude ascriptions to map annotations to d-reps instead of to s-reps. If an ascription of the form

(7) All during hour h, John believed that S

is used to claim that John has undergone Kaplan-style retention, then the ascription, taken in a context c, is true iff there is some correlation f, obeying c's restrictions, such that for every time in the hour h the RAM that S represents one of the RAMs in John's RS under f. Note that it thus turns out that Kaplan-style retention of belief is a matter of continuing to be directly related to a RAM: Since p represents q under f only if f is defined on all the annotations in p, p can represent only one RAM under a fixed correlation f.

This, in outline, is what I have to say about belief retention. (I repeat what I have just said later, a bit more slowly.) It remains to go back and fill in the details. Here is the order in which I will do so: In Section A, I will consider some objections to the name perpetuation (NP) account of belief retention. In Section B, I will say how I mean to construct d-reps from s-reps. In Section C, I will discuss some subtleties that arise as a result of the way I have just proposed to assign truth conditions to sentences of the form of (7).

A. Name perpetuation

In the Venus example above, there is a sort of transtemporal overlap of terms. At t_1, I use 'that' to represent Venus; at t_2, a "trace" of an earlier token of 'that' exists on my blackboard, one grouped with 'Venus'. At t_3, there remains on the blackboard a trace of 'Venus'. The example thus involves a temporal chain of terms, with each link in the chain either a trace of an earlier link or grouped with such a trace. The NP account takes the existence of such a chain as a necessary condition of belief retention.

Some will say that this sort of overlap is not essential to belief retention. Consider a case in which I retain a belief by switching from accepting 'Today is hot' to 'Yesterday was hot'. Surely there is no time at which I think of the day in question as both 'today' and 'yesterday'. Here there need be no overlap at all.

I am not sure that it wouldn't be correct to insist that there is always some overlap of terms, at least if we take belief retention to be Kaplan-style retention. Let me first observe that, if there weren't *some* sort of "interior connection" between the uses of 'today' to hold a belief and the later uses of 'yesterday', there wouldn't be interior continuity. This is easier to see in the case of perceptually acquired beliefs. Accepting throughout an interval 'That is a pencil', never moving the eyes from a certain object, is not sufficient to retain a belief: I might think (falsely) that different pencils keep materializing in the place at which I am looking.

Someone might well observe that this doesn't show that we need to have the sort of overlap just mentioned. John Perry has claimed this is not so. Indeed, he claims that retaining a belief about an object doesn't require retaining *any* name of the object(s) the belief is about. Perry (1980) writes:

I think it is perfectly possible that I continue to believe [x is a dean, Halsey] . . . even though I have no way of referring to [Halsey, who Perry has seen and has had described to him as *a* dean, but for whom he has no name. Suppose that Halsey] is "indexically inaccessible" – 'you' and 'he' and 'that man' will not reach him. I know nothing about him that does not apply equally well to many others. I might, of course, remember enough about the circumstances [in which he was seen] to think of him with a description like 'the man who was near the bar while I was talking to Julius', but I need not remember this, so far as I can see.

Perry observes that he might nonetheless later see Halsey on the quad, recognize him, and say, 'You are a dean'. He continues:

The information about Halsey [that he is a dean and looks as he does] seems to have been retained in my mind without the benefit of singular terms. . . . It seems, instead, to be . . . [a] cluster of predicates, that provides [for belief retention].

Predicates do not need a singluar term to be knitted together. A quantifier phrase serves this purpose: 'Some man wears bolo ties, rumpled suits, . . . and is a dean'. Such a sentence among [those which I accept] we would naturally think of as that in virtue of which a general belief would be held, rather than a belief about a particular person. Yet this seems a mistake (*or perhaps better the phrase I use next can be considered a singular term*). Consider 'a certain man'.... If I say 'A certain man wears a bolo tie and rumpled suits,' I would ordinarily be thought to have someone in mind.... 'A certain man' functions here... as an ersatz name. (pp. 327–8; my emphasis)

Perry goes on to suggest that causal relations between ersatz names and earlier events (in this case, his earlier observation of Halsey in bolo tie and rumpled suits) make it the case that the belief that 'a certain man wears a bolo tie and rumpled suits' establishes is a belief about a particular individual.

Perry clearly says that he opposes the sort of view I endorse, which sees retention of a belief about an object as requiring retaining a name of the object or having a "chain" of such names. But he seems to accede to the view he opposes. The ersatz name 'a certain man' that Perry invokes in accounting for his retention of his belief that Halsey is a dean is, of course, not a singular term of English. But as Perry himself suggests, it is *functioning* like such a term. Its use in thought is prompted by being in a situation in which he does have a term to refer to an object (Perry's tale begins with his seeing Halsey and accepting '*He* is a dean') and a need to "store" information about that object in such a way that the information can be reliably carried from context to context. So far as I can see, there is no real difference between Perry's proposal and one on which we suppose that Perry in effect has introduced a name ('a-certain-man$_i$') to go proxy for 'he', once Perry leaves Halsey's vicinity. But if this was what Perry did, then the case he presents is exactly parallel to the 'that'/'Venus' case above.

If this is an acceptable view of the matter, then we can say something parallel about the 'today'/'yesterday' case. If I accept 'Today is hot' and intend to hold onto this information, then it is perfectly apt to see me as also introducing a nonindexical device – 'a-certain-day$_i$' – to help me refer to and think about this day when it becomes "indexically inaccessible." I thus accept 'A-certain-day$_i$ is today' and 'a-certain-day$_i$ is hot'. Although the day remains "indexically accessible," I have several ways of referring to it. Today, I can refer to it as 'today' and 'a-certain-day$_i$'; tomorrow, I can use either 'yesterday' or 'a-certain-day$_i$'.

But then the sort of overlap of names that was present in the 'that'/'Venus' case is present here, too.

Here is another worry one might have about the account of belief retention I suggested. Let's return to the example of John, who at first accepts 'Jabbar is now on the court' and later changes his mind, accepting 'Alcindor was then on the court'. All the while John rejects 'Alcindor is Jabbar'. On the above account, John does not retain throughout the game the belief that Jabbar was on the court at game's beginning. There isn't a chain of representations of Jabbar throughout the interval that constitutes a d-rep of Jabbar and that is involved in the right way in John's beliefs about who is on the court when. One might observe, however, that it seems correct to say at the end of the game, 'Throughout the game John believed that he [we point at Alcindor] was on the court at the beginning of the game'.

I agree that we might say this. It is a somewhat odd claim, since it seems to imply that John didn't undergo a change of mind about whether he (point at Jabbar again) was on the court at game's beginning. Clearly John did have a change of mind about this. Nonetheless, I think we should probably allow that it can be truly said that throughout the game John believed that he (point at Jabbar) was on the court. This is why I hedged in the outline above by saying that I was giving the truth conditions for 'Throughout hour h, John believed that S' when used to make a claim about Kaplan-style retention. At the end of this section, I will show how we may assign a reading to the claim about John and Jabbar on which it turns out true in the envisioned case.

B. From s-reps to d-reps

Assume that the above gives a basically correct account of belief retention. We need now to give a somewhat more precise account of the notion of a d-rep. Note first that there may be a number of d-reps, d_1, d_2, ..., d_n, such that for some t, $d_1(t) = d_2(t) = \cdots = d_n(t)$. Equivalently, at a single time t, one expression token may determine a number of distinct d-reps. Cases like Peter's require something along these lines. Before Peter learns that there is only one Paderewski, he has two representations, or ways of thinking, of the pianist, $w1$ and $w2$ call them. One corresponds to the set P_t of Peter's talented tokens, the other to P_u, the set of untalented tokens. It's tempting to say that, after his discovery, Peter has but one way of thinking of Paderewski, call it $w3$, corresponding to the sum of P_t and P_u.

But if we say this, we won't be able to say that there is a representation of Paderewski that Peter has throughout the story. And thus we won't be able to say that throughout the story Peter retained the belief that in 1889 Paderewski played the piano, since it would be arbitrary to identify $w3$ with one of $w1$ or $w2$ as opposed to the other. But we can't identify it with both, since $w1$ and $w2$ are themselves distinct.

After he learns that there is only one Paderewski, Peter still has two ways of thinking (i.e., d-reps) of Paderewski, $w1$ and $w2$. They have been "unified" insofar as, for times t after Peter learns there is but one Paderewski, $w1(t) = w2(t) =$ the sum of P_t and P_u.[15] This means that, after his discovery, Peter's 'Paderewski' tokens determine two (diachronic) representations. So when he thinks, 'In 1889, Paderewski is talented', Peter in a sense thinks two things. His accepting a token of this sentence will require us to put two RAMs in his RS, one in which the annotation $\langle w1, \text{Pad} \rangle$ appears, the other containing $\langle w2, \text{Pad} \rangle$. One of these RAMs will have been present in his RS since the beginning of the story; the other won't.

As well as allowing that an s-rep may be a part of several d-reps, we will allow that s-reps of "different types" – for example, demonstrative s-reps and s-reps composed of proper names – may be parts of the same d-rep. Intuitively, a d-rep is a temporally extended way of thinking of a single object, one that is "unified from the inside." Over time, as an object becomes indexically inaccessible (to borrow Perry's phrase), we may go from using a demonstrative to represent an object to using a proper name. For example, I may keep track of a day as 'today', then as 'yesterday', then . . . as 'Feb. 6, 1957'. All else being equal, in doing this I may preserve a belief about the day using such a sequence of representations. So we ought to allow d-reps to correspond to such sequences. The same sort of thing can happen with

---

15 I assume for simplicity that Peter's blackboard always contains the same total set of 'Paderewski' tokens.

just proper names: I learn 'Alcindor'; later I learn 'Alcindor is Jabbar'; finally, I forget the name 'Alcindor', all of its traces having already been "overwritten" with 'Jabbar'.

I will try to give a recipe for constructing d-reps from s-reps. In giving it, I will make use of a notion of one mental name token being a *trace* of another mental name token from some earlier time t. We write: $\langle a, t' \rangle$ is a trace of $\langle b, t \rangle$; it is to be understood that, if $\langle a, t' \rangle$ is a trace of $\langle b, t \rangle$, then t' is later than t.

Intuitively, there are two ways in which token a at t' may be a trace of token b at t. First, a token may perdure from t to t', in which case it is a trace at the later time of itself from the earlier time. Second, a token, though it ceases to exist (it is "erased from the mental blackboard"), may be causally responsible for a later token's existence in certain ways, ways that make the later token a trace of the earlier one. The idea here is that a token's later traces are memory traces of the token. I won't try to define the trace relation in terms of some other notion. I suppose that it satisfies analogues of the interior and exterior conditions on sameness of representation. So if $\langle a, t' \rangle$ is a trace of $\langle b, t \rangle$, then a and b refer to the same thing. And a trace, being a memory trace of a term, will behave as if it were "diachronically grouped" with what it is a trace of.

I assume that each mental term token determines only one s-rep at a time. Where a is such a term token, write $[a]_t$ for *the s-rep that a determines at t*. Say that a term token a is new at t provided that there is no term token b and time t' such that $\langle a, t \rangle$ is a trace of $\langle b, t' \rangle$. We inductively define *sequence S is a d-rep*. First of all, if a is new at t, then $S = \langle [a]_t, t \rangle$ is a d-rep. Now suppose that the sequence $S = \langle \langle r_1, t_1 \rangle, \langle r_2, t_2 \rangle, \ldots, \langle r_n, t_n \rangle \rangle$ is a d-rep, and that S' is the result of extending S with $\langle s, t \rangle$. Then S' is a d-rep just in case

1. s is an s-rep, s represents at t what r_1 does at t_1, and t is later than t_n;
2. s contains a term a, r_n contains a term b, there is a term b' such that $\langle b', t \rangle$ is a trace of $\langle b, t_n \rangle$, and at t, a and b' are grouped together (i.e., they satisfy the interior condition on sameness of s-representation);
3. for each r_j, $1 \leq j < n$, if a member of r_j has a trace at t, then a member of s is grouped with at least one such trace.

A sequence is a d-rep iff it qualifies as such in virtue of the above definition.[16] When useful, I will identify d-reps with the partial functions from times to s-reps associated with such sequences.

16 Here are some observations on this definition. First, at any time t, a term token

This is not quite as complicated as it sounds. Condition 1 is transparent enough. What condition 2 requires for

$$\text{Time 1:} \quad \text{s-rep}_1 = \{a_1, \ldots, a_j\}$$

$\uparrow\downarrow$ are parts of the same d-rep

$$\text{Time 2:} \quad \text{s-rep}_2 = \{b_1, \ldots, b_k\}$$

is that one of the a's leave a trace at t_2 with which one of the b's is grouped:

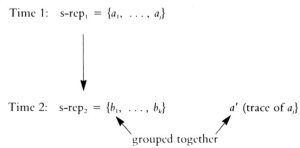

$$\text{Time 1:} \quad \text{s-rep}_1 = \{a_1, \ldots, a_j\}$$

$$\text{Time 2:} \quad \text{s-rep}_2 = \{b_1, \ldots, b_k\} \qquad a' \text{ (trace of } a_j)$$

grouped together

For example, suppose that I see you. I close my eyes and I hear you. Then I open my eyes and see you again. In a normal version of such a case (I don't think that there are two people, one heard and one seen), I am keeping track of you throughout the interval, associating my visual experience with my aural one, and then the aural one with the visual one: If I didn't do this in some way, I wouldn't take the person heard to be the person seen. So my visual and aural experiences add up to a d-rep of you. If we suppose that I retain some trace of the visual experience when I have the aural one, and a trace of the aural with the later visual, my experience can be represented as follows:

a is grouped with itself. (This is necessary for clause 2 to work properly.) Second, the definition must be understood as being implicitly relativized to an individual. Finally, the definition could be complicated a bit, in order to cut down on the number of d-reps it generates. In general, if $\langle s_1, \ldots, s_{i-1}, s_i, s_{i+1}, \ldots, s_n \rangle$ is a d-rep, then so is $\langle s_1, \ldots, s_{i-1}, s_{i+1}, \ldots, s_n \rangle$. I didn't see any point in making the text more complicated than it already is.

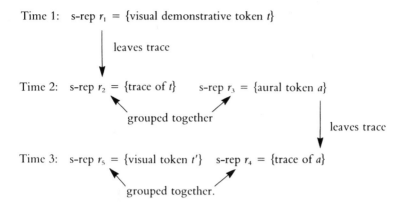

Time 1:   s-rep r_1 = {visual demonstrative token t}

leaves trace

Time 2:   s-rep r_2 = {trace of t}   s-rep r_3 = {aural token a}

grouped together

leaves trace

Time 3:   s-rep r_5 = {visual token t'}   s-rep r_4 = {trace of a}

grouped together.

So the sequence $\langle r_1, t_1 \rangle$, $\langle r_3, t_2 \rangle$, $\langle r_5, t_3 \rangle$ satisfies condition 2.

What work does condition 3 do? Roughly, it guarantees that "from the inside" d-reps seem to represent the same thing. Consider the following scenario: At t_1, I accept '$h = p$'; at t_2, I reject '$h = p$'; at t_3, I reject '$h = p$'. I don't want a sequence of s-reps corresponding to

t_1: h,
t_2: p,
t_3: p

to be a d-rep. At t_3, 'p' will not seem to me to represent what any traces of 'h' represent. So the above sequence doesn't have the sort of psychological continuity that I think is necessary for Kaplan-style belief retention and thus shouldn't qualify as a d-rep.

The last point can be brought out as follows: Suppose that I accepted 'h is bright' at t_1 and t_2, but rejected it at t_3 and that I accepted 'p is bright' at t_1 and t_3, but rejected it at t_2. It seems to me that then it would be wrong to say that I had retained throughout the interval a belief, that h is bright, or the belief that p is bright. To ensure this, we need to prevent the above sequence from determining a d-rep. Otherwise, there will be a single d-rep of the planet that I used throughout the period to fix a belief that what it represented was bright.

Assuming that $\langle$'h', $t_1\rangle$ leaves traces of itself at t_3 – which would be natural to assume if, for example, I have memories from t_1 at t_3 – condition 3 does the necessary work, for if I reject '$h = p$', then, we may assume, I do not group 'h' and 'p' tokens together at t_3, though there will be 'h' tokens about which are traces of earlier 'h' tokens. Condition 3 requires such a grouping for d-reps, and so the above sequence won't determine a d-rep.

As I said, once we move from s-reps to d-reps, we need to generalize the account of how the RS is determined by accepted sentences. In the simplest case, if I accept 'a is F now' at t, 'a', 'F', and 'now' determine the d-reps r, r', and r'', respectively, at t, then the RAM

$$\langle\langle r'', t\rangle, \langle\langle r', \text{ the Russellian referent of } 'F'\rangle, \langle r, \text{ the Russellian referent of } 'a'\rangle\rangle\rangle$$

goes into my RS. Analogous principles apply to other sentences. The only difference is that expressions now typically determine a number of representations at a time. So we will put a number of RAMs in the RS for each sentence accepted.

I think the preceding account of RAMs and the RS to be a fairly natural generalization of that offered in Chapter 3. As I remarked, old RAMs turn out to be temporal parts of the new RAMs. A new RAM – say, $\langle\langle d, x\rangle, \langle d', y\rangle\rangle$ – will find itself in my RS at t according to the generalized account only if the old-style RAM $\langle\langle d(t), x\rangle, \langle d'(t), y\rangle\rangle$ was in my RS on the old account.

C. Assigning truth conditions

Some adjustments and generalizations of the account of truth conditions provided in Chapter 3 are now needed. A relatively minor point is that the restrictions on correlations that contexts provide now apply to mappings to d-reps instead of to s-reps. This isn't much of a change from Chapter 3. Suppose, for example, we are focusing on beliefs thought to be held using sentences containing proper names. We say, for example, that Ham always believed that Hesperus rose in the evening. Then usually we mean to say that Ham always held this belief using the conventional translate of 'Hesperus'. Before, we would have roughly expressed the restriction the context imposes thus: $\langle 'H', H\rangle$ is to be mapped only to $\langle e, H\rangle$, where e is the (representation determined by the) conventional translate of 'H'. Now the restriction is expressed: $\langle 'H', H\rangle$ is to be mapped only to an annotation $\langle e, H\rangle$, where e contains only (representations determined by) natural translates of 'Hesperus'.

This is a natural generalization of the instantaneous case. In general, a restriction abbreviated before as

'Hes' → 'Hes'

is typically a restriction to those mappings that take ⟨'Hes', Hes⟩ to something whose first element d has the following property: For any t for which d is defined, $d(t)$ is composed solely of tokens of the public language type of 'Hes'.

When we are interested in the how of someone's belief at a particular moment, restrictions are keyed to that moment. Return, for example, to the case of Jeff. Jeff is asked if Odile realizes that *Twain* is dead. Jeff knows that she accepts 'Twain is dead' and says, at t, 'Odile thinks that Twain is dead'. Colloquially speaking, in saying what he said, Jeff used 'Twain' to represent a way of thinking of Twain involving Odile's current uses (namely, uses at t) of 'Twain'. So Jeff's intentions establish the following restriction: ⟨'Twain', Twain⟩ can be mapped only to annotations ⟨r, Twain⟩ such that $r(t)$ contains tokens of 'Twain'.[17]

None of this changes in any substantive way what was said in Chapter 3 about the truth conditions of sentences of the form

a believes that S.

Such sentences continue to be true, taken in a context c, provided that for some f respecting c's restrictions, the RAM that S represents one of a's RAMs under f. The account of Chapter 3 can be seen as a special case of the present account, the case in which d-reps are allowed to extend only over a single instant of time.

Earlier I said that a normal use of

(7) All during hour h, John believed that S

is true in a context c iff there is a correlation f obeying the restrictions c provides, such that, for each time t in hour h, the RAM that S represents under f a RAM in John's RS at t. Note that in stating these truth conditions, the quantifier over correlations takes wide scope over the temporal quantifier. For John to retain his belief during the period, it must be true that there are representations ... such that at each time in the period ... ; it is not enough that at

---

17 Given this, perhaps the best format for characterizing restrictions is a collection of trios ⟨x, a, S⟩, where x is an individual, a an annotation, and S a collection of conditions on annotations.

each time in the period . . . there are representations. . . . We must assign such truth conditions to (7) if we want it to have a reading on which it implies that John underwent Kaplan-style retention of a belief.

There is an analogy here to something remarked upon in Chapter 3. Consider

(8) Pierre believes that London is pretty, and he believes that London is not pretty.

This would most naturally be taken as saying that there is a correlation f such that the RAMs that London is pretty and that London is not pretty represent, under f, RAMs in Pierre's RS. It is unnatural to read (8) as claiming that there is a correlation f such that the RAM that London is pretty represents, under f, one of Pierre's RAMs and a correlation f' such that the RAM that London is not pretty represents, under f', one of Pierre's RAMs.

As with (7), in (8) we find quantification over correlations, which is associated semantically with 'believes', contributing to truth conditions before the operator that has 'believes' in its syntactic scope. In (7), 'believes' is syntactically in the scope of 'during the last hour' but behaves as if it were not completely "in its semantic scope"; in (8), the same situation arises with 'believes' and 'and'.

(8), for most conversational purposes, is but a stylistic variant of

(9) Pierre believes that London is pretty. He believes that London is not pretty.

Chapter 3 suggested that what we need for sentences like (8) and (9) is an account of the notion of *Conversation C has such and such truth conditions* that would have as a consequence that (8) and (9), when construed as brief conversations or dialogues, may be assigned the truth conditions I say they may be assigned. Given the analogy just pointed out between (8) and (7), one would hope that such an account would also make the sort of assignment of truth conditions to (7) that I have suggested is the appropriate one.

Such an account requires some departure from many semantical accounts in the Frege–Tarski tradition. Many such accounts impose a rigid correlation between an operator's syntactic position in a sentence and its contribution to the sentence's truth conditions. In such accounts, one clause characterizes the truth conditions of a sentence of the form *a believes p*, another characterizes the truth conditions of *During the last hour, A*. In assigning truth conditions to a sentence of the form *During the last hour, a believed p*, the syntactic scope of expressions determines when they contribute to overall truth conditions, the wider-scope expression contributing first. In (7) the temporal operator has wider syntactic scope than 'believes' – at least this is so on any standard account of scope and syntax. So Frege–Tarski accounts, if they read *a believes p* as we suggest, will read (7) as claiming that, for each *t* in the last hour, there are representations . . . , which is what we are trying to avoid.

That some such departure from standard accounts of truth conditions is necessary isn't in itself objectionable. What occurs to one is that, if we were to process or regiment sentences like (7) and (8) a bit before assigning truth conditions to them – say, inserting something that marked where quantifiers over correlations were to be introduced – we might be able to characterize the truth conditions of the result within the context of a traditional theory. It's common enough to think of truth conditions as being assigned to sentences, as well as to whole discourses, that have been regimented or processed in a rule-governed way. For example, in Montague's fragments of English, one component generates syntactic structures for spoken or written sentences; a second component translates these structures into sentences of a higher-order modal logic. Finally, truth (in a model) is defined directly for the structures of the second language, the syntactic structures of the original language inheriting the truth conditions of their translates. And Hans Kamp has proposed an account that maps (syntactic structures of) natural language sentences and discourses to what Kamp calls "discourse representations," syntactic objects for which truth (in a model) is defined directly (Montague 1974; Kamp 1981).

We can think of our task in the following way: What we want is a procedure that, given a sentence that might contain various operators such as 'not', 'and', 'or', or tense operators, can be applied to yield something that states or otherwise determines the sentence's truth conditions (in a given context). Given such a procedure, we could adapt it to dialogues by (roughly) treating them as conjunctions of sentences.

It might at first seem that nothing very elaborate is called for. Examples like (7) and (8) might make it seem that any sentence in which an attitude verb occurs should be assigned truth conditions so that the quantification over correlations that the verb imports takes precedence over the other operators in the sentence. So why don't we just note this fact and be done with matters?

Consider

(10) Odile doesn't believe that Twain is dead.

Sentence (10) surely doesn't say that there is a correlation f, obeying the appropriate restrictions, under which the RAM that Twain is dead doesn't represent one of Odile's RAMs. For one thing, if (10) is to be read in this way, then it is not the negation of 'Odile believes that Twain is dead'. This also makes it far too easy for (10) to be true: As long as a context is silent about the treatment of some expression or other in the t-clause, there will be some correlation under which its RAM fails to represent one of Odile's RAMs. The correct truth conditions for (10) are clearly as follows: It's not the case that there is a correlation f that respects the relevant restrictions, such that the RAM that Twain is dead represents one of Odile's RAMs under f.

Here is a natural second proposal about the relative scope of quantification over correlations and sentence operators. Quantification over correlations "rises" as high as it can in a sentence or dialogue. However, 'not' (and certain other operators, like 'never') act as barriers above which such quantification cannot rise.[18]

Let me describe a somewhat wooden version of this proposal; I will eventually endorse a slightly less wooden version. A simple way to spell out the proposal is to introduce an algorithm that assigns to a representative of a sentence something that states its truth conditions in an arbitrary context. In giving it, I will at first pretend that truth conditions are sets of worlds at a time.[19]

Suppose our object of study to be a propositional language L with negation ('$-$'), conjunction ('&'), disjunction ('$\vee$'), a conditional ('$\rightarrow$'), tense operators corresponding to the simple past and to 'during hour h' ('P', 'H'), a 'that', and a predicate 'B', corresponding to 'John believes', that takes 'that'-terms as arguments.

18 Irene Heim (1982) proposes an account of indefinites as free variables bound by quantifiers that generally are inserted in logical form; she takes 'not' and allied operators to form barriers to the quantifiers binding such variables in a way such as that suggested in the text. I have profited, in thinking about the issues discussed in the text, from Heim's discussion, as well as the discussion in Kamp (1981).

19 The commitment to eternalism voiced at the beginning of the section requires that truth conditions be identified, in this context, with sets of worlds. I clean things up later.

We want to characterize the truth conditions of its sentences. Let's write things like 'pwt' ('p is true in w at t') for each of L's propositional variables. (We assume that we have already defined models for the language, which, among other things, assign sets of worlds at a time to these variables as semantic values. The model theory also assigns sets of RAMs to contexts, representing the RS of the context's agent and sets of restrictions to contexts.) We also write in our metalanguage

Ofc: f is a correlation obeying context c's restrictions,
$Rpfwt$: p represents under f a RAM that is in John's RS in w at t,
$t < t'$: t is a time earlier than t',
$H^h t$: t is a time in hour h.

Let us treat 'that'-terms of L as being (in our metalanguage) names of the RAMs they determine in the object language. Finally, we may suppose that the metalanguage contains the connectives '$-$', '$\rightarrow$', '$\vee$', and '$\&$' with their usual truth-functional interpretations, as well as standard objectual quantifiers.

Suppose that the variables of our metalanguage have been sorted (for times, worlds, contexts, and correlations); use t, w, c, and f, respectively, to represent such variables. Suppose each sort to be ordered; use a prime on a representative of a variable to represent the next variable in the ordering. Let 'w_1' be a fixed world variable, 'c_1' a fixed context variable, each sitting outside of the ordering. Now consider the procedure *, which associates with a sentence of L and a time variable of our metalanguage an open sentence of the metalanguage:

$$*(p, t) = pw_1 t, \text{ for any propositional variable } p,$$
$$*(B(\text{that } A, t) = Ofc_1 \ \& \ R(\text{that } A, f, w_1, t),$$
$$*(-A, t) = -\exists f(*(A, t)),$$
$$*((A \ \& \ B), t) = (*(A, t) \ \& \ *(B, t)),$$
$$*((A \vee B), t) = (*(A, t) \vee *(B, t)),$$
$$*((A \rightarrow B), t) = (\exists f(*(A, t))) \rightarrow (*(A, t) \ \& \ *(B, t)),$$
$$*(PA, t) = \exists t'(t' < t \ \& \ *(A, t')),$$
$$*(HA, t) = (t')(H^h t' \rightarrow *(A, t')).$$

The clause for $-A$ represents the idea that negation acts as a barrier to quantification over correlations. In effect, this clause ensures that the quantification over correlations that an occurrence of 'B' imports never gets outside of a negation sign's scope.

If we apply this to a sentence of L and variable 't', we get a sentence open in 't', 'w_1', and possible 'c_1'. For example, from 'p & $-B$(that q)', we get successively

$(^*(p, t)$ & $^*(-B(\text{that } q, t))$,
$(pw_1t$ & $-\exists f(^*(B(\text{that } q), t))$,
$(pw_1t$ & $-\exists f(Ofc_1$ & $R(\text{that } q, f, w_1, t))$.

If the procedure gives a sentence S', when applied to a sentence S of L and a variable 't', then

For any context, c_1, S, taken relative to c_1, is true at those world times $\langle w_1, t \rangle$ such that, for some f, S'

gives the truth conditions of S. For example, 'p & $-B$(that q)' turns out to be true at wt, when taken relative to any c, iff, for some f, pwt and for no f, Ofc and R(that q, f, w, t). (I have relettered some bound variables here.) In this case, the initial quantifier is vacuous, since 'f' is bound by the quantifier 'for no f'. So the original sentence is said to be true at w and t iff p is true at w and t and, at the world and time, John has no belief represented by the RAM that q (relative to the context's restrictions). This seems correct.

The procedure does well with the other examples we have considered. To

$-B$(that q),
B(that q) & B(that r),
$H(B$(that q))

the procedure assigns, relative to a context c, respectively,

the world times $\langle w, t \rangle$ such that there is no f such that Ofc and R (that q, f, w, t),
the world times $\langle w, t \rangle$ such that, for some f such that Ofc, R(that p, f, w, t) and R(that q, f, w, t),
the $\langle w, t \rangle$'s such that there is an f such that, for every t during the last hour, Ofc & R(that q, f, w, t).

These are truth conditions we want to assign to these sentences.

Earlier, I called this a wooden implementation. In saying this, I had in mind such facts as that the implementation makes it impossible to assign to a sentence of the form

B(that p) & B(that q)

the truth conditions that there are correlations f and g (obeying the relevant restrictions) such that p under f, and q under g, represent RAMs in John's RS. Such sentences, as well as more complex

240

conjunctions that have 'B(that p)' and 'B(that q)' as individual conjuncts, must sometimes receive such truth conditions.

This becomes clear if we consider arguments that involve such sentences. Consider, for example, the argument form

$p \vee B$(that q),
$-p$,
Thus, B(that q).

It seems to me that, no matter what context we imagine ourselves to be in, it is possible to argue validly using this argument form. So it ought to turn out valid in some central sense of 'valid'.

In *a* sense of 'valid', the above proposal makes this argument valid. Suppose we define consequence so that a sentence T is a consequence of sentences $S_1, \ldots, S_n$ provided that, for any context c, the truth conditions of a conjunction of the S_i's in c include those of a conjunction of the S_i's and T in c. It is a routine exercise to show that most of the natural deduction rules for '$-$', '$\vee$', '&', and '$\rightarrow$' then come out valid. For example, the following rules are valid: From A, B, infer A & B; from A & B, infer A, B; from $A \vee B$, $-A$, infer B; from A, infer $A \vee B$; from A, $A \rightarrow B$, infer B; from $-B$, $A \rightarrow B$; infer $-A$.

However, these rules fail to be valid in a wider, somewhat more important sense of 'valid' in which a rule of inference

$A_1, \ldots, A_n \vdash B$

is valid iff (to put it intuitively) no matter what *additional* premises $C_1, \ldots, C_m$ we may accept, the A_i's and the C_i's jointly entail B. For example, if we say *only* 'p or he believes that q; and $-p$', the above assignment of truth conditions guarantees that what we said entails what we will say if we continue by saying 'and (so) he believes that q'. However, this guarantee does not extend to the case in which, before drawing our conclusion, we say 'of course, he believes that r'; for there may be no correlation, obeying the context's restrictions, under which both q and r represent one of his RAMs.

We should allow that the classical logical laws are in some important sense unrestrictedly valid. If

(V) $A_1, \ldots, A_n$; thus B

is classically valid (where B and the A_i's are surface forms of English), then, no matter how we spell out the details about the context, it ought to be possible for the speaker of the context to argue validly using (V).

To achieve this, we need to allow that quantification over correlations sometimes takes the widest possible scope and sometimes takes the narrowest possible scope. So some alteration in *, the proceduure we used to assign truth conditions, is called for. The correct alteration would seem to be to change the algorithm above so that it maps object language sentences to metalanguage ones in a one–many fashion. The algorithm is thus to be seen as one that is used to generate possible readings of a sentence or a dialogue, as well as to assign it truth conditions.

Consider, then, the operation @. It is like *, save that, where we always had

$$*(B(\text{that } A, t) = Ofc_1 \ \& \ R(\text{that } A, f, w_1, t),$$

the operation @ gives us a choice: We may have either

(a) $@(B(\text{that } A, t) = Ofc_1 \ \& \ R(\text{that } A, f, w_1, t)$

or

(b) $@(B(\text{that } A, t) = \exists f(Ofc_1 \ \& \ R(\text{that } A, f, w_1, t)).$

Let us call the metalanguage sentences that @ associates with an object language sentence S S's *@-forms*; if F is an @-form that @ associates with S, and the generation of F from S involves no use of (a), call F an *n-form* of S. Let A be any object language argument form (i.e., any argument form characterized in terms of the surface syntax of the object language, not in terms of @) that is valid in classical propositional logic. Then A represents a valid argument form in the sense that, for any context c, the intension in c of an n-form of a conjunction of its premises includes that of a conjunction of its premises and conclusion therein. Clearly, argument forms obtained from A by adding to its premises will be valid argument forms if A is. This seems to justify the claim that any classically valid propositional argument form A is such that, no matter what context we may consider, and no matter what we consider as being said in the context, it is possible for the speaker of the context to use A therein to reason validly: No matter what has already been uttered in a context, if A is a classically valid argument, it is possible to interpret a use of A by the speaker of the context as the use of a valid argument.

If we use @ to assign truth conditions to sentences, we also validate the intuition that one may truly say,

Throughout the game, John thought that he [Jabbar] was on the court at the beginning of the game

in a case in which John accepts 'Jabbar is on the court at game's beginning' for the first half of the game, accepts 'Alcindor is on the court at game's beginning' for the second half of the game, but rejects 'Jabbar is Alcindor' throughout the game. This is so because the n-form of the ascription will be equivalent to

For each t such that t occurs during the game, there is a correlation f such that f obeys c's restrictions and the RAM that Jabbar was on the court at the beginning of the game represents, at t, one of John's RAMs,

which is true in the envisioned circumstance (assuming that no restrictions on correlations are present, of course).

It appears straightforward enough to extend this account to more complex languages. For example, in the context of a language with propositional quantifiers, a clause like

$$@((p)A, t) = (p)(@(A, t))$$

appears to give intuitively satisfactory results, with the b-form of

$(p)(\text{John believes } p \rightarrow \text{Odile believes } p)$,
John believes that Smith is here,
Thus, Odile believes that Smith is here

coming out valid.

For simplicity of exposition, I have pretended that the circumstances of evaluation of sentences would be sets of worlds at a time. At the beginning of this section, I suggested that we should take propositions to be "eternally true," that is, if a proposition is true at tw for some t, then it is true at $t'w$, for all t'. Of course, we want to keep the truth conditions we assign to sentences in tandem with the truth conditions of the propositions they express. Perhaps the simplest way to do this is as follows: We said that, when our procedure took us from an object language sentence S to a meta-language sentence S', the sentence

For any context c_1, S, taken relative to c_1 is true at those world times $\langle w_1, t \rangle$ such that, for some f, S'

gave S's truth conditions. In order to "eternalize" this assignment of truth conditions, we make a small alteration:

243

For any context c_i, S, taken relative to c_i is true at those worlds w_i such that, where t is the time of c, for some f, S'.

So long as the assignment of RAMs to t-clauses is properly relativized to contexts, this assigns truth conditions in an adequate way.

4. TRUTH AND RAMS

Traditionally, the objects of the attitudes are identified with the bearers of properties such as truth, falsity, and necessity. We apparently ascribe such properties to propositions when we say, for example, that it is true that Mars is farther from the sun than is earth, or reason that, since everything Mary ever says is false but it's necessary that I am a man, Mary has not said that I am a man.

Are RAMs apt candidates for the office of bearers of truth? The best way to address this question would be to investigate the prospects for introducing into a language implementing the proposal of the past six sections a predicate 'it's true' taking 'that'-clauses and propositional variables as arguments. The aptness of RAMs as truth bearers would be measured by how satisfactory the results were.

But how to introduce such a predicate is a delicate issue, since there is little agreement about the right way to give a paradox-free account of 'true'. I have nothing new to add to the issue of the paradoxes. Here, I want only to suggest that the approach to the attitudes I have been sketching can make good sense of the idea that the objects of attitudes are bearers of truth. I will do this in a rather stodgy way, by gesturing (quite informally) at a way in which the approach I have sketched could be embedded in a Russell–Tarski-style hierarchy of languages, with each containing the truth predicate for the language beneath it.

I invoke this approach because it is relatively simple and very familiar. I don't insist that the way to solve the paradoxes is to use a hierarchy of languages. So far as I can see, the approach to the attitudes taken in this book would mesh well with (propositional versions of) other approaches to the paradoxes. But I don't try to establish that here.[20]

20 I might mention in particular Tyler Burge's (1979) approach to the paradoxes, in which the truth predicate is taken to be indexical. Burge's approach takes sentences to be bearers of truth. Although I have not investigated it in detail, it appears to me that his approach can be adapted to present purposes in a relatively straightforward way.

Certain delicate issues concerning truth and propositions arise *because* of the account of propositions I have given. For the purposes of giving an account of 'true', many RAMs can be considered to be nothing more than Russellian propositions with some extraneous material in them. For example, the RAM that Hesperus is hot is just the Russellian proposition that Hesperus is hot with some extra material in it, material that can be ignored for the purposes of assigning truth conditions.

However, this is not true of RAMs corresponding to sentences containing verbs of propositional attitude. The RAM that Ham believes that Hesperus is hot, for example, is constructed from the context-invariant meaning of 'believes', and not from one or another of its contextually varying contents. To try to assign a truth value to such a RAM, without supplementing it in some way or taking it relative to a context, would be like trying to assign a truth value to the sentence type 'I'm still reading this', without supplementing it with referents for 'I' and 'this', or taking it relative to a context.

We have two reasons for treating propositions about attitudes in this way. First, it is only on such a treatment that we can assign the same truth conditions to iterated attitude ascriptions and their translations when they are taken relative to contexts with different restrictions. Consider, for example, uses of 'John believes that Hans believes that Cologne is dirty' and its German translation, 'John glaubt, dass Hans glaubt, dass Köln schmutzig ist', where each of the speakers is trying to get across that John's belief is held under a sentence in which 'Köln' is used to refer to the relevant city. Such uses ought typically to have the same truth conditions. Now, in a case such as this, the English is used with the restriction 'Cologne' → 'Köln'. The difference in restrictions results in different contents for 'believes' and 'glaubt'. If we used the verbs' contents to construct RAMs for the t-clauses to name, the results would be RAMs that differed not just in vocabulary items, but in the semantic values paired with these. And this can be expected to result in an assignment of different truth conditions to the original sentences. Using the verbs' meanings instead of their contents allows agreement in truth conditions.

Besides securing truth-conditional agreement for translations, this treatment of attitude verbs in RAMs is necessary to get the truth conditions of iterated attitude ascriptions correct to begin

245

with. My use of 'John says that Ham thinks that Hes is hot' ought typically to be true when I hear John utter, 'Ham thinks Hes is hot', and make my utterance an attempt to report what he said. This is so even when John's and my contexts contain different restrictions. If they do, then the content of 'believes' in our contexts will be distinct. In order for my use of 'Ham believes that Hes is hot' to represent a RAM that John asserts in virtue of his utterance, 'believes' in my RAM must be paired with a value identical with what it is paired with in John's RAM. So 'believes' can't be paired with its content. Thus, we use the constant meaning of the verb in constructing both RAMs.

This is the explanation for the incompleteness of this sort of RAM. To deal with it, we take predicates of propositions like 'true' to be indexical, as we have the verbs of attitude. So 'is true', just like 'is domestic' or 'is foreign', is a predicate that determines a different intension in different (simultaneous) contexts. There is thus a contextual relativization of truth. A RAM like the RAM that Ham believes that Hes is hot will be true in some contexts – ones such that, relative to their restrictions, the RAM that Hes is hot represents one of Ham's RAMs – and false in others. (RAMs that are not incomplete, like the RAM that Hes is now hot, don't suffer from such contextual relativization of truth value.)

So far as I have been able to determine, there is nothing too complicated about giving a model-theoretic account of truth for RAMs along such lines, or with introducing a truth predicate that applies to t-clauses. I will outline a procedure that seems to me adequate. Readers with no interest in such details might want to skip across the following.

Excursus

The approach gestured toward here involves sorting propositions as well as languages into various levels, with the semantic value of attitude verbs and truth predicates of a language of a particular level defined only on propositions that appear at lower levels. It is (very loosely) modeled on the sort of hierarchy found in ramified-type theory or that which would be associated with a Tarskian hierarchy of languages. (See Church 1976 for an illuminating comparison of ramified-type theory and a Tarskian hierarchy.)

By invoking this approach, we take care of the two complications mentioned in the initial excursus of Chapter 3, Section 2. Once we employ a hierarchy, we assign different semantic values to the different occurrences of 'believes' in

John believes that Hammurabi believes that Hesperus is hot,

which ensures that the semantic value of 'believes' doesn't contain itself as a part. Likewise, the existential quantifiers in

$\exists f$(believes (John, that $\exists g$ believes (Ham, that Hes is hot, g) f)

will range over different domains, with the embedded quantifier's domain being a proper subset of the embedding quantifier's domain; indeed, '$\exists f$' in the above will have a domain that includes that of '$\exists g$'. So we are not required to have correlations operating on annotations that contain those very correlations.

Let us revert to ignoring time and tense. Start with a first-order language L_0 in whose sentences 'true' doesn't occur and that contains no attitude verbs. Let a model for the language contain sets of individuals, worlds, contexts, a set of "extra vocabulary" (for constructing RAMs that represent the RAMs determined by languages other than L_0), and an assignment function V. Define appropriate semantic domains for the sorts of vocabulary in L_0 itself (including connectives and quantifiers), and let V make appropriate assignments from these domains to L_0's vocabulary.

Now, continuing to characterize L_0's models, characterize the RAMs determined by L_0's sentences (by induction on logical complexity of L_0's sentences), and let V assign each sentence its RAM. [Strictly speaking, we assign RAMs to logical forms that are associated with the sentences of L_0; likewise for succeeding languages. In the case of L_0, the forms can be identified with L_0's sentences. If the object language's surface structure has attitude verbs as two-place predicates, then, for sentences of later languages, forms can be identified with sentences that come from the object language's sentences by replacing verbs of attitudes – and truth predicates – with predicates containing an extra argument place (for correlations) and by inserting quantifiers over correlations. This complication doesn't materially affect the following, and so I suppress it.]

Now define a general notion of an L_0 RAM: It is what is obtained from a RAM of a closed sentence L_0 by substituting in the extra vocabulary that the model contains for L_0 vocabulary and/or substituting semantic values for semantic values (replacing a value from semantic domain d with a value from the same domain, of course). Some care must be exercised in stating the definition: No piece of vocabulary should end up in different syntactic positions in a RAM, and substitution for variables must not take a "closed RAM" to an open one.

In defining the notion of an L_0 RAM, we will have defined the notion of an L_0 annotation, such annotations simply being the appropriate members of L_0 RAMs. Language L_0 correlations are simply (partial) functions that map L_0 annotations to L_0 annotations while preserving reference. Observe that, in the language L_0, we don't quantify over L_0 RAMs or over L_0 correlations, though such are definable in terms of an L_0 model. It is only in languages "above" L_0 that we will so quantify.

As well as making the assignments mentioned above, V is understood to assign sets of L_0 RAMs to contexts, as well as sets of restrictions thereto, the latter being trios of a member of the domain of individuals, an L_0 annotation, and a set of L_0 annotations. The first assignment represents the RS of the agent of the context.

One can now define *sentence S of L_0, taken in context c, is true at world w in model M* in a straightforward manner. Function V's assignments of RAMs and annotations to contexts are actually irrelevant to this definition, but are used to define truth for languages higher in the hierarchy. We also define *the L_0 RAM p, taken in c, is true at w in M*. In the case of L_0, which has no predicates of RAMs, we suppose that the contextual relativization for RAMs is vacuous. The definition of truth for RAMs is then completely straightforward and recapitulates the definition of truth for sentences.

We may now build a series of languages atop L_0. Given a language L_n, L_{n+1} is obtained from it as follows: We extend L_n's vocabulary to include a set of propositional variables (which will range over L_n RAMs); a propositional quantifier to bind such variables; new existential and universal quantifiers (ranging over what L_n's quantifiers did, and over L_n correlations); the expression 'that$_{n+1}$'; a two-place predicate 'B_{n+1}' (which takes an individual term and either a t-clause formed from 'that$_{n+1}$' and a sentence of L_n or a propositional variable of any language up to and including L_{n+1} as argument); and a predicate 'T_{n+1}', which takes the sort of t-clauses and propositional variables 'B_{n+1}' takes as arguments.

Models for L_{n+1} are always extensions of models of L_n. To the domain of individuals we add L_n correlations, so that we can quan-

248

tify over them. In characterizing the models and defining truth, we go through the same series of steps as we did for L_0:

1. Characterize semantic domains. In general, the semantic domains of L_{n+1} are those of L_n plus (a) functions from contexts to functions from correlations, individuals, and RAMs of lower levels to sets of worlds; (b) functions from contexts to functions from lower-level RAMs to sets of worlds. The first addition yields a semantic domain for attitude verbs introduced in L_{n+1}, the latter a domain for the truth predicate of L_{n+1}.

2. Assign appropriate semantic values to new vocabulary items (save variables and the syncategorematic 'that'), letting the old vocabulary retain its assignment from the model we are extending. For the belief and truth predicate, assignments are always determined by the model we are extending. For example, to 'T_{n+1}' we assign, in an extension of a model M for L_n, the function that takes a context c to the function that maps an L_n RAM P of M to the set of worlds w such that p, taken in c, is true at w in M.

3. Assign RAMs to L_{n+1} sentences on the basis of step 2, again by extending the assignment of RAMs to sentences made by the model we are extending.

4. Define L_{n+1} RAMs in the way characterized above; define as well L_{n+1} correlations.

5. Extend V's assignments to contexts to include L_{n+1} RAMs and restrictions involving annotations in which new vocabulary and semantic values occur.

6. Define truth, both for a sentence in a context at a world and for an L_{n+1} RAM in a context at a world, in a model.

In the definition of truth for a RAM, we assume that RAMs can be characterized in terms of some measure of logical complexity. Among "atomic RAMs," we will distinguish between those whose "predicate" (namely, annotation "in predicate position") contains a meaning (function from contexts to intensions) and those whose predicate does not. Since we have limited the sort of values that such predicates can contain (in step 1), we can then deal with these in two clauses. An atomic RAM whose predicate contains a value from the semantic domain of attitude verbs will be a RAM corresponding to an atomic sentence of the form

$B(a, \text{ that } S, f)$.

The RAM will be of the general form

$$\langle\langle b, b'\rangle, \langle\langle a, a'\rangle, p, \langle f, f'\rangle\rangle\rangle,$$

where p is a RAM of a level less than $n + 1$. Taken in c, the RAM is true at w just in case b' applied to c maps $\langle a', p, f'\rangle$ to a set

249

containing w. The value of $b'(c)$ is, of course, as characterized in the first excursus of Chapter 3, Section 2. RAMs with truth predicates are treated in an analogous fashion.

For example, a RAM of the form

$\langle\langle$ 'B_1', the semantic value of 'B_1'$\rangle$, $\langle\langle$ 'a', the semantic value of 'a'$\rangle$, a RAM p of level 0, $\langle$ 'f', correlation $f_1\rangle\rangle\rangle$

will be true in c at w iff the semantic value of 'B_1' applied to c – that is, supplemented with c's restrictions – maps $\langle$the referent of 'a', p, $f_1\rangle$ to something containing w.

(Note that in the case of higher-order iterations – for example, in the case of the RAM corresponding to 'John believes that Mary believes that Fred believes that frogs are funny' – the embedded verbs are not evaluated at c in order to determine whether the RAM is true at a world, when taken relative to c.)

The guiding idea of all of this is that, in a model M_n of L_n, the RAM we assign to a sentence S of the language should turn out to be related to S as follows: For any context c and world w, relative to c, S is true at w in M_n iff, relative to c, the RAM assigned to S is true at w in M_n. Given this, for any model of a language L_{n+1} and c and w in the model, if S is a sentence of L_n, then S, taken relative to c, is true at w in M iff $T_{n+1}(that\ S)$ is true, taken relative to c, at w in M.

End of excursus

On my view, 'Odile believes that Twain is dead' can vary in truth value from context to context. So can 'It's true that Odile believes that Twain is dead'. And I do not stop with allowing a contextual variation in the truth of the sentence; I allow a contextual variation in the truth of what the sentence says.

I expect that some will find odious the contextual variation in the truth of truth bearers. I am unaware of a principled argument that such variation is objectionable. In any case, once we grant that 'Odile believes that Twain is dead' can vary in truth across contexts, we are headed for the sort of contextual variation I have introduced. Suppose, for example, that both Mutt and Jeff can express beliefs by saying, 'Odile believes that Twain is dead', and that it is thus true that both believe that she believes that Twain is dead. We agree that one of them may speak falsely, the other truly, in expressing this belief. So we are already committed to saying that, in some sense, their common belief, that Odile believes that Twain is dead, may be true in one of their contexts but false in the other. If we can agree on this much, then it is not clear what point there is in denying that truth bearers (not sentences, but what they express) may be true in some contexts while false in simultaneous contexts. There is a long tradition which holds that the bearers of truth may shift truth value across contexts. Some have wanted to say that a proposition like the proposition that a Republican is president can shift truth value across time. I disagree with the view that a mere shift in time affects the truth value of a truth bearer. But just because truth bearers don't shift truth value in response to certain contextual variations doesn't mean that they don't shift truth value in response to others.

My account requires that we be careful about how we treat factive verbs like 'know'. When we say that Smith knows that Odile thinks that Twain is dead, the object of Smith's belief needs to be "true in two places": in Smith's context and in ours. The correct treatment of such a verb, I think, is as follows: Ignore the fact, irrelevant for present purposes, that knowledge is more than mere true belief. Then among the RAMs (of a particular level n) that are in the RS of an individual u at a world w will be some that are true, taken relative to u's context, at the world of his context. Let $k(u, w)$ be the function that assigns to each individual and world the relevant set. We can introduce into a language L_{n+1} a predicate 'K_{n+1}', to represent 'knows', with syntactic properties like those of 'believes'. Its semantic value will be the function that, applied to a context c, returns a function that maps an individual u, a RAM p, and correlation f to the set of those worlds w such that p taken relative to c is true at w and, for some q, q is in $k(u, w)$ and p represents q under f. Assigning such a value to representatives of 'knows' (and otherwise treating them like 'believes') will then validate arguments such as that from 'He knows that S' to 'It's true that S'.

5. REFERENCE AND CONTENT

Someone says, 'Rex wishes that Mike were running'. On my view, what is said is true only if Rex is in a state with constituents that determine, in an appropriate sense, the referential values of 'Mike' and 'is running', namely, Mike and the property of running.

In general, before

x wishes that S

or any other attitude ascription involving 'that S' can be true, there has to be a sort of isomorphism of referential content between 'that S' and some state of x. With only one exception – the verbs of attitude – if an attitude ascription's that-clause contains a (syntactically simple) expression whose Russellian interpretation is R, then the ascription is true only if the ascribee is in a state with a part that determines, in an appropriate manner, R. And the departure from this rule in the case of attitude verbs is not very great. Although the truth of 'John wishes that Mary believed that snow is white' doesn't require that John be in a state with a constituent that *in his context* determines the same referential content as does 'believes' in ours, it does require that John's state have a constituent that, taken *in our context*, determines the same referential content as 'believes' does in ours.

Let us use 'referential agreement' to name the relation between the t-clause (in a context c) and the state (in a context c') that obtains when, for each simple constituent x of the t-clause that isn't (is) a verb of attitude, there is a constituent x' of the state such that x' determines in c' the Russellian interpretation of x in c (x' determines the same function from contexts to interpretations as does x).

The notion of referential agreement remains rather vague, since I haven't tried to say what it is for a part of a state to determine, relative to a context, a particular referential value. Spelling this out, of course, is a rather large philosophical project. A complete answer would be something that told us when a word or a part of a mental state was about or meant an individual, property, or relation; it would be a solution to what is sometimes called the problem of intentionality.

I am not going to pursue *that* project here, for we can discuss the requirement of referential agreement without presupposing a particular account of intentionality. The requirement should be discussed, since many philosophers think it is obviously wrong. They claim that we can successfully ascribe attitudes to animals, children, and those, like aborigines, whose culture or belief systems are very alien to our own. They argue that such animals, human

252

and nonhuman, do not always have the concepts associated with predicates in t-clauses of successful ascriptions. Dogs don't have the concept of bone or of chewing, though some want to chew on bones; small children don't have the concept of osteopath, though some believe their mothers to be osteopaths. But someone or something without the concept of chewing or osteopath cannot be in a state that determines, in any interesting sense, the referential content of the English 'chewing' or 'osteopath'. So there is no referential agreement between t-clauses in successful ascriptions to these creatures and the creatures' states.[21]

I will first say something in defense of the claim that the truth of an attitude ascription requires referential agreement between its t-clause and some state of the ascribee. (For short, attitude ascription requires referential agreement.) I will then say something about versions of the above objection that involve ascriptions of attitude to higher nonhuman animals such as dogs. My defense of the requirement of referential agreement is quite simple. I want only to observe that we have fairly strong intuitions that suggest that this *is* a requirement on successful ascription.

Suppose, for example, that we encounter someone speaking an alien language. She utters something we can determine to be an indicative subject–predicate sentence. Let's say it is 'Glug lxit', with 'glug' the subject, 'lxit' the predicate. Perhaps we know that 'glug' is a demonstrative that refers to us. And we know that 'lxit' has an extension close to the English 'are treacherous'. But it is not exactly the same extension, since some things satisfying it aren't treacherous. Then surely this person did not say that we are treacherous. This seems to me obvious: Whatever she said we were, it couldn't have been treacherous, for, ex hypothesi, something is what she said we were, but not treacherous. And even if some philosophers don't think this is obvious, it is a very widely held, and quite strong, intuition.

The point is quite general. If someone assertively utters a sentence of the form Fa, and F does not have the extension of the English predicate E, then it would be false to say that the speaker said of something that it E's. Indeed, if F does not have the *in*tension of E, the same holds true. Return to the example above, supposing

21 These sorts of objections can be found in Dennett (1969), Grandy (1986), Stalnaker (1984) and Stich (1983).

only that something *could* be a 'lxit' but not treacherous. Then surely the same conclusion, that our friend didn't say we were treacherous, can be drawn and supported by similar observations.

The point generalizes beyond subject–predicate sentences. Given the truth of the kind of sentientialism I defended in Chapter 1 – on which having an attitude requires being in a sentential state whose structure is isomorphic to that of a t-clause ascribing the attitude – such examples strongly suggest that we suppose that successful ascriptions of assertion require referential agreement. The reason that our friend didn't say that we are treacherous seems to be that his utterance didn't have a component that determined the property of being treacherous.

Similar points can be made about attitudes such as belief. For example, Stitch (1979) gives an argument that dogs do not have beliefs that are ascribable using the word 'bone'. Many people find the argument compelling, if somewhat unsettling. What gives the argument its power, I think, is the tacit assumption that belief ascription requires referential agreement.

Stitch's argument is quite simple: Consider a dog, Fido. An ascription of the form

(1) Fido believes that... bone...

(e.g., 'Fido believes that there is a bone behind the couch') is true only if Fido has the concept we associate with 'bone'. But Fido doesn't have such a concept. Stitch gives three reasons for thinking that the dog lacks the concept. (a) He does not have enough of the same beliefs about bones that we do. (b) Nothing about the dog's behavior suggests that he groups bones into a single class. The dog does not, for example, have a propensity to chew unusual bones. (c) The dog is not able to distinguish ersatz from real bones. So ascriptions of the form of (1) are not true.

One might dispute that (a) through (c) give us a good reason for accepting the claim that the dog lacks the concept bone. Note, however, that the suggestion that, for whatever reason, the dog does lack the concept suggests very strongly that Stitch's conclusion is correct. Most people who encounter the argument, I think, are not inclined to challenge it at this point. And this suggests that most of us suppose that belief ascription requires referential agreement; since if possession of the concept bone is necessary, in order to have a belief that qualifies as the belief... bones..., this is

presumably so because a state, in order to qualify as the belief that
... bones ..., must involve this concept in some significant way.
Given that the concept bone determines the same ex- and intension
as the the English 'bone', it follows that, to believe that ...
bone ..., is to be in a state with a constituent that mirrors 'bone'
in referential properties. And this strongly suggests that attitude
ascription requires referential agreement.[22]

Let us consider some other reactions to Stich's argument. Stalnaker (1984) has claimed that the argument functions in effect as a
reductio of the idea that beliefs are realized as

linguistic items or as quasi-linguistic complexes stored in the mind or the
brain. The problem [the argument poses], on this assumption, would be
to translate as accurately as possible the dog's mental language into English.
... it is not very plausible to hypothesize such linguistic or conceptual
structures [in a dog]. (p. 63)

I disagree. Surely the dog does have distinguishable abilities to
recognize and discriminate among objects, and surely it does have
perceptual images of objects in its environment. Such abilities and
representations seem apt candidates for the constituents of belief and
desire states that correspond to terms and predicates. So long as we
confine ourselves to "atomic" beliefs (e.g., this is a bone, that is in
this) ascribing a linguistic structure to the states of the animal that
constitute its beliefs requires us only to say such things as the following: The dog's belief that we call the belief that this is a bone involves
a certain coordination of a perceptual representation (of this) and a
particular discriminatory ability (which is involved in other beliefs
we characterize using 'bone'). This doesn't seem at all implausible, as
long as we allow that the animal's "bone concept" may be so different from ours that it doesn't even have the same extension. And
surely we can justify the ascription of, say, existential or conjunctive
beliefs on the basis of certain kinds of (functional) modes of organization of such mental structures, as we suggested in Chapter 1, we
might for the case of humans. The problem that animal attitudes

22 In order to support the claim that belief ascription requires referential agreement,
one must make out that anything that counts as the concept bone determines
the *in*tension of the English 'bone', and not just its *ex*tension. It seems that we
can do this by joining Stich's argument with such observations as the following:
If the dog's belief would be true iff something fell under such and such a concept
of the dog's, and something other than a bone could be in the extension of that
concept, then the dog's belief is not that there are bones.

present is *not* that they are realized nonsententially – at least this is not so given a broad enough notion of sentence.

Perhaps all Stalnaker means here is that the argument functions as a *reductio* of a position like my own, which requires referential agreement for successful attitude ascription: It is supposedly *obvious* that some dogs think that bones are fun to play with. All I can say is that many people cease to think it is obvious that dogs have such beliefs upon hearing the argument, and most people at least acknowledge being made uncomfortable by the argument. And this seems to show that we feel a commitment to referential agreement in attitude ascription.

Stich himself does not react to the argument in the way I suggest we should react. Stich thinks that the primary hindrance to identifying the content of any of Fido's states with the content of any of our sentence tokens in which 'bone' occurs is a failure of ideological similarity:

Our difficulty in specifying the contents of animals' beliefs derives . . . from a basic feature of the way we go about assigning content to a subject's beliefs: *We are comfortable in attributing to a subject a belief with a specific content only if we can assume the subject to have a broad network of related beliefs that are largely isomorphic with our own.* (Stich 1979, p. 22, italics in original)[23]

Stich has misdiagnosed the problem. The problem with saying that the dog believes that . . . bones . . . is that it seems that no discriminatory capacity of the dog's, which we might be inclined to identify as his concept bone, determines an extension even remotely close to the extension determined by our use of the word 'bone'. And, of course, no such capacity determines anything remotely like the *in*tension of our use of 'bone'. Since the dog's capacities are presumably responsible for the extension (and intension) of its concepts, it thus seems unlikely that any of Fido's concepts have the same extension (intension) as that expressed by our 'bone'. The unease that we feel about ascribing a belief about bones to Fido once we hear Stich's argument results from uncertainty about

---

23 Stich's views about animal attitude ascriptions changed after he wrote Stich (1979). In Stich (1983), he argues that we can successfully, i.e., truly, ascribe animal beliefs. This is because, he says, attitude ascriptions say only that the ascribee is in a state similar to that which would prompt, in the ascriber, a declarative use of the ascription's content sentence. He continues to hold that ideological similarity is an important component of determining such similarity. Some of the criticisms of Fregean similarity accounts made in Chapter 3 can, I think, be turned against Stich.

whether Fido could really be said to be thinking about *bones*, as opposed to (what to our mind is) a miscellaneous collection of small- and medium-sized bones of a certain general shape, cleverly designed mixtures of dog food and rubber, the odd stick, and so on. Our uncertainty is a result of a doubt as to whether the component of Fido's state that corresponds to our use of 'bone' has the same intension, or even extension, as does our use of 'bone'. The problem is not with Fido's ideological impurity.

Consider what happens to Stich's argument if we stipulate that, *mirabile dictu*, Fido discriminates between bones and nonbones about as well as we can. Suppose, for example, that he is trained to bark when presented with a bone and prompted 'bone?' and to whine when presented with a nonbone and prompted 'bone?' After training, he turns out to distinguish the bones from the nonbones about as well as we do. There is no longer a very good case for denying to Fido beliefs such as that which might be ascribed with the sentence 'This is a bone'. Most people find Fido's lack of anatomical knowledge no barrier to ascribing such beliefs to Fido.

Compare the case of a child who would sincerely say, 'Clouds are alive'; who wants to know if clouds can talk; if they are awake or asleep during the evening, and so on.[24] So long as the child can discriminate clouds as well as we can, I think that we would not hesitate to ascribe to her the belief that clouds are alive. In this sort of case, there is a rather large ideological difference between the child and ourselves, but it doesn't interfere with the attitude ascription.

I would say that this is because the child's discriminatory ability, combined with her membership in a community of English speakers, serves to fix the intension of her use of 'clouds', so that it is the same as ours. There is thus an identity of intension, component by component, between the child's state and the sentence we use to ascribe belief to the child. This again suggests that it is not ideological difference per se that prevents attitude ascription, but a difference of intension between the constituents of an attitude and the constituents of the sentence we use to ascribe the attitude.

One might point out on Stich's behalf that, in any natural fleshing out of this case, we would find that there was considerable verbal agreement between the child and ourselves: The child and we agree,

---

24 This example, put to other purposes, is found in Partee (1982).

for example, that clouds appear in the sky, that clouds have a certain customary appearance, that there is no rain without clouds, and so on. One might say this indicates that we presuppose a sufficient similarity in ideology between the child and ourselves. This is the reason we find no difficulty in ascribing the belief to the child.

I do not know whether Stich himself would endorse such a response.[25] In any case, once one develops the case in such a way as to remove the verbal agreement, it becomes implausible that the child picks out clouds with her use of 'clouds'. After all, once the child stops assenting to such things as 'Clouds are in the sky', it becomes puzzling as to what, if anything, she could be picking out with the term. So this defense makes it seem once again as if there is nothing about ideological difference per se that is a barrier to attitude ascription.

I think the appropriate moral to draw here is that a very large difference in ideology is very often accompanied by a difference in reference. So we can grant that a very large difference in ideology will very often lead to a breakdown in our ability to ascribe an attitude, even when there is verbal agreement between ourselves and the ascribee. But to say this is *not* to say that the truth of an attitude ascription requires such agreement in ideology, or that it doesn't require referential agreement.

There is another reaction to Stich's argument, again one of his own, that should be addressed. Stich (1979) seems to suggest that it would follow from the claim that we couldn't ascribe beliefs to Fido that Fido's belief states wouldn't have truth conditions and therefore wouldn't really be beliefs:

What are we to say of these . . . states that . . . lack specifiable content? Are we to count them as beliefs? . . . If we opt for an affirmative answer then we are, of course, committed to accepting beliefs without specifiable content. If a subject has one of these beliefs we cannot attribute it to him with a sentence of the form

The subject believes that _____.

There is no saying what the subject believes, thus no way of filling in the blank. An equally uncomfortable feature of contentless beliefs is that we cannot assign them a truth value. . . . what are we to say of a belief whose content we cannot specify? Under what conditions is it true or false? There

---

25 Stich (1983, p. 57) suggests that he would not be comfortable with such a defense.

is no obvious account of truth for such beliefs. In depriving beliefs of expressible content we have also deprived them of truth values. (p. 26)

We may agree that a belief without truth conditions is not a belief, even if it is a state that plays the sort of role in the causation of behavior characterized by folk-psychological principles, like "belief + desire = action" schemata. But it is one thing not to have truth conditions, quite another not to have truth conditions captured by any of our sentences. To infer that the states of the animal associated with bone perception, which we tend to call beliefs, are not beliefs because *we* can't assign them truth conditions, is somewhat like inferring that there is no life outside of earth because *we* can't find any. Why should all the beliefs there are have content that is captured by one of our sentences? I see little reason for thinking that our inability to say exactly what an animal believes or desires gives us reason to say that they don't believe or desire anything at all.

So far, I have avoided committing myself to whether animals such as dogs have attitudes. I have been trying to make clear that our intuitions about the truth conditions of ascriptions of attitude and our reactions to certain arguments seem to commit us to the view that referential agreement is necessary for successful attitude ascription.

It seems reasonable, nonetheless, to grant that animals like dogs do have beliefs and desires. It seems to me that we may even be in a position to ascribe some of them. For example, it is not wildly implausible to think that a dog has, on the basis of its perceptual abilities, the same concept of one thing's being behind another as do we. So it seems plausible enough to think that an ascription like 'The dog thinks that the bone is behind the couch', when read 'For some x and y such that x is the bone and y is the couch, the dog believes that x is behind y', is literally true.[26]

But I suspect that a great many of our workaday attitude ascriptions to animals are literally false. For example, I suspect that ascriptions of attitude like 'The dog believes that this is a bone' are false, since there fails to be referential agreement with respect to 'bone' and the relevant states of the dog.

At this point some will disagree with me. They will insist dogs indeed have our concepts; thus, there is often enough referential

26 Sydney Shoemaker pointed out to me the plausibility of saying that such ascriptions are true.

agreement between animal belief states and the sentences we use to ascribe them. Those who say this offer one or another causal, or teleological, or other naturalistic account of how a state comes to have its content. They claim for example, that the discriminatory ability or concept that bones activate in the typical dog is to be assigned the very same content as that of the English 'bone'.[27]

I have no quarrel with the claim that we must eventually give a naturalistic account of content. If such an account turns out to make the better part of our workaday ascriptions of attitude to animals true, so much the better. But I tend to doubt that it will. So I accept no naturalistic gifts from the audience. Instead, I want to consider how embarrassing it would be for the account I have been sketching if we were forced to say that the vast majority of animal attitude ascriptions were literally false.

Given our apparent committment to the view that successful attitude ascription requires referential agreement, I don't think this is clearly embarrassing at all. If dogs *don't* have our concepts, and we are committed to a view that implies that, by and large, we can't ascribe attitudes to those who don't have our concepts, where is the embarrassment?

There is one aspect of ascribing attitudes to animals that calls for some comment. Most such ascriptions seem to be made in an attempt to explain animal behavior. And this sort of explanation seems to be fairly successful. When Fido is digging madly in the yard and you ask me why, I tell you that he's doing it because he thinks there is a bone buried where he's digging; I add that he's hungry. If Fido *is* hungry, if he *does* usually go bone digging when he's seen a bonelike thing hidden in the ground and is hungry, and if Fido's behavior has been caused by the appropriate sort of belief state (along with his hunger), then I have presumably explained Fido's behavior. At least this seems so if human attitude ascriptions typically explain human behavior.

But how can this be so on the view I am defending? It seems as if I am implicitly invoking a law of "folk ethology" to give an explanation of the dog's behavior, an explanation like the following:

27 Causal theories of content are championed in Stampe (1979), Stalnaker (1984), and Fodor (1987); Milikan (1984) proposes a teleological account. Fodor (1987) contains a frank discussion of some of the problems causal theories face. Not all of these philosophers would necessarily, or even contingently, endorse the suggestion in the text about the content of animal attitudes.

For most dogs d and place p, if d is hungry and d believes that there is a bone buried at p, then ceteris paribus, the dog will dig at p,
Fido is hungry, and he believes that there is bone buried there,
Hence, as ceteris is paribus, Fido is digging there.

The problem is that the "law" invoked here is at best vacuously true, since we are assuming dogs don't have the sort of beliefs invoked in the antecedent. And the second premise itself isn't true, Fido not being in a position to have such a belief. So it seems as if I have to say that most attempts to explain animal attitudes are failures and are based on a confused view about what attitudes animals have. And that would be somewhat embarrassing, since, as I have just admitted, it doesn't seem to be a failure at all.

I want to point out that there is a sense in which, even if most animal attitude ascriptions are false, it doesn't follow that most attempts to explain animal behavior by attitude ascriptions are failures. First of all, note that even though the "law" invoked above is vacuously true, the same need not be the case with other laws formally similar to it. Consider, for example, the following:

(D) For most dogs d, there is an R and S such that R is true of typical bones (i.e., ones typical in d's experience); S includes in its extension many pairs $\langle x, y \rangle$ such that x is buried at y, and for any place y, if d is hungry and d believes that, for some z, Rz and Szy, then, ceteris paribus, d will dig at y.

The quantifiers here on 'R' and 'S' are second-order ones whose variables take functions from tuples of individuals to sets of worlds as values. If it is reasonable to think that folk-psychological laws are approximately true of us folks, then it seems reasonable to think that some folk-ethological laws like (D) are true, or roughly true. And it seems reasonable to think that we are justified in believing in the truth of such laws.

We are justified on the basis of our observations of animals in thinking that they have beliefs and desires. Observation justifies our thinking that (a) animals have states that are connected with their environment, with one and another, and with behavior in a way very much like human beliefs and desires are and that (b) these states involve classifying or conceptualizing objects in some way, and hence the states can be said to be correct or incorrect, that is, can be said to have truth conditions. This makes it appropriate to call the states in question beliefs and desires.

Even without knowing how an animal classifies objects – without knowing what the extensions of its concepts are – we can know, or at least make reasonable inferences, about when it is classifying an object in the same way as it did on past occasions. Such inferences are justified by the same sort of evidence as they are for humans. Similar appropriate reactions to things that we have reason to think (on the basis of what we know of the animal's physiology, history, etc.) appear the same to the animal justify these inferences. Perhaps the inference from Fido's repeated tail wagging and dash to the door whenever I put on my sweater to the claim that he has the same sort of belief whenever he notices me put on my sweater is not *quite* as secure as the inference from your repeated exclamation 'Oh, no, not macaroni and cheese again' on seeing the yellow stuff on the table to the claim that you have the same sort of belief whenever you see the yellow stuff on the table. But it is a reasonable inference nonetheless. It is a reasonable first step on the road from folk ethology to cognitive ethopsychology.

Something similar is true of the desires of animals. Let us suppose that, for reasons that Stich brings out, it can't be quite right to say that Fido wants a bone. But we can presumably be justified in saying that Fido's state today, which is a desire and would be satiated by a bone, is the same as the one he was in yesterday. The identification is justified in terms of satiation: Roughly, if the same things would satiate the states, then they are the same. A little less crudely, if the same things would satiate the state, given the same beliefs and concurring desires, they are the same.

Finally, even though we can't say what the contents of Fido's beliefs and desires are, we are often justified in positing a coordination of content between them. In part, we are so justified by observations that the presence of certain things tends to bring on the belief state, while the same things tend to extinguish the desire. Likewise, we are often justified in positing a regularity between Fido's being in a state and his being disposed to behave in certain ways.

In summary, we are often justified in (a) identifying an animal's state as a belief state, one typically activated by a certain kind of state of the world; (b) positing a certain sort of coordination of content between the belief state and a desire state; (c) positing a regularity between the animal's being in the two states and its being disposed to act in certain ways. If all this is plausible, then, I think, it is also plausible that we can know things like principle (D) above.

In fact, our evidence for (D) is very much like our evidence for analogous principles about human beings.

If I can be said to know principles like (D), then when I try to explain what Fido is doing by saying, 'He thinks that there is a bone buried there', I can be seen to be implicitly invoking such a principle. If it is granted that Fido is one of the many dogs to which (D) applies, then when I say that he thinks a bone to be buried there, I may be taken to be getting across that Fido is in a state covered by (D). That is, when I say or suggest that Fido believes that there is a bone buried there and he is hungry, in the attempt to explain why he is digging, my claim suggests the following:

(D') There is an R and S such that R is true of typical bones (i.e., ones typical in Fido's experience); S includes in its extension many pairs $\langle x, y \rangle$ such that x is buried at y, and, for any place y, if Fido is hungry and he believes that, for some z, Rz and $S(z, y)$, then, ceteris paribus, Fido will dig at y; *and* Fido is hungry; *and* Fido believes that, for some z, Rz and $S(z,$ there$)$.

This is something that might reasonably be held to be true. Furthermore, it makes the claim that Fido is digging at the relevant location a reasonable belief, in just the way that the premises of a normal belief/desire explanation make the belief in its conclusion a reasonable one.

My point is that, when we seem to be able to explain an animal's behavior by ascribing attitudes to it, our success can at least sometimes be explained as follows: Our explanation suggests, in a straightforward manner, (a) a principle like (D) that we know or at least are justified in believing, to be nonvacuously true, and (b) a claim, related to the principle as (D') is to (D), that we have reason to think true and that, if true, would form the basis of an explanation of the animal's behavior. But all of this is consistent with the literal falsity of the ascription we actually make.

It seems to me that it does not follow, from the fact that most of our ascriptions of attitude to animals are false, that they fail to serve their primary purpose: to explain the behavior of the animal to which attitude is ascribed.

Conclusion

This is very much a work in the tradition of Frege and Russell. Perhaps as good a way of ending it as any is to remark on a few of the ways in which its conclusions fit in with Russell's and Frege's views of attitudes and their ascription.

Painting with a broad brush, we can contrast Frege and Russell's views on attitudes as follows. Frege thought that attitudes were not the sort of thing that could be characterized simply in terms of the objects and properties that they are intuitively about. Indeed, he thought ordinary objects and properties were simply the wrong sorts of things to use, in saying what someone believes or wants. Russell, by contrast, thought that workaday objects and properties were essential to attitude characterization. In fact, some of his comments about the multiple-relation theory of belief occasionally suggest the view that a correct characterization of an attitude refers to *nothing* but the objects and properties that it is about.

These differences are reflected in their views of the behavior of expressions within attitude ascriptions. For Frege, expressions governed by an attitude verb shift their reference from workaday objects and so on to the sorts of things appropriate for attitude characterization. For Russell, expressions within the scope of an attitude verb behave no differently than without. There is no need for them to do so, since they already name the sort of thing we need to refer to in order to say what someone thinks.

In certain ways, the story I have told agrees with those told by both Russell and Frege. With Russell and against Frege, I think that our attitudes are to be characterized by reference to things that they are intuitively about. Like Russell, I see expressions continuing to contribute their workaday semantic values to a sentence when they are within the scope of 'believes' and other attitude verbs. With Frege and against Russell, I do not think an attitude is characterized simply in terms of objects and properties. And like Frege, I see this as requiring a sort of reference shift when an expression is embedded. Of course, the reference shift I see occurring is quite different, in form and function, from that which Frege saw.

Frege and Russell, at least the Russell of *Principles of Mathematics* (1903), thought that a (central aspect of a) sentence's meaning provided a useful tool for individuating the states with which attitude ascriptions are concerned. I do not think it a distortion to say that they thought that semantic natural kinds (thoughts, propositions) were able to yield psychological natural kinds. Both thought that attitudes were in some important sense direct, unmediated relations to a sentence's meaning, or at least to something definable therefrom in a straightforward way.

I am not much in sympathy with this view. In a sense, my insisting that in an attitude ascription we use a sentence to *represent* what someone thinks is tantamount to denying this. If forced to pick a candidate for meaning, I would pick something like Kaplan's characters, construed as functions from contexts to possible-worlds intensions, or to (complexes of) individuals and properties. I don't think that it is particularly useful to try to individuate psychological states like belief in terms of the characters of the sentences that realize those states. Character is a function from context to reference, and thus is no more psychologically transparent than reference. In fact, the set of things satisfying a predicate like 'believes that this is a dog', when this is taken relative to one or another context, isn't much of a psychological natural kind either.

Contemporary truth-conditional semantics traces its lineage back to the work of Russell and Frege. It should be obvious that I think that this tradition provides an appropriate arena for giving an account of central aspects of meaning. This work departs very little from the contemporary tune of such semantics. It does urge that we make the unit for assigning truth conditions conversations or dialogues, instead of simply sentences, but this has been in the wind for a while now. It urges that we abandon Leibniz's law; but, as I have argued, this is little loss, since the law is no law to begin with.

One way in which this book's position departs from *some* contemporary approaches to truth-conditional semantics is in its insistence that, among the contextual factors that can affect what a sentence strictly and literally says, are the intentions, expectations, and other intentional states of its participants. If what I have said here is correct, not only can our intentions affect the semantic value of a verb like 'believes' (by contributing restrictions on how we represent beliefs), but they can affect the very syntax of our sentences (by affecting the distribution of quantifiers over correlations in the way suggested in Chapter 4).

I am conscious of having provided less than a full theory of this. I certainly haven't provided a full theory of what sorts of intentions and so forth can have this kind of effect. Nor have I tried to say what observable aspects of context hearers use to determine what the speaker's relevant intentions and so forth are. This is something someone needs to give a theory of. This is something which, in David Kaplan's playful phrase, is left as an exercise for the reader.

Bibliography

When a work is cited in the text and a republication of it is mentioned, an asterisk indicates the source whose pagination is followed.

Aczel, P. 1988. *Non-well-founded Sets*. Stanford, Calif.: CSLI Lecture Notes No. 14.

Almog, J., J. Perry, and H. Wettstein, eds. 1989. *Themes from Kaplan*. New York: Oxford University Press.

Asher, N. 1986. "Belief in Discourse Representation Theory." *Journal of Philosophical Logic 15*, 127–89.

Audi, R. 1982. "Affirming and Believing." *Mind 91*, 115–20.

Austin, D., ed. 1988. *Philosophical Analysis: A Defense by Example*. Dordrecht: Reidel.

Barwise, J., and J. Perry. 1983. *Situations and Attitudes*. Cambridge, Mass.: MIT Press.

Bealer, G. 1982. *Quality and Concept*. New York: Oxford University Press.

Boër, S., and W. Lycan. 1986. *Knowing Who*. Cambridge, Mass.: MIT Press.

Burge, T. 1979. "Semantical Paradox." *Journal of Philosophy 76*, 169–98. Reprinted in Martin (1984).

Carnap, R. 1947. *Meaning and Necessity*. Chicago: University of Chicago Press.

Cartwright, R. 1979. "Indiscernibility Principles." In French et al. (1979b).

Church, A. 1950. "On Carnap's Analysis of Statements of Assertion and Belief." *Analysis 10*, no. 5, 97–9.* Reprinted in Linsky (1971).

    1954. "Intensional Isomorphism and Identity of Belief." *Philosophical Studies 5*, 65–73. Reprinted in Salmon and Soames (1988).

    1976. "Comparison of Russell's Resolution of the Semantical Antinomies with that of Tarski." *Journal of Symbolic Logic 41*, 747–60. Reprinted in Martin (1984).

Cresswell, M. 1978. "Semantic Competence." In Guenthner and Guenthner-Reutter (1978).

    1985. *Structured Meanings: The Semantics of Propositional Attitudes*. Cambridge, Mass.: MIT Press.

267

Davidson, D., and G. Harman, eds. 1972. *Semantics of Natural Language.* Dordrecht: Reidel.

Dennett, D. 1969. *Content and Consciousness.* London: Routledge & Kegan Paul.

  1975. "Brain Reading and Mind Writing." In Gunderson (1975); reprinted in Dennett (1978).*

  1978. *Brainstorms.* Montgomery, Vt.: Bradford.

Devitt, M. 1981. *Designation.* New York: Columbia University Press.

Donnellan, K. 1972. "Proper Names and Identifying Descriptions." In Davidson and Harman (1972).

  1974. "Speaking of Nothing." *Philosophical Review 83*, 3–31.

  1979. "The Contingent *a Priori* and Rigid Designators." In French et al. (1979a).

Evans, G. 1981. "Understanding Demonstratives." In Parret and Bouveresse (1981).

Evans, G., and J. McDowell, eds. 1976. *Truth and Meaning.* New York: Oxford University Press.

Field, H. 1977. "Logic, Meaning, and Conceptual Role." *Journal of Philosophy 74*, 379–409.

Fodor, J. 1987. *Psychosemantics.* Cambridge, Mass.: MIT Press.

Forbes, G. 1987a. "Indexicals and Intentionality: A Fregean Perspective." *Philosophical Review 96*, 3–31.

  1987b. "A Dichotomy Sustained." *Philosophical Studies 51*, 187–211.

  1989. *The Languages of Possibility.* Oxford: Blackwell Publisher.

  ms. 1. "Indirect Contexts in Unideal Languages." Unpublished manuscript.

Frege, G. 1892. "Uber Sinn und Bedeutung." Translated as "On Sense and Reference" in Geach and Black (1952).*

  1918. "Der Gedanke." Translated as "Thoughts" in Geach (1977).

  1980. *Philosophical and Mathematical Correspondence,* ed. G. Gabriel et al. Chicago: University of Chicago Press.

French, P., T. Uehling, and H. Wettstein, eds. 1979a. *Contemporary Perspectives in the Philosophy of Language.* Minneapolis: University of Minnesota Press.

  1979b. *Midwest Studies in Philosophy IV: Studies in Metaphysics.* Minneapolis: University of Minnesota Press.

  1981. *Midwest Studies in Philosophy VI: The Foundations of Analytic Philosophy.* Minneapolis: University of Minnesota Press.

  1989. *Midwest Studies in Philosophy XIV.* Notre Dame, Ind.: University of Notre Dame Press.

Geach, P., ed. 1977. *Logical Investigations,* tr. P. Geach and R. Stoothoff. New Haven, Conn.: Yale University Press.

Geach, P., and M. Black, eds. and trs. 1952. *Translations from the Philosophical Writings of Gottlob Frege.* Oxford: Blackwell Publisher.

Grandy, R. 1986. "Some Misconceptions about Belief." In Grandy and Warner (1986).

Grandy, R., and R. Warner, eds. 1986. *Philosophical Grounds of Rationality: Intentions, Categories, Ends.* New York: Oxford University Press.

268

Groenendijk, J., Th. Janssen, and M. Stokhof, eds. 1981. *Formal Methods in the Study of Language*. Amsterdam: Mathematisch Centrum Tracts.

Guenthner, F., and M. Guenthner-Reutter, eds. 1978. *Meaning and Translation: Philosophical and Linguistic Approaches*. New York: New York University Press.

Gunderson, K., ed. 1975. *Language, Mind, and Knowledge* (Minnesota Studies in the Philosophy of Science VII). Minneapolis: University of Minnesota Press.

Gupta, A., and L. Savion 1987. "Semantics of Propositional Attitudes: A Critical Study of Cresswell's *Structured Meanings*." *Journal of Philosophical Logic 16*, 395–410.

Hahn, P., and P. Schlipp, eds. 1986. *The Philosophy of W. V. Quine*. La Salle, Ill.: Open Court.

Harman, G. 1973. *Thought*. Princeton, N.J.: Princeton University Press.

1982. "Conceptual Role Semantics." *Notre Dame Journal of Formal Logic 23*, 242–56.

Heim, I. 1982. *The Semantics of Definite and Indefinite Noun Phrases*. Ph. D. dissertation, University of Massachusetts.

Hinrichs, E. 1986. "Temporal Anaphora in Discourses of English." *Linguistics and Philosophy 9*, 63–82.

Hodes, H. 1982. "The Composition of Fregean Thoughts." *Philosophical Studies 41*, 161–78.

Kamp, H. 1981. "A Theory of Truth and Semantic Representation." In Groenendijk et al. (1981).

1985. "Context, Thought, and Communication." *Proceedings of the Aristotelian Society 85*, 239–61.

Kaplan, D. 1977. *Demonstratives. Draft No. 2*. Dittograph. Published in Almog et al. (1989).*

1986. "Opacity." In Hahn and Schlipp (1986).

Kazmi, A. 1987. "Quantification and Opacity." *Linguistics and Philosophy 10*, 77–100.

Kripke, S. 1976. "Is There a Problem about Substitutional Quantification?" In Evans and McDowell (1976).

1979. "A Puzzle About Belief." In Margalit (1979);* reprinted in Salmon and Soames (1988).

1980. *Naming and Necessity*. Cambridge, Mass.: Harvard University Press.

Levin, H. 1982. *Categorial Grammar and the Logical Form of Quantification*. Atlantic Highlands, N.J.: Humanities Press.

Lewis, D. 1970. "How to Define Theoretical Terms." *Journal of Philosophy 67*, 427–46. Reprinted in Lewis (1983).

1972. "General Semantics." In Davidson and Harman (1972); reprinted in Lewis (1983).

1979a. "Scorekeeping in a Language Game." *Journal of Philosophical Logic 8*, 339–59. Reprinted in Lewis (1983).

1979b. "Counterfactual Dependence and Time's Arrow." *Nous 13*, 455–76. Reprinted in Lewis (1986).*

1983. *Philosophical Papers. Volume I*. New York: Oxford University Press.

1986. *Philosophical Papers. Volume II.* New York: Oxford University Press.

Linsky, L., ed. 1971. *Reference and Modality.* New York: Oxford University Press.

Loar, B. 1981. *Mind and Meaning.* Cambridge University Press.

Lycan, W. 1982. "Toward a Homuncular Theory of Believing." *Cognition and Brain Theory 4*, 139–59.

Marcus, R. 1962. "Modalities and Intensional Languages." *Synthese 27*, 303–22.

Margalit, A., ed. 1979. *Meaning and Use.* Dordrecht: Reidel.

Martin, Robert L., ed. 1984. *Recent Essays on Truth and the Liar Paradox.* New York: Oxford University Press.

McGinn, C. 1983. *The Subjective View: Secondary Qualities and Indexical Thoughts.* New York: Oxford University Press.

Millikan, R. 1984. *Language, Thought, and Other Biological Categories: New Foundations for Realism.* Cambridge, Mass.: MIT Press.

Minsky, M. 1987. *The Society of the Mind.* New York: Simon & Schuster.

Montague, R. 1974. *Formal Philosophy.* ed. by R. Thomason. New Haven, Conn.: Yale University Press.

Parret, H., and J. Bouveresse, eds. 1981. *Meaning and Understanding.* Berlin: de Gruyter.

Parsons, T. 1981. "Frege's Hierarchies of Indirect Senses and the Paradox of Analysis." In French et al. (1981).

Partee, B. 1982. "Belief Sentences and the Limits of Semantics." In Peters and Saarinen (1982).

1984. "Nominal and Temporal Anaphora." *Linguistics and Philosophy 7*, 243–78.

Peacocke, C. 1981. "Demonstrative Thought and Psychological Explanation." *Synthese 49*, 187–217.

Perry, J. 1977. "Frege on Demonstratives." *Philosophical Review 86*, 474–97.

1980. "A Problem About Continued Belief." *Pacific Philosophical Quarterly 61*, 317–22.

Peters, S., and E. Saarinen, eds. 1982. *Processes, Beliefs, and Questions.* Dordrecht: Reidel.

Pitcher, G., ed. 1964. *Truth.* Englewood Cliffs, N.J.: Prentice-Hall.

Putnam, H. 1975. "The Meaning of 'Meaning'." In Gunderson (1975).

Quine, W. V. 1956. "Quantifiers and Propositional Attitudes." *Journal of Philosophy 53*, 177–87. Reprinted in Linsky (1971).

1960a. "Variables Explained Away." *Proceedings of the American Philosophical Society 104*, 343–47. Reprinted in Quine (1966).*

1960b. *Word and Object.* Cambridge, Mass.: MIT Press.

1966. *Selected Logical Papers.* New York: Random House.

Richard, M. 1981. "Temporalism and Eternalism." *Philosophical Studies 39*, 1–13.

1982. "Tense, Propositions, and Meanings." *Philosophical Studies 41*, 337–51.

1983. "Direct Reference and Ascriptions of Belief." *Journal of Philosophical Logic 12*, 425–52. Reprinted in Salmon and Soames (1988).

1987a. "Attitude Ascriptions, Semantic Theory, and Pragmatic Evidence." *Proceedings of the Aristotelian Society 87*, 243–62.

1987b. "Quantification and Leibniz's Law." *Philosophical Review 96*, 555–78.

1988. "Taking the Fregean Seriously." In Austin (1988).

1989. "How I Say What You Think." In French et al. (1989).

Russell, B. 1903. *Principles of Mathematics*. New York: Norton.

1912. *The Problems of Philosophy*. New York: Oxford University Press.

Salmon, N. 1981. *Reference and Essence*. Princeton, N.J.: Princeton University Press.

1986. *Frege's Puzzle*. Cambridge, Mass.: MIT Press.

Salmon, N., and S. Soames, eds. (1988). *Propositions and Attitudes*. New York: Oxford University Press.

Schiffer, S. 1987. *Remnants of Meaning*. Cambridge, Mass.: MIT Press.

Sellars, W. 1954. "Some Reflections on Language Games." *Philosophy of Science 21*, 204–28.

Soames, S. 1985. "Lost Innocence." *Linguistics and Philosophy 8*, 59–71.

1987a. "Direct Reference, Propositional Attitudes, and Semantic Content." *Philosophical Topics 15*, 47–87. Reprinted in Salmon and Soames (1988).

1987b. "Substitutivity." In Thomason (1987).

Stalnaker, R. 1984. *Inquiry*. Cambridge, Mass.: MIT Press.

Stampe, D. 1979. "Towards a Causal Theory of Linguistic Representation." In French et al. (1979a).

Stich, S. 1979. "Do Animals Have Beliefs?" *Australasian Journal of Philosophy 57*, 15–28.

1983. *From Folk Psychology to Cognitive Science: The Case Against Belief*. Cambridge, Mass.: MIT Press.

Taschek, W. 1987. "Content, Character, and Cognitive Significance." *Philosophical Studies 52*, 161–89.

Thomson, J. J. 1987. *On Being and Saying: Essays for Richard Cartwright*. Cambridge, Mass.: MIT Press.

Index